until it rains again.

RUCHIKAA BHUYAN

First Published in December 2021

ISBN: 978-93-5472-547-0

BLUEROSE PUBLISHERS

www.bluerosepublishers.com

info@bluerosepublishers.com

+91 8882 898 898

Cover Design:

Muskan Sachdeva

Typographic Design:

Ilma Mirza

Distributed by: BlueRose, Amazon, Flipkart

Dedicated to the nebulous stars flickering

away in some corner of the cosmos—

We shall rise again.

Acknowledgements

It has always been my dream to write a book. To tell a story. To sandwich my thoughts and musings and fantasies between two rectangles of hard paper. I thought that stumbling upon an idea for a story that people would relate to or be willing to read— something different— would be the most confounding part, as I sat on my desk on a rainy May morning, a blank white document glaring at me dauntingly, tapping my fingers on my temple, I realized that I couldn't have been more wrong. A book does write itself. I'd be lying if I said that the story I present to you is identical to the one I had framed in my mind that morning in May. Writing a book is like traversing through a new tangent of emotions and experiences altogether that one creates for oneself, and traversing through that journey isn't plain sailing. The words you will read are mine but the effort put into weaving them as a story is a collective one. Firstly, I would love to extend my profound gratitude towards my parents, who have been with me every step of the day. To my father, who would always keep nudging me not to relinquish by perpetually checking in on my progress, thank you, for even if at the time I'd found them irksome, I know now that without your nudges, I wouldn't have been able to complete my story within the timeline that I did. I am also immensely beholden to you for being my ray of hope when dubious clouds blurred my vision when the matter of publishing came into being. I will always be grateful for the passion and involvement you have invested in my project. To my mother, thank you for always reminding me of my caliber and pushing me to be my best at times when I drooped down to self-doubt and apprehension. Thank you for the scrumptious meals and the cups of coffee you made to make the writing process more seamless than it could ever be.

As with most writers, I had my share of writer's blocks in composing this story. Plotholes and missing links were the biggest demotivators for me, but thanks to Nishka, my best friend for three years (and some months now?) and an avid reader, for having helped me in linking ideas when it seemed impossible. I am ever-indebted to you for having received my calls at odd hours, helping me design the perfect cover, listening to my abrupt bursts of bliss at a successful chapter, or whining over a lack of inspiration. Thank you so much for your genuine criticisms every now and then which helped me turn this story into one worth reading. Your knowledge of books continues to baffle me.

To Sukanya, my soul sister and writing mate, words simply do not suffice in expressing my love and gratitude for you. You have always been there, even if miles apart, to inspire me. Thank you for the constructive criticism on my word choices and brevity, and your prudent advice on catering a book to its target audience. There were times when I felt insecure about my writing, when I wanted to discard everything, but you were there to help me through those low periods. Thank you so much.

Bringing my words to life and this story to the hands of readers wouldn't have been plausible without the BlueRose Publishing House. Ilma Mirza, Pranavi Jha, Muskan Sachdeva, Shreya Kapoor, and Sania— I couldn't have asked for a better team. From endless calls for arriving at the perfect aesthetic for the book to brainstorming cover designs, I am indebted to you all for having supported me each step of the way and providing my story with wings to fly.

I wrote this story during a transformative period of my life, a departure from homeostasis and an open embrace of changes. Moving schools is one thing but moving cities requires you to adjust to two new sets of customs and habits: of the school and of the city. The experience was not easy and anxiety rippled at my fingertips and toes for the first few days as a new student and as a new resident in this dreamy city, Mumbai, where the story is set. It is an indubitably scary experience but the fear was allayed by the companionship of my mother every step of the way. Ma, my love and respect for your endurance and efforts to realize my dreams amplify every second. I had presumed that making friends would be impossible and I would find myself out-of-place for two whole years, but boy was I wrong. Soumil and Adeetya, thank you for hyping me up and being more enthusiastic than me for the launch of the book. Keishaa, Diya, Trayi, Advit, and Arishta, thanks a ton for being my motivators. I love all of you so much.

To my brother, Rohaan, despite us being segregated in age by thirteen years, I never find you distant or unrelatable. Rather, you are the best sibling I could ever have. Thank you for reviewing my writings and being there for me during one of the most stressful and difficult times in my life. Thank you for letting me intrude into your room when I wanted a change of environment while writing when the tones of my own room began seeming humdrum.

Armaan, my best friend of many years, thank you for always uplifting me from periods of dejection and encouraging me with positive phrases of affirmation that helped me remain motivated to complete this story. Thank you for the beautiful songs you shared with me(and still do), for some of them have inspired some of the emotions expressed in this book.

My list of acknowledgments would be incomplete without thanking my English teachers, Manna Nurani Ma'am, who taught me that it is brevity which constitutes the foundation of writing and not necessarily rich vocabulary; Ankita Das Ma'am, who guided me towards the direction of creative writing; Scharada Dubey Ma'am, who taught me how to inculcate my voice in my writings and the nuances of composing a novel; and Miss Lorraine Rodrigues, whose expertise on analysis helped me build the characters in my story and whose impactful words, "the power of editing" will always be imprinted on my mind.

Faith in oneself is largely influenced by the kind of faith and confidence others implant in you, and nobody could have better made me realise this than my Heads and now, sisterly figures at

GlobalShala(where I work), Ananya Kumar and Sonu Mehtha. I look up to both of you as my sources of inspiration to become better and grow everyday. Your words of motivation never fail to bring a smile to my countenance. It's a blessing to have you as my mentors.
To Bugmita, Shruti, Abhilasha, Sunny, Sanjuri, Kaushiki, Vatsal, Aaditya, Fareeha, Chandanika, Banashree(Maina Baa), Aakshi, Boni Dada, Swapnali Mahi, Riyaa, Iffat, Shatakshi, Kabir, Shambhavi, Debargha, Dr. (Mrs.) Banashree Phukan Ma'am, Mrs. Rashmi Baruah Ma'am, Nandini Kataky Ma'am, Sanjay Purkayashtha Sir, Mrs. Anjali Kumar Ma'am, Mrs. Abhijita Kashyap Ma'am, Mrs. Banita Agarwal Ma'am, and Himashree Aunty, who always motivated along the journey of writing, thank you very much.

Finally, I would like to thank my readers, those who picked up this book and found something in the cover, or in the title, or in the synopsis, or all of them, or anything else, that intrigued them or embark upon a quest for meaning in Alaina's story.

Thank you, all.

The Girl on the Typewriter

Ruchika Rashya Bhuyan is a 15-year-old budding writer from Guwahati, Assam. To her, writing is not all about structuring sentences with the correct grammatical framework but about being able to bring to the life stories and emotions everyone experiences but doesn't pay enough heed to or hushes down to silent tones. Her writings have been previously featured in popular Instagram-based writing platforms like 'The Scribbled Stories' , 'The Untold Tales' and 'The Amateur Writers'. She also writes occasional articles for 'The Sentinel', a local daily in Assam. Currently studying in the 11th grade at Dhirubhai Ambani International School, she aspires to pursue Economics and Creative Writing in the future. 'It might not be the most conventional combination,' she says, 'But I've learnt to follow the prompts of my heart.'

Synopsis

'Perhaps we were more metaphors than we were skin, flesh and blood.'

When seventeen-year-old Alaina was caught in a deluging whirlpool of emotions— battling with a staggering relationship, a pernicious friendship and a conventional Indian family that was perpetually at a conflict of interest with her unconventional mind— one glance from across the classroom threshold sufficed to dissolve the massive frenzy in her life and in her mind.

Until it only amplified the dilemma enfolding her.

Was it wrong to unabashedly desire to fiddle with those brown ringlets or long to discover what dreams and stars shone behind those spectacles?

Was it wrong to feel a tingling nervousness for someone who nearly cost two hearts?

Ride along this unputdownable voyage in the quest of identity and self, where raw thoughts from an unveiled mind will knock at the walls of your heart and prompt you to let the hurricane of emotions drench you.

Knock. Knock.

Are you ready to unlock the gates to the crude beauty of being and feeling human?

Contents

ONE

Dreamy City

One summer can change your life. I never believed in that. No doubt that I had watched countless movies where one day you're on the streets and the next thing you know, there's a limo waiting to take you to your million-dollar business office. Then there's the classic rom-com sequence where a nerdy, shy, quiet, and reserved girl suddenly starts dating the popular guy of the school, the one whom all the girls (and guys alike) have a crush on and he either plays soccer or basketball, and then she is transformed into a confident, popular and formidable fashionista. These tales are fun to watch for a pastime sport, but they have fantasy and imagination written all over them—unreasonable and highly unlikely to play out in real life. While these still fit into the category of 'too-good-to-be-true', one summer can actually turn your life upside down, as cliche as that may sound. It really depends on the things happening around you and how they're timed. I know that, *now.*

Mumbai is a *happening* city. They call it the *city of dreams,* where folks from different parts of the world amalgamate in quest of their aspirations and in hope of realising them. In most movies, web series, and even books that are set in the city, Mumbai is painted either as a dreamy place, like an escape to utopia, or as the nerve centre of thriving business activities or a dangerous land of crime. These demonstrations are not wholly inaccurate. The liberating feeling of walking along Marine Drive, glaring into the vastness of the waters, the waves dancing periodically, circled by towering skyscrapers that prance their heads towards the cerulean sky— a gorgeous treat to the eyes— is nothing short of a utopia indeed. But mostly, it's crowded with either tourists or other residents like me who can never get enough of the view or the desire to escape the woes of life. So, the real sense of a dreamy world is only felt when you stand there, gentle zephyrs rustling through your hair, past midnight. But then the dread of crime creeps in and draws out any sense of serenity because your mind is constantly counting down the seconds left before you get robbed, kidnapped, raped, and/or murdered. Escalated to morbidity too quickly, didn't it? I've just grown up in a way that the most irrational fears manage to reign over the forefront of my brain.

Being born in this city, I could never really grasp what others came *seeking* here. Yes, there was the city life, the muffled sounds of late-night parties crawling in through your casements at midnight, the sense of belonging to a larger world rendered while gazing into the starry skyline canopied by stars at night, and the fact that the city never sleeps. But my life was pretty well-defined and constant. I would wake up (groaning most mornings because my eyes refuse to unfasten at five. What an ungodly hour to break your slumber!), get dressed for school, have breakfast, set out for school, find Alisha and Sasha (my best friends), and attend tedious classes. During breaks, though, school was not so tedious after all. Our trio would rule over the cafeteria and every corridor. We were the centre of gossip and attention. While most people weren't very fond of us, they feared us. Or so Alisha would tell Sasha and me. Then school would get over and I'd be back home, study a little, complete assignments, Skype with Alisha and Sasha to make plans for the weekends, talk to my boyfriend, Arj, till one in the morning (now you know why I cannot for the life of me wake up at five), and before I know it, the alarm would go off in a revolt the next morning. Weekends were different from weekdays, certainly, but every weekend was the same. They were usually squandered away in partying, either in someone's house from our friend circle, or in a club (we'd use our fake IDs, duh). Every day was pretty much the same, and every week was repetitive, except during vacations. During the summer, our family would always go on a vacation to a foreign country. It was like a tradition we celebrated annually. Last year, we went to the Bahamas and I would've almost hooked up with a stranger unless my brother, Sparsh, had not reminded me that I was in a committed relationship. I had genuinely thanked him for saving my relationship, only to realise his generosity and endeavour to keep my virtues in place were part of an act. He had only wanted to hook up with the Bahamian guy himself, and he did, since he had no pre-existing romantic strings restraining him.

Life was normal, I guess, to some extent. Although I did occasionally feel frustrated by the humdrum routine that repeated every day, I was okay with it most of the time. Like I said, life was *normal,* not *perfect*. It can never be for anyone. Despite how unblemished and put-together we may appear externally, I think we all are a little broken inside, because there will always be at least one thing that we wish were better than it is now or we wish were different than it is now. Some of us have not yet discovered those fragile places, some resolutely ignore their existence and choose to dwell in pretence, while others are trying to fix them, trying to build themselves up again.

Yes, I am from a reasonably affluent family so I never faced the problems of not having access to quality education, or the clothes, books, accessories, phones, laptops, and other luxuries that joined my bucket list from time to time. And I am grateful for that. I understand the privilege that I was born into, but don't expect me not to utilise it. At the same time, I am not one to brag about my parents' earnings and wealth to others. I am not stupid, nor am I a snob. Although I am friends with some. Well, more than some. What was *broken,* then? Home. Yes, the home that I described as *nearly* perfect was not-so-perfect, after all. One may have all the wealth in the world and still feel broken inside. Desolate and empty, like there's something missing. Peace of mind? Well, one can't truly have that till reaching the grave. Happiness? Maybe. Money can buy some happiness, not all. While

Mom and Dad gave Sparsh and me whatever we needed, or wanted, it was always materialistic. We had their money, but not *them.* Every year on parent-teacher meet day, I would see so many of my classmates arrive with their parents, whether in perturbation or excitement. Sparsh and I, on the other hand, like Alisha and Sasha, and some other snobby kids, would have our parents come only for five minutes, collect the reports and leave. Most of the time, we came with our aunts or uncles. The last time our parents had set foot into the school was probably when I was fourteen. Three years ago!

It never felt like a family at home. It was just four people, who somewhat knew each other, living under the same room in peaceful co-existence, each not bothering much about the other. Things were not pretty at home. While I had a somewhat stable relationship with my brother, the equation between my parents and me was nearly non-existent. We never talked about things that really mattered. They didn't even *know* me, and the worst part was, after a certain period of trying, I had given up trying to open up to them whatsoever. Until I was doing okay at school, they didn't really care about who I was befriending or canoodling or killing. Seriously. It was in a way very conducive to me because I know how nosy and strict the parents of some of my friends are, but I still dreamt of having an intimate equation with them, what some would label as being best friends with them.

I sought the feeling of home.

I realise that there are more glaring and grave problems that the world has been combatting, without triumph, for centuries, like poverty, war, human trafficking, unemployment, and so on. I am not belittling them, for I cannot even imagine the struggles people have to fight through without any external support, having to go weeks without food, or being bought and sold in a market like a commodity. Like I said, we are all broken a little inside, in different ways, and one day or the other, we must deal with the flaws of the rude world, in different ways.

TWO

The New Arrival

Today marked the beginning of the last week of school before the summer holidays would begin. The crowd at school seemed heavier than regular days. Noise pollution was at its peak, with students whispering secrets, gossiping about nasty hearsays and roaring with laughter at the most unhumorous topics, all adding up to a loud, irritating indistinct chatter penetrating into my eardrums like poison. I was so busy finding my way through hundreds of bodies while also trying to save myself from the noise that I ended up entering the wrong classroom. As soon as I crossed the threshold, my eyes met with the sight of a stranger. She looked slightly taller than I am. Her hair was up in a high ponytail which, by the looks of it, probably reached till her hips when open. Her ovally round face was flanked on either side by strands of frizzy ringlets parted in the middle. She was biting her lips in nervousness. They were shaped nearly like a heart, plumpy and glittering with a gloss that I could spot from nearly a metre away. She was wearing rounded, Harry Potter-like spectacles that had a metallic frame. Behind those lenses, her eyes were lost, scanning around the room back and forth anxiously, as if they were waiting for something or searching for something that would bring her an instant wave of relief. Would they find it? Before they could find it, they found mine. They caught mine and clutched onto them for a while. My heart began thumping faster. I did not fancy first-encounters. I was miserable at them. What on earth are you supposed to do when a stranger looks you right in the eye, even if it lasts for just a second? If you look away, it might seem too adamant. I did not wish to come off as rude to a newcomer or make her day begin with a wrong turn. On the other hand, if you keep glaring irrationally, you might end up looking like a creepy stalker. Beads of sweat broke out on my head. Before this perplexion could intensify any more, I felt a tap on my shoulder.

'Babe, what's up? Your face is flushed. Are the air-conditioners not working properly here?'

That was Alisha. *The* Alisha Kumar, with her chiseled countenance and hazel eyes, perfectly-arched dark brown eyebrows and pink juicy lips that were today covered in a nude lipstick shade, and her shoulder-length bob-cut chestnut hair designed with golden highlights, glimmering against the radiating sun. She stood there for sonic moments, staring at me in amusement, her gorgeous curves running down her waist and along her hips. She stood with a straight back, body raised to just the ideal height, neither too short nor too tall, looking at me, bumfuzzled, with that classic raised eyebrow expression set on her perfect face. Everything about her seemed just perfect; she was the 'IT' girl after all. There was not a girl in the whole city (could be an exaggeration, let's say the whole school) who did not want to look like her and be like her. She was not just a person, she was a whole trend. A statement of confidence. She was genetically blessed with the optimum-sized breasts and butt, with the most beautiful features complementing her golden-peachy complexion. To top it all, she was daring and universally talented: the list of her talents was endless: she was a dancer, singer, athlete, got good grades (I usually scored higher than her, but that doesn't count because I could do literally nothing else), got every guy that she laid her eyes upon to helplessly fall in love with her, and, this one baffles me the most, was simultaneously feared and liked by everyone. She was all that I could only dream of being. She was like one of those enchanting models you see on your Instagram feed, except this one even stood the chance of going to an Ivy League. Don't get me wrong, I'm comfortable in my skin and yada yada. I was not exactly jealous of her. She was my 'bestie' after all. I was just in awe of her and may have some feeling of envy toward her simultaneously, despite the fact that we had grown up in each other's company since we were two and were next-door neighbours for nearly six years until her father launched a very successful enterprise and with all the gains, they moved into a more posh area in the city.

'Are you listening?', she asked, with her soft, sufficiently-pitched voice that was well-acquainted with such speech that would stand out even in a commotion of countless raging voices, and in a manner that you'd never forget her. She snapped her finger in front of my face in a zigzag motion, and that's when she finally interjected my train of thought and caught my attention.

'I'm sorry, babe. I was dazed and I zoned out from all the lack of sleep these past couple of weeks. Arj made me stay up till three this morning! Can you believe it? Not that I was not entertained by his anecdotes of how poorly his team plays on the field and how he always ends up taking up the responsibility of the entire game, but that cost me half an hour extra in the morning to conceal these bags under my eyes. Ugh.'

'Tell me about these boyfriends! They rant about how excessively girls talk but it's them rambling on through the night. Not gonna lie, it gets on my nerves sometimes. Ray and I were supposed to have a movie night last night, but he kept interrupting every five minutes to add some commentary and then would talk about stupid things like the water crisis.' Ray was Alisha's ninth boyfriend. She was sixteen and had already had nine boyfriends! I could never pull so hard. Three of them were long-term; the boys were decent but apparently, she grew too bored of their 'niceness'. Five of them were short-termed heated fiery romances with a lot of drama. As for Ray, she had been dating him for five months now, and this was the first time she ever complained about his talkativeness. Looked like a red flag to me. Sasha and I had always teased her regarding how Ray could go on chattering without break for the remainder of his lifetime, but Alisha would always say, 'I like listening to him!' in a defensive tone. It was adorable nonetheless. She was one of those people who felt tired of monotone. She could not stand the same people for too long a time. So, it was strange how she had not yet gotten tired or bored of Sasha or me yet. But we were both pretty sure that nice guys like Ray don't last very long with our queen bee, and this pretence of 'I like listening to him!' would end soon.

'Well, umm, the water crisis isn't exactly stupid but I get your point. Anyway, where's Sasha?'

Hardly had those words been voiced when Sasha sidled up to Alisha from behind. They were both now standing opposite to me. 'What's the tea?', she asked in anticipation of hearing about something remarkable.

'Eh, nothing much, babe, just ranting about common boy problems, you wouldn't relate.' Alisha didn't say the last three words in ridicule. On the contrary, she could not have been more to the point. Sasha didn't roll like us. She was openly and proudly a member of the LGBTQ+ community, using the label of queer publicly but among the three of us, we knew that she was still confused between being queer and lesbian. While queer had more flexibility, Sasha was by the day amplifying her contempt for men and her love for women. When the time would be right, she'd probably figure it out. She had the coolest personality I had ever come across. To begin with, she went by the nickname 'Sash', concise, convenient, and classy. Period. Moreover, the fact that it nearly resembled the word "sass" couldn't have been more accurate to her persona. She had lavender roots and bases tainting her naturally black hair— basically, ombre with a twist. And she had the most beautiful brown eyes ever, with her eyelids bordered by long, divine eyelashes that never needed mascara. What I envied about her the most were her Cara Delevingne-like eyebrows, shaping her visage into near perfection. Sash's family moved into the city four years ago, and when I had first met her at school, we instantly clicked. There was no sense of awkwardness that usually hovers in the conversation between any two strangers, no what-should-I-say-next or how-do-I-respond-to-that. While Alisha and I had been inseparable since forever, it didn't take much time for a bosom bond to spring to life among the three of us. I know that in popular thought, in a trio or "throuple", two of them are always more intimate than the third was with either of them. But I never felt any air of being unwelcome or FOMO. It was a strong friendship, I guess, although neither of them knew that I had a proportion of life unrevealed besides everything else I told them about, which to them seemed like it was everything there can be to know about me. There are just some feelings that are too difficult or too personal or too embarrassing to express to someone else, despite the history of exemplary friendship or whatever other relationship you might have with him/her/them. Then there are some things which you cannot comprehend yourself— things which you can't figure out why you feel, things which are so unconventional or unheard of in popular chatter that you almost think that it's proscribed or erroneous to feel them, even if you are not voluntarily giving birth to those feelings.

'Speaking of boyfriends, have you seen Arj?' I asked both of them.

'No,' they replied in unison.

'Forget Arj, who was the *other dude* you were gaping at five minutes ago?' Alisha asked with a smirk.

'Nobody. I told you that I completely zoned out. My brain isn't functioning today. Anyway, we're late for class. Let's hurry!'

*****

We were already at the last class of the day: Business Management, which I liked to abbreviate as BM because I was too lazy to utter any word more than a syllable long after it hit noon. My mind was heavy, and my eyes were nearly shutting as I strained them to peruse the words in my BM textbook. I felt as though I could swoon at any moment, partly because the lack of sleep was evident in my teary eyes, and partly because I had failed to put my mind to any class today, and in trying harder to focus, I had only given myself a pounding headache. I felt very distracted and that was unusual for me. I rolled in class in only one of two ways: either I would pay complete heed to the teacher and be absorbed into what was being taught because in all honesty, I did enjoy learning despite being opposed to the idea of exams (why do I need to memorise a book to prove that I am knowledgeable about a concept?), or, I would engage myself in meaningless gossip, not focusing on the class whatsoever. Both of these, on any day, were voluntary and conscious decisions. But today, I found myself subconsciously dwelling on one person: the stranger I had exchanged a gaze with earlier. The inquisitiveness that sparked in me after I broke eye contact with her was unbearable. She looked so enigmatic. *What were her eyes seeking out? Why did she look at me like she wanted to keep looking? Did she want to keep looking or was she also under the confusion I was? Where was she from?* I wanted to know so much about a stranger. I didn't even understand why. Throughout the five classes I had today, I could think of nothing else but her: those wandering eyes scanning the room in anticipation, those curls hanging divinely from her head, her eyes meeting mine.

Would I get to see her again? Would we be friends?

This strange curiosity disturbed me but I enjoyed it simultaneously.

Minutes stretched to hours until finally, at what seemed like the hundredth hour of the same BM class, the clock ticked to two, the bell rang in a resonant 'ding-dong', and my mind eventually dawdled back to the present. I was depositing my books, laptop and other stationery into my backpack when I heard my name being called out.

'ALAINA!'

I heard for a second time.

It was Mrs. Whayton. She was our English teacher. The thing about her, by which she was known in our school, was that she was unusually and unnecessarily loud, and she was uncontrollably impatient— two qualities which I detested in people in general. But English happened to be my favourite subject, and I was the leader of the Literary Club at school, so I felt obliged to be nice to her. She was also in charge of our batch, or 'class teacher' as we term it— all the more reason not to fall into her bad books. But I couldn't help but wonder why she would call me at the end of the school day when we did have English class today and she could've conveniently called me then. Moreover, the Literary Club had no new events lined up, nor were any creative writing competitions being held in my knowledge. Before I could entertain any more overthinking, my feet were already set in motion. There was just something in her voice that was so commanding that one would spontaneously feel bound to listen to her and follow her.

We were in her office and she said that we were waiting for another student to come. I didn't bother asking who he/she/they was/were. I would know in a couple of seconds anyway. Or minutes. But the wait was killing me. I was slightly curious about whom we were waiting for, but mainly, I was desperate to go home, hop onto my bed, and slumber away the exhaust that was presently draining all energy out of me. There was a knock at the door and Mrs. Whayton, in a surprisingly subtle tone, said 'Come inside, dear.' As I turned my head around, I once again met the eyes that my mind could not let go of for the whole day. It was now that I could scan her frame with closer observance. Behind her Potter spectacles rested two elegant pearly black eyes, not roaming about with perplexity anymore. There was a certain calmness in her pupils that pacified me too, and just for a moment, I felt the exhaustion letting go of me.

'This is Myra Sibal, a new girl. She's joined one grade lower than yours, which would be grade eleven. And it so happens that she's an avid writer too. I've read some of her compositions, and I must say,' addressing Myra directly this time, 'Your style is unique. I like it. That's Alaina, the leader of the Literary Club in our school. Alaina, I'd like you to count Myra as a new addition to the club. She *belongs* there.'

Seldom did Mrs. Whayton compliment a student on their writing abilities. Only a few students from the club were recipients of her approbation, and in the seven years that she's been my English teacher, she has only praised my work thrice: the first time when I was in fifth grade and I was the only student in class who composed poetry, the second time in ninth grade when my analysis of Bennet and Darcy's dynamic in Pride and Prejudice had 'stood out' compared to the other analyses she had read, and for the third time and what now seemed like the last, in the eleventh grade, when she was 'proud' of me for having published an anthology of poems. She clearly already had a new favourite, because it was very rare for her to grow fond of newbies. I know that it was bold of me to presume that I used to be her favourite, but at least I was in her good books. I failed to subdue the dirty green jealousy tainting my face. Perhaps the exhaust didn't give way for the jealousy to show. It's funny how just a few hours ago I could not suppress the curiosity I had about her whereabouts, and now I could not suppress the jealousy I felt towards her. Probably it was not that big of a deal, though, right? One compliment against three for me, I was still leading the tally. But for how long, though?

Here's the thing about me: I am ruthlessly competitive. I've tried multiple times not to let that nature get the better of me, but it always does. And jealousy branches off as an organic consequence of it. Dad's one of the most successful entrepreneurs in the city and Mom has had a thriving musical career, so the competitiveness runs in the family. Despite how toxic it is, Sparsh and I have more than once been victims of comparison to our peers, which has instilled in me a constant battle for being good *enough,* even if not the best. But here's another thing about me: I am not the best person for being honest about how I feel towards someone. I may dislike certain people but I feel bound to be nice to them still. I don't exactly enjoy bitching about them behind their backs. I only dread the awkwardness that might creep in after a confrontation. In simpler times, I am a people-pleaser.

Before I knew it, we went from Myra being a new addition to the club, to deciding that I would give Myra a tour of the school and some history about our club tomorrow. While I cursed under my breath at my fortune, I also thanked Mrs. Whayton's rare generosity in silence. At least *not today*.

When the two of us made our ways out of her office, our shoulders rubbed against each other. 'Sorry,' she uttered nervously.

'It's okay,' I mumbled.

And even if they might've lasted a millisecond, goosebumps rose up both my arms and I could feel an unfamiliar heat in my cheeks.

THREE

An Uneasy Car Ride

It was Friday and I had no will to get myself up and get ready for school.

The week went by in a blur of events. The school tour with Myra did not turn out to be as uneasy as I had anticipated. I managed to make it through. We simply walked around the school, with her following my lead, and I made sure not to have eye contact with her. She tried her best to stimulate small talk— I could tell— by asking me questions every now and then, often about me rather than the school. I tried to deal with them gracefully, although to think about it now, I might've come off as unapproachable. It's just that it was weird. I could not fathom out why I had goosebumps the other day. It was almost as if I was nervous when I looked at her. The jealousy didn't add up to a desirable amalgamation of feelings either. I found it difficult to weave words into sensible sentences. Did I feel intimidated? I could not tell. It was a wholly unfamiliar nervousness, nothing like the sudden rush of heat that ascends to your thorax when you're nervous before a test, or when lying to your parents, or before your first kiss. It was a tinkling nervousness that made my stomach curl into a ball, made my cheeks flush, and made my heart race faster. And I felt uncomfortable with that tinkling nervousness because I did not know why I felt the way I did. I loathe dwelling in oblivion. This not-knowing set my mind at unrest for the whole week. So, later in the day, I kept the information session about the club brief and invited a few members in an attempt to get rid of the tinkling nervousness.

I cannot recall much of the days that went by. To describe them as scattered pieces of a puzzle: there were late-night calls with Alisha and Sash (we were planning on how we'd spend the summer together), making out in a parking lot with Arj, a whole lot of schoolwork, a handful of brother-sisterly scuffles with Sparsh, and oh, a thirty-minute breakdown session after reading 'The Fault in Our Stars' for the umpteenth time, not only because I absolutely craved the storyline, which is indubitably quite tragic, but also because I'd finally arrived at the conclusion that I could never write like John Green. Petty, I know.

Summer break would commence in a day but there wasn't much exhilaration in me. Mom and Dad were going on a business trip which they described as 'utterly significant for maintaining cordial relations with your partners', and while they were benevolent enough in suggesting that Sparsh and I could tag along, we refused to spend two weeks in New York enfolded by middle-aged people wearing suits instead of exploring the Big Apple. While I was a little disappointed on hearing the news, I didn't throw a tantrum or cry over it like a baby. I could comprehend where Mom and Dad were coming from. I'd read about the 'Favour Bank' in Paulo Coelho's 'The Zahir', which basically is the conception that if you make a conscious effort to be in people's good books, connect with them every now and then preferably help them with a thing or two, they will feel the obligation to return you a favour or more back. And when you seriously ponder upon it, the Favour Bank holds true not only in the professional world but in day-to-day life as well. We all have acquaintances whom we turn to when we need a favour, and they turn to us when they need it back. You don't necessarily need to have an emotional attachment with them, and there exists an unspoken consensus between them and you that you're all debtors and creditors in the Favour Bank, switching between the two roles as circumstances change.

Mom and Dad were taking an early flight at seven and had probably left by the time I woke up. I hugged them goodbye last night though. Since our usual ride wasn't available and we never really took the bus to school, we were riding to school with Alisha today. I was still combing my hair out of knots when there was a loud honking breaking the silence of the tranquil morning.

'Oh my gawd, can you chill? We have an hour till school starts and besides, the campus is only fifteen minutes away!' I screamed downward, after unlocking the window and thrusting my head into the openness of the neighbourhood.

'But we have a lot to chat about! Plus, your brother's coming too. I need to gossip about his class!'

'Argh!'

I slammed the window shut and continued styling my hair at the pace of a turtle. This was one thing I did not particularly fancy about Alisha. All she craved was gossip. It was as if her entire life revolved around gossip and drama. She was so influenced after watching the show *'Gossip Girl'* that she began being driven by the goal to inculcate a few elements of the show into her own high school experience. I did not mind engaging in conversation about other people, especially when it involved some steaming hot tea, given that my own life tasted so bland, because it was an escape from my own problems. It kept me distracted when I simply didn't want to deal with life. But of late, I found myself growing sick of talking about other people, comparing ourselves to other people, mocking others because they didn't do things like we did, and attempting to derive pleasure from that. I guess I was peer pressured into a gossip gang, but over time, I've come to understand its futility.

We eventually ended up leaving for school forty-five minutes early, because Alisha had sparked a wave of revolt against her presence in the neighbourhood by aggravating all our neighbours through continuous honking and screaming. Bowing our heads down in embarrassment and humiliation to say the least, Sparsh and I entered the car as rapidly as one could. The chauffeur was driving slower than usual. Clearly, he had been instructed accordingly by Alisha. The first few minutes seemed tediously long and we sat in awkward silence, with the driver's eyes on the road and the three of us looking out through the glass. Being the big talker that she is, Alisha broke the silence and said, 'I'm sorryyyyyy! I really am. You know I was getting irritated sitting alone under the scorching heat of a Mumbai summer. Mom strictly warned me not to use the AC when the car wasn't running. I shouldn't have gone all haywire, though. There won't be a next time, I promise. C'mon A, I am really sorry.'

That was quite a long apology to be admitted by *the* Alisha Kumar. Maybe she was maturing and changing. Hopefully, she'd give up gossiping one day too.

'It's okay, A. And you better keep the promise.'

'The sister hath forgiven! And the brother?', she asked, with her eyes looking apologetically at Sparsh.

'Yeah, it's fine. I wasn't mad anyway. I actually enjoyed the look of disgust on our neighbours. Never seen them like that.'

'Now that's a fun-seeker! Take lessons, A. I might just start hanging out with him instead of you if you continue to remain this serious-faced-judgemental-aunty all the time.'

'Ugh! I'm nothing like a judgemental aunty, okay? Don't infuriate me more than you already have, or else I shall renounce the forgiveness I had just granted,' I replied in a tease.

'Woah, big vocab alert! Anyway, let the man talk today. What's up with you, Sparsh? How's that thing going with Miss I'm-too-shy-to-post-a-picture-with-my-boyfriend-on-Instagram ?'

'Umm, firstly, she has a name: Ira, and secondly, it's going just fine. There's no 'tea', so nothing that might interest you.'

'What about her friend, Neha? I heard she's been wrapping her fingers around some guy called Darsh? Never heard of him.'

'I dunno. I don't keep nosing into other people's businesses unnecessarily.' Burn. This was one of those rare moments when I was proud of my brother.

'Wow, putting on a coat of roasting today, are we? Have the two siblings vowed to seal their li—'

'Stop it,' I interjected. 'If he doesn't know, then he doesn't. If he doesn't care enough to keep track of other people's lives, then he doesn't. I don't either. Can we please talk about ourselves instead of others?' The moment the words left my mouth, I realised this was the first time I called out Alisha on gossiping. I felt baffled for a couple of seconds until the conversation continued and my train of thought was naturally interrupted.

'Okay, A! I get your point. No more of others. So, Sparsh, you were talking about Ira?'

'Forget about Ira and Sparsh. Their relationship is as dry as his DMs. Let's talk about you and your loquacious little Ray.'

'What does that even mean?' she replied aggravatedly.

Sparsh glanced at me with a grateful sigh and I answered with an 'Anytime, brother'.

'It means that I am referring to your boyfriend whom you ranted about throughout the week for being excessively talkative. What's up with that? Are you sick of him? Is everything okay with you two?' I asked genuinely, not being sardonic anymore.

'I don't know, Alaina. Things have been pretty weird lately. Just when I was starting to think that I might be onto something that'll last, it appears that we're on the edge of the cliff again. Or at least, I am. Yeah, he's talkative, which is still fine. But it's like he only wants to talk about himself and wants me to be a trash can to be dumped with all of his stupid anecdotes. And all he wants to do, besides talking, is sex,' she sighed out a deep breath of relief after this unannounced burst of frustration.

Sparsh utilised the pause to remark snarkily, 'Sounds to me like what was your general norm with your past boyfriends.'

'Not the time,' I replied in a stern tone, warning him not to go further.

The remnant of the car ride passed by in silence. While Sparsh had been warned by me not to utter the wrong things at the wrong time, I didn't know how to respond to Alisha or console her. I could sense an inch of hurt in her voice, which I had never heard when it came to her talking about her romantic affairs. It was also mutually understood between the two of us, even in silence, that a better time to converse would probably be tonight (we had planned a sleepover), for we neither did we want to enter school on the last day before the summer break in a vinegar temper nor did we want to leave Sasha out of an important conversation.

Sparsh was still closeted and Ira and I were the only two people who were aware of this of all the people in his life. In fact, Ira and him were not dating at all. They were best friends, and they put up a pretence of dating because 1. All of Sparsh's friends had girlfriends and he was bullied for not having one till he got one and 2. Ira wanted to keep Sparsh's secret safe while concurrently making her friends jealous (yeah, my brother was pretty good-looking, whatever).

I still remember the day when he came out to me. He was twelve and I was a few months away from turning fourteen. I'd barged into his room without warning when he was putting some makeup on. He started in his stationary position and jumped around to see who'd come. I had looked at him with a gape mouth and eyes wide in shock, like I'd seen a ghost. 'I-I am gay!', he said like a bolt from the blue, and as far as I can recall, his cheeks had flushed a deep magenta in embarrassment and fear more than the blusher could ever achieve. At the time, I did not know what to say because my knowledge about the LGBTQ+ community was as non-existent as the rights for the community in our country. Our society has always treated (and a proportion of it still does) gay people with disdain. It dictated that loving who you want was not normal, but promising vows of marriage to a stranger was. It addressed them with slurs and degrading language. And although I had watched a few progressive movies, my brain seemed to be programmed to disdain gay people or feel uncomfortable when I was around them or heard about them. Naturally, I had no idea how to react when those words mumbled out of him. I slammed the door, hastened to my room, shut my door, and stood there like a gypsum statue for fifteen minutes straight, still trying to process and fully comprehend the situation. I had heard of terms like 'gay' and 'lesbian' before, but I had no notion of their implication. It was nearly forbidden in our house to speak such words or acknowledge any emotion of attraction towards people from the same gender or just be anybody other than straight and binary. And in spite of having heard of the term 'gay' before, when Sparsh voiced the word, it sounded so unfamiliar and unknown that I felt tempted to fire up my laptop and indulge in extensive research. I had only typed 'gay' in Google's search bar and after three hours of my eyes being glued to the screen, I was balling my eyes out. The internet has information about everything. I'm not being hyperbolic. I actually mean it. Literally, EVERYTHING. I went from reading a blog about homosexuality, to learning about how broad the LGTBQ+ spectrum is, to abruptly stumbling upon articles and photos of hate crimes against the community. I had only begun to understand, even if by an infinitesimal magnitude, what the various types of sexual orientations and genders were when I saw a picture of people being beaten up because they were of the same gender and were holding hands together in public. My heart broke a little and guilt gathered around my throat in a lump. What had I done? Had I just dismissed my own brother? Without thinking further, I ran out of my room and started knocking vigorously on his door. He unlocked it open, with his hands slightly trembling, and eyes glazed over in regret, with a look that said: '*I shouldn't have told her. This was all a mistake. Something's wrong with me*'. With my eyes welled with tears and my mouth finding it difficult to form words that would attenuate his expression of sorrow, I embraced him into a tight hug. We probably had not had a real hug before that time, and as we held onto each other, we were both balling this time. I stayed through the night in his room that day, talking to him and listening to him. I apologised to him probably ten times till he threatened to slap me if I did not stop. He told me about how his blood curdled and how beads of cold sweat broke out on his temple when he saw me with no alarm. He panicked and was caught off-guard, so he couldn't lie on the spot. We gushed over boys together and he told me about the first time he had felt the slim possibility of having a crush on a boy. He had been suppressing these feelings for many months, trying to convince himself that it was just a 'phase' and hormonal activity naturally causes such emotions. We conversed incessantly for four hours until our eyes felt drained and begged for us to go to sleep, and even if today in the car was probably the first time in several months that Sparsh and I had engaged in conversation except for the necessary table talk during meals, we had realized that night itself that we'd always have each other's backs.

Most of the time, at least.

FOUR

Pushing Back

'Why aren't you two uttering a word? What's wrong? This is very odd.'

We were in the school cafeteria, Alisha, Sasha, and me. It was lunch break but for us, it was usually a 'gossip break'. Alisha would usually gather her fanbase around our table, 'minions' as she called them, and would gossip about everything, from why Sneha from sixth grade is trying to be promiscuous to the new affair of the security guard. Sometimes she would make ignorant comments that reflected misogyny or racism which rubbed me the wrong way, but I chose to remain silent, letting them pass under the excuse that her intentions weren't impure. In addition, she would talk so rapidly that the chances of anybody interjecting her were getting thinner by the day. Not today, though. Today the entire cafeteria resonated in the silence that hung in the air and all around us, like an unwelcome burden. I felt distinctly uncomfortable because I had no idea whether to speak or not, and if I did, what should I include and avoid addressing. As the silence grew exponentially unbearable, and the people around us, even from the table right across the room from us could discern that something was wrong, Sasha spoke up. She asked what was wrong. In all honesty, I was as clueless as her. I had never seen Alisha so dull and down. I failed to comprehend how easily she let down her gloss of confidence and sway because a guy didn't acknowledge enough how amazing she was. I felt bad for her and I wanted to pull her into a tight hug but I knew she hated being sympathised with. Why on earth did I think it was a good idea to bring up her relationship problems, even if in a jocular manner, early in the morning?

'Nothing, Sash. Alisha had a really bad sleep last night and is drained, aren't you, A? We'll talk tonight at the sleepover when the surroundings are a little more, umm, confidential,' I responded to Sash's searching questions, knowing that Alisha wouldn't speak on the theme for a long time. Surprisingly, Alisha's eyes lit up at the sound of 'sleepover' and she said, back with her gloss of confidence and sway, in a voice that just made you want to listen to her, 'No, Alaina. Sleepovers are for noobs. We're having a full-on SLUMBER PARTY! Also, I was thinking that it'd probably be a better idea for us to come over to your place, you know since your parents are out of town.' While I was relieved that she finally found some words, I was horrified by her proposition and cut in before Sash would add her support to the idea, 'No! Absolutely not. After what happened in the morning today, our neighbours are likely to murder you if you step foot anywhere near a meter within our area. It's best if it's at your place cause what's a fun summer slumber party without a hot tub? The one at our place is under repair. Trust me, your place is literally begging for a slumber party.'

'The idea of wearing sleek swimsuits and sipping cocktails in a hot tub is making me want to skip to the evening already!', Sasha exclaimed excitedly.

'Looks like we have a fun night to look forward to.'

*****

I had one more class left for the day and a meeting after that with the members of the Literary Club.

While Sash and Alisha had a class right after the lunch break, I had thirty minutes free, all to myself. Very few people in our batch had the subject choices as I did, and so I'd have breaks at times when the majority of others would wreck their heads with organic chemistry or calculus. While solitude is not popularly regarded as bliss, and often at times mistaken with being depressed, I enjoyed it. Without any disregard intended to people *actually* diagnosed with depression, as far as I've seen, you can be depressed even when you're surrounded by a crowd every day and you can be mirthful even when you choose to be alone. I did enjoy some lone company every once in a while, and during such breaks, I usually spent time reading in the library or musing in a bathroom stall. Sounds gross, but it actually isn't because whether good at other things or not, our school has a commendable record of hygiene maintenance.

Anyone from my friend group would find it impossible to even entertain the thought remotely that I had a life beyond what I'd shown them. But I'm sure they, too, had things about themselves that I didn't know. There are parts of ourselves which we would prefer to keep within us, tucked away in unsearchable depths of our souls discreetly, because we dread judgement, we dread being an orange in a pile of apples, we dread talking about stuff that has not seen the face of general conversation yet, but most of all, we dread losing ourselves if we give away too much of us to the world. So, there I was, staring at myself in the wide rectangular mirror that spread across almost the entire breadth of the front wall facing the doors of the stalls in the washroom, glaring endlessly into my insecurities, at those asymmetrical eyebrows that grew with no particular shape, at those lips that were not plumpy enough, those cheeks that were too chubby, those collarbones that were visible so vaguely that you could regard them as non-existent, that waist that was quite slim but not slim enough, that belly fat hiding beneath my skirt because I was neither completely skinny nor completely fat but I had an odd body with no proper figure, when suddenly, I detected some movement behind me in the looking glass. Before I could even register what had happened, somebody grabbed me by the arm and dragged me into a stall. I almost opened my mouth to scream in horror when a soft palm pressed against my lips and a familiar voice whispered, 'Shush! It's me.'

Unfastening my eyes slowly, in the hope that if it was a kidnapper of some sort, I would kick him in the balls while he'd be anticipating me to open my eyes fully, I met with the lovely beaver eyes of Arj. I scanned his face from head to chin to ensure that my brain wasn't playing a trick and the person standing in front of me was actually him and not a kidnapper.

'What are you doing here?', I asked, baffled. He was supposed to be in soccer practice.

'Well, we haven't been talking much lately. You've been ignoring my calls and seem resolute on replying to my messages with no more than three words. You are gone before I even reach our table at lunch and when I call you in the hallway or on the grounds or wherever I see you, you either pretend not to hear or you have serious issues with your hearing. And, I just miss you and would rather miss soccer practice than miss you anymore. It's killing me. Did I do something?'

I felt caught without a signal. I didn't know how to answer. He was right. He was right about all of the things he'd just said. And no, he had not done anything wrong that could reasonably upset me. In fact, he had been a really good boyfriend. I know that I was groaning over his chitter-chatter not five days ago to Alisha, but what I didn't mention was that he actually had had a terrible day and had asked me thrice if I was okay with just talking and not watching the movie we'd planned to because he was upset and wanted to vent. When I would get upset, even at the silliest of matters, he'd not just listen to me. He'd get me flowers and send over chocolates and cheer-up cards to our place. He was the ideal boyfriend. And for some reason, I was not satisfied with that. I bitched about him to my best friends out of nowhere, with no real reason at all. Nothing was wrong with him. It was me. And I know that I had the opportunity then to express to him how I felt and resolve our problems in peace, but I didn't. I failed to comprehend my own emotions and behaviour, let alone explain them to him, so I played the victim, despite knowing that it would only make things more difficult later.

'I'm sorry. I just have a lot going on now, you know, with my parents away and with this new girl, Myra or something, trying to steal my spotlight in the Literary Club. I just feel exhausted and all over the place.'

'It's okay. You don't need to be sorry. I knew that not going on a vacation might have you in low spirits but I had no idea about this Literary Club thing. I just heard of a new girl coming in but nothing specific. And don't say that she'll steal your spotlight. She can't. Nobody ever can.' Having said that with every sign of tender affection, he curled his fingers around my face ever so gently, looking me in the eye with an: 'I'm here for you', and slowly brushed his soft lips against mine. He draped both his arms around me lovingly and we smooched for around two minutes. I could feel his heart racing in his chest as it pressed against mine, and his kisses gradually glided from my lips down to my neck. But instead of feeling any sparks of electricity or passion like usual, guilt washed over me like a tide that was long overdue and perhaps being boycotted by me because I hated dealing with reality. There was love in the way he kissed me and held his arms around my waist, but I simply couldn't requite. 'It'll all be okay,' he whispered into my ear as he licked my earlobe. Before I knew it, tears slid down my cheeks, reached my neck, and found his lips. He detached his lips from my neck and looked at me, concerned. I didn't say much, except pulling him into an embrace and lying, 'I've missed you.'

There were ten minutes for the bell to ring and our Economics teacher to finally stop lecturing us on the crippling economy of India and what we must learn from other developed countries. Arj and I were sitting on the same bench, next to each other. Economics and English were the only two classes we had in common. While the two of us fixated our eyes on Mr. Agarwal, it was but a mere pretense of concentration. His right hand was on the table in a triangle, resting chin on his palm and balancing his elbow on the table, while the left one rested on my right thigh, stroking gently to comfort me after our emotional moment in the washroom stall.

'You see, inflation in our country occurs now more frequently than floods in Assam. It's truly a shame. We just have five minutes left. Any que— are you alright, Alaina? You've been staring at me blankly for the past thirty minutes. Are you facing any difficulties with this unit?', asked Mr. Agarwal in a pitiful tone, breaking my train of thought.

Frankly, I was not alright. I was miles from being anywhere near the station of 'alright'. The talk in the washroom stall with Arj was not just emotional, but it was a confrontation with myself and my feelings. Feelings that I had been subconsciously running away from for more months than it should've been. It was not that I had not cried in front of him before. But I had never been vulnerable— not in the complete sense of it— in front of him ever before. I had met with the epiphany which I should've found months ago, but me being me, I procrastinated encountering my feelings. It was not just about a dearth of communication in our relationship, but the fact that I was not willing to put any effort to fight the dearth. I was not willing to fight for us. I realised at that moment when he kissed me, more beautifully and tenderly than I'd ever been kissed before, that I had lost feelings for him. He was the most attractive, hot, and handsome athlete that any girl would feel infatuated towards. And so did I. But you'd expect these athletes to be hard on the inside, available physically and not emotionally, from the image of them engendered by popular media. However, Arj was different. I had never been with someone *different* before. As fantastic an athlete as he was, he was also a fantastic lover. He was loyal, kind, caring, and very affectionate, so much so that I could never bring myself to truly believe that I was dating such a gentleman. I was lusting for him for so long that it was the only thing I was holding on to. And since being single was treated as being a loser, the peer pressure suppressed any questions of whether I was actually happy or not; whether I actually wanted it or not. And

I know that I have no right to play the victim anymore. I was seventeen years old— mature enough to make my own decisions. I could no longer go hunting for excuses when reality stood right in front of me, ready to slap me across the face and unfasten my eyes from dreaming of an imaginary utopia. But for that, I'd have to take his bonafide and benevolent heart and stab a dagger into it. So, throughout the Econ class, I was staring at our teacher because I'd nowhere else to look. Every head around the classroom would, in some distant way or another, remind me of how bad a person I was. In addition, my mind was so caught in a labyrinth of contemplation that I barely was conscious of where my eyes were looking. But I was not a lunatic that I'd say all of that to my teacher, so I white lied again, 'Everything's okay, Sir. Just a little tired.'

'Well, don't hesitate to reach out to me if you have any doubts.'

'Sure thing, Sir.'

*****

We were assembled around Mrs. Whayton in a circle, all the members of the club. Myra was sitting diametrically across from me. I avoided eye contact with her as much as possible, but she kept stealing glances from me intermittently. Mrs. Whayton was not one to trifle time, so as soon as she saw that we had all settled down and were readily seated for a discussion, she began speaking with an accent that sounded like American sprinkled over with some drops of British and said, 'I hope that you all are well-aware of why we've all gathered here today. My dear budding writers, it's the time of the year when we begin working on the school's annual magazine publication. This year, after several rounds of discourse, the principal, along with the management, has agreed upon the theme of 'Artem', meaning, of course, 'Art'. With this comes tremendous responsibility on our shoulders and we expect to receive over a hundred submissions of poetry, plays, prose, articles, and so on. However, the restrictions of the number of pages do not sanction any more than sixty pieces of writing. Now, we are fifteen members here, excluding me, obviously. I want fifteen of the sixty pieces featured to be from the members of our club mandatorily. If possible, even more. So, put your creative caps on and get the ink flowing on paper. Write about anything you like, but make sure that it's worth reading. If you have queries or seek my reviews before finalising on a submission, email me anytime during this vacation. I will certainly respond. You may leave now, except Miss Myra and Miss Alaina.'

Not again. What now? Just when I thought I'd not have to see her for another forty days, Mrs. Whayton really had to add her element of surprise.

I stood up from my seat and waited in a stationary position there till the room contained only the three of us and Mrs. Whayton addressed us, in the hope that I could leave without having to exchange words with Myra. But by now I was pretty sure that either this bitch was obsessed with me or she had been planning my murder because she walked across the room towards me and stood beside me. Could she not discern the flags? I did not want to speak with her. I wanted nothing to do with her. But she would come to hobnob with me at every chance she got.

'So, ladies,' started Mrs. Whayton, in a valley girl accent this time, 'you both are two of the best writers in our school and I think the respective styles of your writing will beautifully complement each other for the theme in hand. I want the two of you to team up for the editorial board for this year's magazine, as well as contribute three pieces to it, one each to be written individually, and the third, a collaborative composition. You have quite a long break ahead of you, and I'm sure you'll be able to find plenty of time to work together. Coordinate among yourselves. All submissions that I receive will be emailed to both of you. I hope that you're willing to help me with editing and shortlisting the writings.'

One thing I knew with absolute certainty about Mrs. Whayton was that she derived immense pleasure from breaking into long, tedious oration in situations that did not call for it. I was waiting for Myra to respond but she didn't for about a solid minute, and I figured that she must've been puzzled by the amount of content Miss. Whayton can inundate into a single speech. So, I took charge of filling the uncomfortable silence with some sound, and said, 'Yes, Ma'am. We'll be happy to work in the editorial team and I cannot begin to tell you how beholden I am to you for this opportunity. Thank you,' I paused for a few moments, and turned to my now co-editor, and continued, 'from both of us."

With a smile of approval, Mrs. Whayton left the room, leaving behind just the two of us. Although I had no desire to talk to Myra, it seemed like the universal law of attraction had played a UNO reverse card on me. She finally seemed to be finding her voice again, and said to me, 'Thank you for that. I mean, for responding to Mrs. Whayton. I was just so bumfuzzled by her words that I could hardly process any of them.' There was a hint of nervousness in her voice that her deliberate way of speaking had failed to obliterate. One part of my mind thought, 'She's cute!', while another groaned in disgust for even entertaining such a thought.

'It's all good. So, we should exchange our numbers now, I think. We'll coordinate the rest of it later,' I replied as civilly as possible, trying to conceal the haste in my voice for I desperately did wish to run homeward and just go to sleep, in an attempt to evade the chaos which was today.

We exchanged numbers on small pieces of paper torn from the corners of a notebook which I was sure to lose in a matter of minutes, given my careless and forgetful nature, but she'd still have my number, so I was not much fretful about whether or not we'd maintain contact over the summer. But I definitely was fretting over *how* that would go.

FIVE

Slumber Party

The slumber party had completely slipped out of my mind. In fact, the car ride and the morning at the cafeteria seemed to be occurrences of weeks ago. The only two things fresh in my memory and consciousness were Arj and Myra, while the two didn't have anything to do with each other, but at the same time, it felt like they *could* have everything to do with each other. I would've slept through the evening and seen daylight the next morning had Sasha not rang me up four times, for the sound of the call woke me up from sleep only the fourth time. I was convinced, for the first three times, that there was music in my dreams. After having Sash shriek into my eardrums to hurry up and rush downstairs, I rose from bed with painful effort, barely repressing the desire to just fall back on the bed again. She had apparently been waiting to pick me up for over an hour. My head was still reeling from the dream I had just seen, with little fragments of it still flashing across my subconscious mind. It was a peculiar dream, nothing like I'd ever seen before. Usually, my dreams were an escape from reality, which, now that I read it, is the most basic definition of a dream. But it's true. I wasn't addicted to sleeping but I was addicted to dreaming. I'd sleep excessively to simply try and forget about what's actually happening and delve into a state of feeling light-headed, free, and serene. It was getting unhealthy and if I really thought about it carefully, it could be potentially growing into an addiction to sleeping itself. But today, as far as I remember, my dream more reminded me of reality than assisting me in forgetting about it, even if temporarily. I vaguely remember the presence of Arj and me, the scene including us fighting and sobbing. I cannot tell for sure if Alisha and Sash were there too. I didn't want to pressure my mind to recall more of it, because I only got all the more anxious in realising that now, even my dreams were dictating me to get my shit together.

The drive to Alisha's house was all over the place. I felt dazed and my vision was all hazy, despite having washed my face twice, splashing water vigorously to quash any remnants of a terribly realistic dream. I pulled down the car window and poked my head out into the busy nightlife of the city, all the while looking at the exquisite skyscrapers painting the dark firmament with golden and silver, and allowing the wind to ebb all the tension out of me. Sash was speaking to me throughout the forty-five minutes that the drive lasted, but her voice reached me in fuzzy words that I could only partially understand. So, I kept my answers brief, mostly in 'Yes' or 'No', even if it didn't sensibly answer most of her questions.

We got down the car and I finally took stock of the situation, i.e., my life. In short, for the next few weeks, I would have to communicate and work with someone I nearly despised, my relationship was on the verge of stability, and I was now finding myself incongruous at a slumber party that I had hardly even arrived at and to which I had not been looking forward whatsoever. The chaos made me just want to go to sleep and never have to wake up again, not in the implication of death but simply running away, like I always have, from my feelings and problems. But now it seemed to me that I couldn't anymore. Everything that I did, everywhere that I went, every person I encountered, was in some way reminding me of my cowardice, and in the back of my mind, I knew that there were more things that I had been boycotting for a long time that may not be slapping me in the face currently, but soon might be.

'Dude, are you okay? You look sick and dehydrated,' said Sasha in the elevator as we were ascending towards an absolute nightmare.

'I don't think so. I just feel so discombobulated and every thought in my head is adding up to a wilderness.'

'Do you wanna talk?'

'Yeah,' I replied wearily, as the elevator came to a halt and we both stepped out in sync, knowing in silence that the conversation would be continued once we were with Alisha.

The slumber party was very much like the image I had sketched in my mind, but just ten times over-glorified. There were neon lights of all colours glimmering around the house and disco lights shooting circular and other strange patterns on the walls. There was resonantly loud music playing, the one that would aggravate you had your neighbours been partying crazily adjacent to your house, and the kind that blocked your ears from perceiving any other sound, even if someone was screaming their lungs out into your ears, echoed through the house. Usually, Alisha didn't go too overboard with the lights and decoration. So, it was with some surprise that we entered her lavishly embellished house. As we made our way to Alisha's room, we came across their humongous dining table holding more dishes than the three of us could ever devour, and we saw all sorts of party decorations hanging around the house. It looked like we were expecting more company. *Exactly what I had been looking forward to, of course.*

Alisha was wearing a glittery silver short dress with a deep back cut, almost exposing her butt. Her hair was curled in gorgeous beachy waves and her face was glowing with make-up, finished perfectly with a red lipstick that indicated the classic tease of flirtation. Opposed to her, Sasha and I were dressed how you'd expect two girls to be clothed at a regular sleepover. I was anticipating that we'd be watching movies, talking a whole lot, eating, drinking, shouting, dancing, playing games and having a tonne of fun, just like our past sleepovers, because 'slumber party' technically was synonymous to a sleepover. But boy, was I mistaken. It seemed that Alisha had taken the word 'party' in slumber party way too seriously. I was literally in pyjamas and a crop top, with my hair up in a messy bun, the pink scrunchie unstably holding my hair in place, and my face looking half-dead, only saved by the concealer that successfully concealed all the stress under my eyes. I was in flip-flops while Alisha was flaunting her sexy legs in four-inched pencil heels. Sasha, holding a much similar perspective about a slumber party as me, was wearing a basic tee paired with denim jeans and a pair of slippers, with her hair down and her face devoid of any cosmetics. In order of ranking, it would be Alisha, followed by Sasha, followed by me, with Alisha looking like she was going to a red carpet and me looking like I had just woken up, which I in fact had.

Sasha and I stood stunned at the threshold to Alisha's room, as she made her way from her dressing table in a catwalk, fixing her beachy waves like a diva and not even taking notice of the homeless beggars standing at her door until walking to a spot right in front of us. The diva expression from her visage dissipated into a bewildered shock. She looked at us from head to toe like we were outcasts. We were playing a 'Who can stare at whom with a more intense expression of bewilderment?' for about three minutes till Sasha finally broke the silence, 'YOU DID NOT TELL US WE HAD TO DRESS UP LIKE BARBIES!'

'Nor did you tell us that we were expecting more company,' I added.

'I-I thought you'd know,' Alisha stuttered, not knowing how to deal with the fiasco of miscommunication she'd brought on, yet continuing still, 'and it's only Ray, Arj and Kiara I've invited. I thought y'all wouldn't mind a little surprise!'

'WHAT THE FUCK, ALISHA?! Have you gone absolutely bonkers?'. Just when I was beginning to think that I could unwind tonight and forget about what happened in school today with Arj, not more than six hours ago, my dear best friend invited him over.

'Why on earth would you invite Kiara? You don't even know her!', Sasha barked.

'Well haven't you been *talking* to her?!'

'That doesn't give you any right to make conclusions about how our private lives are going and if we want to see them or not!'. My brain could actually burst at that point.

'And now we're at this extravaganza of a slumber party looking like we belong to the streets!'. Sasha seemed to be losing it too. Although in scattered pieces, I recall Sasha mentioning in the car about how she didn't appreciate Alisha always trying to sneak a peek into her romantic affairs and popularise the matter, so, I could comprehend where all that rage was stemming from.

'Okay, umm, calm down please. The others don't arrive till another twenty minutes. So, I can quickly give you both a makeover. You can wear my clothes and it'll all be fine.'

'Doesn't look like there's another option here, does it?', Sasha remarked with a waspish air.

'Where are your parents, by the way?', I asked inquiringly, as we walked to her room, because I knew very well that they'd never in a lifetime give sanction for their house to be decorated like a near brothel.

'They have gone out to some lavish business party that will go on until at least three in the morning.'

And with that, we finally crossed the threshold and headed inside her room, knowing that it was going to be a long, long night.

*****

We were in the living room, swaying our hips and swinging our hands to our favourite music. Lights were shining in a bouncing manner and the whole world around me seemed to be revolving. I think Kiara and Ray had come, because I could spot with my peripheral vision two people making out and other two dancing away in madness, and it was easy to guess which pair was involved in what action. Arj probably still had not arrived yet, but at this point I wasn't bothered. In all month, I had not felt as free and relaxed as I did at that moment, with every cell in my body dancing to every beat of the music. I was not a prolific dancer, but I still loved dancing. The slumber party was not so bad, after all. It was surprisingly liberating to be dancing in a club-like environment which was not thronged with sweaty bodies as in an actual club. My vision was hazy, probably because Alisha had made me gulp down two shots, saying, 'Don't be a teeto, you just have one life, babe!'. I might have resisted initially but I cannot recall what followed. My memory was in fragments, flying too haphazardly over the place for me to piece anything together. No sooner than I had presumed that I could escape an undesirable encounter with Arj, I felt his strong arms curl around my waist into a warm hug. I knew it was him because I could feel the cold metal of his bracelet against my bare stomach. I was wearing a set of a pink crop top and pencil skirt, with knee-length boots, silver hoops hooked onto my ears, and my hair was down in the messiest way imaginable. He delicately planted a kiss on my cheek and I could feel the alcohol from his mouth dissolve into my skin in a shiver.

'You look beautiful,' he said in a croaky voice with hints of inebriation, one that would make me swoon within seconds a month ago, but had no effect on me that day. I hated it. I hated not being able to return what he gave me.

'But you haven't even seen me yet.'

'I don't have to see you to know that you are beautiful.'

These are the kinds of sentences anyone would want to hear from their significant other, and usually, be pleased by them. I don't have a count of how many compliments I received that night from him, but I was sure that they were more than enough to have any person levitating on the ninth cloud. But I wasn't, and every time he complimented me, my heart broke bit by bit. Though, I haven't really ever been on the receiving side of a heartbreak, I can bet it must be excruciatingly painful to suffer through. But to be on the giving end wasn't much better either. While the heartbroken are mostly sympathised with and even pitied over at times, the heartbreakers are generally seen as flag bearers of callousness. Well, there might be some who deliberately hurt the sentiments of others without repenting, but I was one of those who was about to break a heart because I had misconstrued attraction as love. I knew that I'd have to do it soon. Break a heart. But not tonight. I was not ready. And maybe I still had some more of my own feelings to confront. And Arj definitely didn't deserve to get his heart broken on a night he seemed to be so happy.

We plunged into the hot tub at around midnight. I had completely forgotten to carry a swimsuit with me, so, I dipped in Alisha's dress. She laughed it off and reassured me that she didn't mind her dressing getting wet, but I knew that when sober, she would be absolutely inflamed. Hopefully, I would leave her house right before she would take notice the next morning. We chatted, drank, and laughed for a while till Ray and Alisha began getting too comfortable once again and the rest of us groaned disgustedly, forcing them to get out of the tub and find someplace more private. For the next few minutes, the remaining four of us— Arj, Kiara, Sash and I conversed about life and school, our plans for the summer, and anything that came up in our intoxicated minds. In the process, I couldn't help but notice how Kiara looked at Sasha— amorously and wistfully— and how Sasha kept playing with Kiara's drenched hair. There was a growing heat in my chest and I couldn't tell if it was the temperature of the water against a satin dress or plausible jealousy brewing in me. But why would I be jealous? Was I only envying the connection that I lacked with Arj? I could not tell. Just as these searching questions were beginning to make my head ache, Arj distracted me by curling his hand around my waist and planting a kiss on my forehead. So, guilt washed over the battling thoughts in my mind once again.

It was nearly one in the morning when the music had stopped playing. Ray, Arj, and Kiara were preparing to leave because they had only come for the 'party', not the 'slumber'. The effect of alcohol gradually abated from my body and my vision gained focus once more. On the couch, Ray and Alisha were canoodling as usual, with pink neon lights glistening delicately on their faces. Sasha looked like she was releasing herself into deep conversations about life with Kiara in the balcony, the two of them staring into the firmament lit with stars and window lights, their hands entangled and playing with each other. Arj was devouring the scrumptious food cooked by Alisha's chefs. I decided to join him. I sidled down to sit next to him at the dining table and watched him eat with every sign of keen joy. If you looked at him for the first time, you'd have an impression that he was one of those athletic jerks that held a lot of arrogance because of their looks and their parents' bank accounts. But on getting to know him, you would realise that his personality and his mien were actually foil for each other. Before we started dating, we had been amazing friends for a year. I remember the first day he had arrived at school. He'd shifted from Vadodara because his father had a transferable job and had had a new posting in Mumbai. He was, by far, the most handsome boy my eyes had ever looked upon. Not even five seconds into glancing at him and my cheeks were tinged with a mix of deep pink and red. I had been too embarrassed to make eye contact, so I'd looked away. Mrs. Whayton had burdened (*blessed)* me with the opportunity to give him a school tour the day after he joined, and that's when we first exchanged words. I had indubitably developed an irrepressible crush on him which only amplified as days passed by. We developed an amazing bond of friendship and trust, which is probably why our relationship propagated strongly for the first few months. I looked at his eyes from the side, at the relish that glimmered in his pupils as he took a mouthful of a slice of cheese pizza, at the purity of his soul, and wished in silence that I wouldn't lose a great friendship. I didn't realise that I was smiling at the sight of him eating until I let out a little laugh when some cheese slid out of his mouth, and he hadn't even noticed my presence till my laughter rang louder than the sound of his chewing.

'Since when were you staring at me, stalker?'

'For the past fifteen minutes, maybe. You chose the smell of pizza over my perfume. I feel betrayed,' I teased in a jocular manner.

‘Forgive me, Princess, for I have sinned. May I make it up to you?’

‘I’m afraid you’ve missed your chance.’

‘I’m afraid that’s not the case.’

He finished eating the pizza slice, grabbed the wooden frame under the seat of my chair, and pulled it towards him. His hands then slowly travelled their way up from my thighs to my waist, resting there for a while, and finally up to my face, all the while locking his eyes with mine. We kissed and made out for a while, with so much passion from his end that regret only magnified in my heart. Every touch of his lips against my skin was a reminder of how wrong I was to lead him on. To lie to him. When our lips parted, we hugged. He said that he loved me and I replied that I loved him too, which I did, with all my heart, just not in the same way as he did.

Once everyone else had left and it was only the three of us, we finally felt relieved. It was a fun night, and when the alcohol kicks in, you automatically forget about all your woes and worries and just want to ‘live in the moment’ (which was a phrase I was strongly opposed to in sobriety). 'That went unexpectedly well,' Sasha said, releasing a breath she seemed to be holding in for quite long.

'So, all the energy that you spent shouting at me went in vain,' Alisha replied, curling her lips in sneer.

'I never said that it was okay for you to throw a party when all we wanted to do was talk. We've lost four hours.'

'Psssht! Stop coming at me always! I know you had a great time with Kiara, Alaina with Arj and me with Ray, and of course, all together. So, let's look on the bright side now, we still have four hours more. It's two now. Let's please change into PJs and go to my room?'

I was not that person who tried finding optimism when things were negatively spoken of, but I was also too tired to go haywire again. So, without revolt, I walked towards Alisha's room, and eventually, Sasha followed too.

The AC was at 16 degrees and the comforter was pulled up to our chins. Faint music found its way in through the casements from a gathering on the other side of the city, probably the party Alisha's parents were attending, having lost most of its intensity in traversing between towering buildings and hanging wires, its presence was nearly null unless you focused really hard on it.

Resuming our conversation from the elevator four hours ago, Sasha asked me, ‘So, why is your life chaotic, Alaina?’

‘So many reasons, where do I start?’

‘When did this happen? What am I missing?’, Alisha questioned, as we had expected her to.

‘Nothing, A. Sasha and I specially paused our conversation to make sure you didn’t miss out on anything. As for my life, it’s a huge mess. I think I might be breaking up with Arj.’ Alisha gasped at this while Sasha furrowed her eyebrows, as if asking, ‘Why, though?’. Ignoring their unspoken comments, I continued, ‘I don’t know if I love him anymore. I don’t think I ever did to begin with. It was mere infatuation and we all know attraction dies before it's even fully born. It isn’t enough fuel to drive a serious relationship. The worst part is that I'm pretty sure he’s in love with me, and I do NOT want to break his heart or pity him, but I also don't want to cage myself into something compulsively nor do I want to lie to someone I care about. But I don't want to lose an amazing friend in the process either. To add fuel to the fire, while I'm still trying to figure out my feelings and the future of this relationship, I've to deal with this new girl, Myra, who is an insufferable teacher's pet and has found a way to make my life more troublesome than it already is! She's just everywhere. I see her in the corridors, in the Literary Club, in the washroom and even in the mornings when I spot her waiting to take the bus. She lives near my house, can you imagine? Plus, she's apparently Mrs. Whayton's new favourite and is on an accelerating path to replace me as the Head of the Club, and if I think more about her or Arj even for one more second, I think my head will burst open!'.

Alisha and Sasha stared at me strangely for several minutes. They appeared to be taken aback with shock, with their mouths open to roughly form an 'O' and their minds trying to process what I'd just said. They were probably not expecting me to launch into such a long rant. On the other hand, I was finally put at ease to some extent. I had been bottling these thoughts up for so long that had I not talked about them to someone, I would've actually lost my mind. I looked at them expectantly for some time, then relinquished, realising I'd have to remind them to tell me something and not just stare at me like I was a nutter.

'SAY SOMETHING FOR FUCK'S SAKE!' That came out way more aggressively than how it had sounded in my head, but it had the desired effect, despite having made the two girls jump slightly from their places.

Sasha took the lead and answered my aggressively long oration, 'Firstly, you bombarded us with a whole lotta info which is difficult to register all at once. A disclaimer would've been nice. Secondly, jokes apart, I don't really know what to tell you about relationship issues because I have never been in a real one. I'm scared of exactly what you described: things going astray or losing feelings. That's why I only have flings. You see, I am taking things very slow with Kiara to figure out my own feelings whether I really like her or is it just infatuation. But since for you, the damage is already done, I'd say the best thing to do is not to delay the break-up. It'll only be more painful by the time you delay it. And about that girl, Mira? Myra? Anyway, I don't think it's that big a deal. It's not her fault she writes well. I think all of this happening together is making you irrational.'

Her words were a massive welt on my chest. Was she lying? No. Did I want to believe her? Also, no. Why is it that dwelling on the truth you want to hear is much easier than facing the actual truth? Also, why can't the truth you want to hear be the actual truth? I don't know much about the Universal Law of Attraction, but one thing I'm certain about is that it will never work in my favour.

Before I could even gracefully accept defeat, Alisha slashed her sword and said, 'Well, I don't agree with what Sash said. Look, even I felt a relationship slump with Ray for the past few days, but today, everything was back to normal again. The sparks were all there. You'll get over it. Just give it some time. And there's seriously something wrong with that bitch you talked about. I noticed her staring at the three of us chatting in the corridor the other day. Very sus. Dunno what she's up to. Don't like her.'

Alisha's perspective was like a sword made of wood. I definitely did not want to hear the first part, nor did I see eye to eye with her on the 'sparks' matter. For her, sparks meant the heat of the physical relationship. To me, emotional attachment secured a higher rank. And although all the kissing and making out was fun, anyone with the right skill and expertise could nail that. But love didn't come from everyone. I don't think she could even comprehend what I meant. That was the sword. The second part of her perspective was the wood, harmless and most welcome.

As an awkward silence crept into the room, I realised that it was now my turn to talk again.

'I think I just want to explore myself, my feelings, and my sexuality for now. I don't even know what *I* want because I've always been so busy doing what others like or what's in trend. And despite the negative vibes that I get from Myra, I have to come to terms with the fact that I have to work with her this summer.' No sooner had I completed the sentence than I registered what I had just said. The words seemed to have tumbled out involuntarily, having surprised me as much as they did Sasha and Alisha. The former had an expression of confusion sitting on her face whereas Alisha looked at me in bewilderment, like I had uttered the stupidest thing ever. 'Have you lost it? You just lost some interest in your relationship and you want to end it all instead of trying to figure out the problem?', Alisha asked in a tone that had judgement written all over it.

'No, I have NOT lost it but I will if I don't do the right thing, which is to find a way to tell him that this cannot work out anymore without breaking his heart. And I HAVE figured out the problem. It's me! I rushed into things. I have just been in one relationship before this and you know why it failed? Because it was all about lust. And this time it's not that, and I don't know how to deal with it!'

Alisha had almost opened her mouth to argue when Sasha interjected, 'You said you'll have to work with Myra this summer. What do you mean?'

'Yeah, that. Mrs. Whayton has placed the two of us in the editorial team for this year's magazine.'

'That must be the last thing you want, but congratulations on getting the position! I know you've dreamt of it since I met you.' At least Sasha made an attempt to understand how I was feeling despite being against my opinion on the theme of Myra.

'Ye—,' I began to answer but Alisha cut me, 'Babe, you are not the problem. You're just jumping to conclusions too quickly. Go on a date with him tomorrow and bring him back to your house and see whether the spark is still alive. I bet you'll come crawling up to me to thank me.'

'Oh my GOD! ALISHA! Are you even listening to yourself? Not everyone is like you! Not everyone just desires kissing and making out and whatnot in a relationship! It's also about FEELINGS. Love, ever felt that? Bet you haven't. Just for once, without being dominating, can you try to look through my lens and understand how I'm feeling? He was almost like my guy best friend and now I have to break his heart just because I misunderstood love as infatuation because that's what all the craze is about, isn't it? That's what teenagers are running after: hookups and losing their virginities before turning eighteen. Maybe I don't want that and I don't want to chase what everyone else is chasing. But I can't, because then I'll be outcast, won't I?'

I don't know if anybody said anything after that because I spontaneously got up and left the room. I think Sasha may have called out and asked me where I was going, and I had answered that I had no idea. Or I probably didn't answer verbally but in my head I did. Finding my way to the living room, I laid down on the couch, too exhausted to think any further. My eyes shut without command and I could faintly hear the click of the door to Alisha's room close, but I was too tired to be bothered. Sleep came to me slowly as I felt less and less conscious of my surroundings till it was pitch black under my eyelids.

SIX

Hot Chocolate Tinkles

A week had passed since the argument. I had not left my room except for meals and I had forgotten to eat my breakfast twice. Whatever chaos I had found myself in a week ago had only amplified to become ten times worse. I felt trapped in a labyrinth of my thoughts, my anxiety, and my fear of dealing with reality. A week had passed by as if at the drop of a hat. I had no idea how. My memory was floating like scattered clouds with no destination. I think Sasha woke me up from the couch at six in the morning, merely two hours after sleep had kicked in, and drove me back home. We might've exchanged a few words and I remember her telling me something about Alisha flying into a rage after I had stormed out of the room and spending the rest of the morning in silence. As soon as I reached home, I made my way to my room and went to bed. I kept feeling groggy and disoriented for the remaining days of the week and completely avoided opening my phone. Sparsh may have infrequently tried to check in on me to know if I was still alive, but most times the door was locked and I was slumbering away in anxiety, or reading Jane Austen, or quoting Shakespeare to distract myself from the commotion in my head.

It was Friday. Exactly a week after. To think of it now, I probably should've apologized right away the next day. While I still didn't see eye to eye with Alisha, I would admit that I uttered some of the most bitter words to her in all years of our friendship (which had probably hit an iceberg now). It's not like we never argued before. We did, several times indeed, because it's impossible for two people to hold a similar perspective on every matter. But we never scuffled nor shouted at each other. Well, I was the one doing most of the shouting. I was still feeling intoxicated on the day right after, even after having slept for over ten hours. I had no will to pick up the phone and ring her up. Ego and pride slithered in as well. *She could've called, but she didn't,* I thought. But I didn't think that perhaps *I could be the bigger person and resolve this thing before it could worsen.* And it did probably worsen for it had been a week and I had not been in contact with anyone or anything else but my thoughts. I may have over-assessed the situation, turning a molehill into a mountain, but it felt good to hide. It felt good to sleep through days straight and not do anything, because I was too anxious about what I'd have to wake up to.

Mom and Dad would be returning home next week and they would be discombobulated to see me in such a disorderly spirit, wearing unchanged clothes on a body that hadn't bathed for over three days and hair looking like a wrecked mesh that hadn't felt the touch of a comb for a week. I had woken up before the alarm clock went off. With all the extra sleeping I had been indulging in the past few days, my eyes voluntarily unfastened at five in the morning. I got out of bed, unwillingly and with painful effort, and took a brief look at myself in the mirror. I looked horrible. There was mascara dripping down my lashes still. Had I cried? I had no idea. Staring at my uncombed hair and filthy clothes, I realized that I had made things more complicated than they already were. Sometimes you don't have your emotions under your sway and you might burst out involuntarily. Now, I am not saying it's okay to go around shouting and screaming at people because your life is a mess and since you're too afraid to blame yourself, you shoot the gun of allegation at them. It probably wasn't okay, but it also wasn't controllable. I had known, even while uttering those words, that Alisha wouldn't get it. Because her views on romance were drastically different from mine. But at the same time, I couldn't help but wonder, *shouldn't true friendship be able to withstand a conflict of interest every now and then?* I knew I was in the wrong but I didn't feel she was in the right either. For some reason, I felt like she was forcing me to feel something that I didn't and wouldn't— like she was forcing me to follow her. Whether or not this was the case, as I was gazing into my own gaze in the looking glass into what seemed like an unending spiral, I understood that I could no more crawl into my hideaway. Maybe I had over-assessed the situation and created a mountain out of a molehill, but it felt good to stay hidden, away from the noise I had brought on myself.

I brimmed the tub with ice-cold water and soaked myself completely into it. The water struck against my body in a splash, hitting every corner of my skin, reinvigorating every cell in my body, hugging all my flaws, and un-knotting the mesh of thoughts that spiraled around my head. All the stress and strain receded out as my limbs floated weightlessly. It was so strange. The coldness of the water rendered me a warmth I hadn't felt anywhere else despite it being summer. I felt relaxed. The first monsoons hydrating the parched earth after a drought; the roots which had lost their ways in quest of a few drops of relief feeling alive once again; rain rattling vigorously against tin roofs; the farmer letting out a bellow of joy as the showers summoned him to the fields where he'd sweated and sweltered for a bountiful harvest. An infant chortling, amused, in the mother's melodies of lullaby. All things beautiful and mirthful. I felt like I was a child again, away from the vile world, feeling invincible in the embrace of my parents. And although I knew in the back of my mind that the peace was ephemeral, much like the calm before the storm, I intended to sink myself into every inch of it before it ended.

No sooner had I stepped out of the shower than Sparsh was knocking at the door, asking in an excessively loud voice if I was going to have breakfast, to which I replied, 'Yes!', and I heard him gasp. I had hardly spoken any words since last Friday, even if the two of us reside under the same roof. He didn't deserve this torture of having to check in on me and not receive any response. I felt guilty and decided to begin my first apology of the day with him. It was not until we were halfway through breakfast when I realised that it was only six in the morning and Sparsh was up early. Way earlier than he should be, considering that it was summer break.

'What are you doing rising and shining at six in the morning?'

'I was expecting more of a 'Thank you so much, Sparsh, for cooking a delicious breakfast, you're the best brother ever' but I forgot that it's you.'

'You cooked this?! Scrambled eggs, grilled cheese, and chocolate-covered strawberries? Are you kidding me? You're right, I owe you both gratitude and an apology. Thank you for taking the pain of checking up on me when I was literally in the worst slump, and I'm sorry for being unresponsive. You're an amazing brother and I love you.'

‘Woah there, slow down. You went overboard, but umm, welcome, I guess? Also, what happened though? At that slumber party, I mean?’

‘It was a disaster. In brief, I have finally come to terms with the fact that I am not in love with my boyfriend of eleven months, I fought with my best friends, well mainly Alisha, and haven’t spoken to anyone for a week. The deets are too tedious to go into.’

‘Damn, the brief was heavy enough. I don’t think I wanna hear the deets anyway. Plus, Mom and Dad have been calling you every day. No wonder you haven’t received their calls either. Call them back, they’re worried.’

‘Oh, fuck! My phone has been on silent and I haven't really opened it. What am I going to tell them?’

‘Tell them you had diarrhoea or something.’

‘Ewww, no!’

‘Do you have any better ideas, then?’

'Diarrhoea it is, then,' I said, accepting defeat, but instantly remembering that he dodged my initial question, 'But why are you up, though?'

'Why can I not be awake at six?'

'Cause you're Sparsh, which basically means a sloth who doesn't open his eyes before noon during summer holidays.'

'Okay, that was a little too harsh!'

'You know I'm just joking! Now, tell me honestly, why on god's green earth are you up at this hour?'

'I've been, uhh, talking to this new guy, and we're supposed to meet now because we're both scared of being seen. We're not ready yet, if you know what I mean.'

'Yes, of course. So, you've been getting all this action while I've been sleeping like a lethargic cow. Oh wait, is that why you were so desperate to talk to me? To get boy advice? Not that you were actually concerned about my existence? I'm offended.'

'Not exactly, c'mon, you're my elder sister. I do care about you.'

'There are lies written all over your face, but okay, I'll let that pass. But you need to tell me everything after this early-morn rendezvous with your supposed lover,' I teased, winking at him.

By the time Sparsh had left, it was six-thirty and I proceeded to my room. I opened my closet and searched for a cute summer dress. Putting on a beige flowy dress, I sat in front of my concave mirror and applied some sunscreen on my face. Painting my lips with a baby pink shade that aligned with the soft blush on my cheeks, I curled my lashes outward in deep black mascara, hooked some earrings on, and hung a pendant around my neck. I was not heading out anywhere, definitely not at seven in the morning. But there was something so satisfying about rising early and delving into something productive, or something that made you feel good about yourself. I didn't *intend* to go outside later either. Physical contact with anyone seemed like a bad idea till I had not resolved my issues. I just dressed up because it made me feel happy on finally emerging out of my hideaway, and it was an additional way to delay checking my phone.

There were fifty missed calls. Fifty missed calls in seven days, of which twenty were from Mom and Dad combined, seven from Arj, ten from Sasha, ten from Alisha and three from an unrecognisable number. The huge numbers piled up at the top didn't intrigue me. It was the unknown number lying at the bottom of the list of missed calls that had rung me every alternative day since Saturday that prompted me to click on it. So, I did. After about a minute of waiting on the line, somebody picked up and said, 'Hello?', in a mellow morning voice, creased with a peculiar hoarseness. I wasn't expecting the call to be answered so early in the day. I didn't respond for a solid thirty seconds because I had completely zoned out. There was something about that voice that evoked a certain longing in me, like I wanted to hear it repeatedly, and like I could never get tired of listening to it. Hearing no response, she spoke again, as if asking the silence to answer back, 'Hello?'. This time her voice lacked the previous hoarseness and I could hear the vibrations of her vocal cord distinctly as she uttered the two-syllable word. 'Hey,' I answered in a tone that struck a chord of mirth, and it was then that I realised that my lips had twisted in a smile on hearing her sweet, raspy voice.

'Alaina?'

'Uh, yes?'

'Oh, hi, it's seven in the morning. I mean, hi, this is Myra, you know—'

'Yes, I know, from the Literary Club. I'm so sorry for having missed your calls. It's just been a really messed up week and I was trying to keep away from toxicity as much as possible,' and at the exact moment I finished that sentence, I realised that I might've spilled too much information to someone I had barely had one proper conversation with.

'Oh,' she answered in a puzzled air.

'So, umm, Myra, why don't we meet up today?' This was the only way I found to divert her attention from what I had just blurted out. Brainstorming is difficult when you're put on the spot.

'Yes, that would be great. How about the Rosé Café in town?'

'Yeah, the place has a soothing aura and isn't very crowded. Rosé Café it is, then.'

'But when?'

'For brunch?'

'Okay. See you later today. Bye.'

'Bye.'

I spent the remnant of the morning starting with some school projects and writing in my journal. It had been a week since I had skimmed through its pages or penned something down on it. It would usually be about some made-up scenario that I'd imagine in my head or about topics that I held staunch opinions about. Picking out a pen from my pen holder, I turned to a fresh new page and began writing. For the first time, I didn't stop in between to think or analyse or critique or gather my thoughts in one place. For the first time, although my thoughts felt like they could be fluttering all over my brain in all directions, they seemed to collectively find their ways back on the paper in curves and straight lines, blotting the dirty white paper in pitch-black ink. And once my brain finally commanded my hand that it was time to stop, that all that had to be said was said and if I said any more, I would fail to understand myself, I placed the pen back in its shed and read the words in front of me. My thoughts didn't seem to be dancing around now. They stood still in one place, sentences giving meaning to them and each paragraph connecting me to three separate feelings which the paper in front of me was screaming out loudly: loss, ego, and confusion. A sense of loss crept in stealthily at first but now hit me like a truck. And I was scared. At stake was losing two people who had both differently shaped my life and made it seem more enjoyable than it'd be without them: Arj and Alisha. Was I ready to let go of them? Life had been hell the past two weeks. I had never questioned if I was in a controlling friendship, had my own words, thanks to the alcohol, not slapped me with an epiphany. But I still was trying to convince myself that I might be over-evaluating the situation. The other loss seemed inevitable and I was holding on to one last string of hope, that maybe it was all imagined, that maybe I indeed *was in love* with him, or maybe I still had time to entertain romantic feelings before we hit rock bottom. But from reading my own words, I realised that I had boarded a ship of lust all along, and I had not known what love could be. In fact, I had anticipated a break-up all along too, because I had foolishly predicted that this would end like my last relationship, with no hearts breaking, just a couple of petty teenage fights which I'd perceive much later to be imbecile and immature, some tears would be shed and after some gossip and bitching about how bad the relationship was anyway, I'd feel better again.

The first time I had encountered loss was when Granny had passed away three years back. I was fourteen. Although I was mature enough then to know what death was, I had not understood what death could inflict upon a person. I still don't understand. There was crying, screaming, burning, excruciating pain, and emotional turmoil to sum it up briefly. Despite having seen Granny's health deteriorate perniciously over two years, despite knowing that her call to mortality was not very far away, we weren't ready that day when we walked into her room in the morning to lend her a hand to get out of bed and have breakfast with us, only to find out that she would never wake up again. Mom mildly shook her shoulders repeatedly and Dad tried to wake her up by splashing water on her face. Sparsh still hadn't woken up and as for me, I just stood there, by her bed, frozen, eyes glaring into the zilch that had become of her soul and my voice lost somewhere in the bottom of my belly, not to find its way up to my throat again for the rest of the day. Loss by death and loss by anagapesis or alienation may not stand in the position to be compared to each other, but they both sting deeply. You still probably won't ever speak with the person, and even if you do, it would be no better than conversing with a stranger. You no longer get to hang out with them or even see them as frequently as you used to. Permanent loss is irreversible but when the loss is right in front of you, breathing and smiling, living and thriving, you wonder what it'd be like if that one bifurcation had not come in your paths, if things would perhaps never get so complicated, if you could've been sharing those breaths and smiles with them. There'll be bittersweet nostalgia and again grounding yourself that whatever happened was meant to be, but you cannot stop your ever-wandering mind from retracing its path back to a time you both didn't seem so distant after all, and wish silently, even if by a minuscule amount, that nothing had changed.

Ego and loss, though sounding like they could possibly have nothing to do with each other, were unendingly intertwined in my respect. I could perhaps prevent one loss from taking action by letting go of my ego, but that also meant compromising on my opinion just so that I could fit into someone else's world. I could relinquish my ego but it'd have to be bilateral. And I felt a strong indication thumping in my chest and causing a churning unrest in my throat that that wouldn't be the case.

Of the three, confusion won the lion's share. I was confused about it all. Should I really be letting go of my ego or wait till she lets go of hers? Should I really be jumping to conclusions or wait to spot any future in the horizon of my and Arj's relationship? But I was most confused about my feelings towards Myra, bolstered by the call this morning. Was I really not fond of her or was it merely childish jealousy that had been driving me insane? Was there really anything suspicious about her or was she just trying to be amiable, much like any new body in an already-established crowd would want to be? If I did dislike her, why did I feel nervous around her?

I despised this state of conundrum I was trapped in for the past two weeks, whose inimical nature I had failed to perceive until it had reached its crux. I was staring blankly into my journal, regretting that I had even entertained the thought of penning down my feelings, because as things became less hazy, I could now understand that my life was not so 'set' after all. The regularity had been disrupted, and although I might've been seeking an adventurous escape from the dull undertones of humdrum, I had definitely not imagined it in this way.

It was only when our house-help had been knocking at my door for ten minutes that I travelled back to the present, out of my musings. He came in with a broom to clean my room which had been, he described and I quote, 'locked like a dungeon for days' and that he must clean it immediately. I chuckled lightly and told him to proceed with his cleaning marathon. He asked me if I would need the car for travel today because Sparsh had returned from his rendezvous and the driver was available for another two hours, after which he wished to go home. I quickly remembered the brunch I had promised to Myra. I said that I would need the car for some time, grabbed my bag with enough money for a brunch, tossed my phone and lipstick and portable deodorant in it, and headed out.

Surprisingly, I arrived earlier than her. The place was neither too crowded nor too empty. Perhaps we would have a peaceful discussion. I took a seat beside a humongous glass window that allowed me to view roads throng with wayfarers hurrying across before the lights turned green again and vehicles halted impatiently behind them. The walls of the cafe were painted in black and white with a vintage theme to them. There was a bookshelf loaded with over fifty books near the billing counter. On the table next to mine was seated a gorgeous couple, fingers playing with each other and smiling away in the delight of youthful love. A waiter came up to me and asked for my order and I answered, 'I'm waiting on someone, so a glass of water would suffice.'

After half an hour of intermittent glances at the streets and trying to muster my words in one place, forming sentences of what I'd say to her because I was completely unprepared for the work in hand, the glass doors of the cafe opened. She came in, eyes travelling around the room until they caught my being. She set her feet free from a stationary stance and walked towards me. A huge bag, like the ones that our mothers carry, swung down from her shoulder as she struggled to keep it from falling. She was wearing a lilac off-shoulder crop top paired with black trousers, her collarbones beautifully resting below her neck. Golden hoops hung down her ears and her lips were glossy with a pink tint. Her hair was down, frizzy and curly, hanging down till her butt, just like I had guessed the very first time I saw her, with ringlets flanking either side of her visage. She was not wearing her spectacles today. A strong lily scent infiltrated my nostrils as she approached. She reached *our* table and sat herself down on the chair opposite to mine, resting her bag on the floor, and with a wide smile that radiated optimism and exuberance, she said, 'Hi!'.

'Hi!', I answered, realising this was the first time I was voluntarily speaking to her.

'I'm so sorry for having kept you waiting. I was stuck in traffic. I had underestimated the time it would take to get here because I stay three blocks away.'

'Yeah, I know.'

'Huh?', she asked, her smile disappearing into perplexion.

'I mean, I saw you waiting at your stop for the bus one day. I stay a block away from you.'

'Oh, I didn't know!', she exclaimed, smiling once more.

But the thing was, I didn't just *see* her *once* waiting at the bus stop. I saw her one day and it grew into a habit to spot her every day, deliberately making sure she didn't spot me back. I could see her eyes distinctly now, not being concealed behind a pair of glasses. They were tranquil and happy. There was a certain spark of glee that you could only see if she wasn't wearing her spectacles, and it made me want to keep looking forever, as if there was something more to discover, as if it was summoning me to delve into its endless spiral and seek something. *What could it be?*

The waiter came once again, noticing that the company I was waiting for had finally arrived, because I can bet from the look of pity in his eyes I had caught some minutes ago that he thought I had been left hanging. He asked for our order, and as if electromagnetic waves travelled across the table, we said in unison, 'Hot chocolate with whipped cream', immediately looking at each other bizarrely, curling our lips into smiles of suppressed laughter until finally moving on to order a dish. She asked for a cheeseburger while I ordered a mac and cheese. Close enough.

'So, I'm not the only one who craves hot chocolate during the scorching summer,' she said.

'And here I was thinking that I was an unusual breed.'

We laughed heartily at this. It was not feigned laughter but a genuine burst of happiness at the congruity of our interests. I failed to comprehend my emotions. I felt excited, nervous, and curious, but simultaneously I felt at ease. We had hardly exchanged two or three sentences and in truth, I knew nothing about her other than her being a good writer and loving hot chocolate. There must be more because those two things alone came very near to my own description. There was no jealousy, not yet, at least. I still wasn't completely fond of her but I did want to get to know her. With all other things going astray, maybe something would find the right direction.

We chatted a while about our favourite books and it turned out we had a lot of common interests. Besides being Potterheads, which nearly everybody in our generation was, we agreed upon the futility of movies that were based on books. 'We write about things we cannot visualise or find difficult to express in words, and such movies negate the whole point of writing about feelings,' she said on the matter, and I felt like it was my inner voice speaking to me after years of being mute. By the time the waiter made his third visit to our table with steaming hot chocolates crowned with domes of whipped cream and delicious-looking cheeseburger and mac and cheese, I had understood that we both loved Jane Austen and Virginia Woolf, admired Shakespeare but were often frustrated at not being able to decipher his words on the first read, and agreed that we all lived in our own little bubbles as a mechanism to distract ourselves from the dawning truth of mortality. And I had also understood that I was beginning to grow fond of this girl.

As we stuffed our hungry stomachs with food, we began conversing about the topic that was uppermost in both our heads but either felt too lazy to refer to it, the annual magazine.

'So, have you come up with any ideas for the magazine?'

'If I'm being honest, no, I haven't. My creative tank has run out of fuel.'

'Oh, thank god, we're on the same page. But what's in that huge bag then?'

'Oh, you thought I had a whole draft ready here? No, no! I just picked out some scrapbooks I had made as a child and thought I'd show you. Maybe we could come up with something *together.*'

'Scrapbook, that sounds interesting. Let's finish eating and then we can brainstorm.'

She flipped through a couple of pages of her scrapbook, explaining the presence of every element on every page. I listened attentively for the first few minutes until I was completely lost in her words. The scrapbook was designed aesthetically, with stickers, sketches and broken poetry spread everywhere. She had kept dried leaves and rose petals that reminded her of how love can wither, and there were also torn pieces of newspaper she'd stuck on the pages, highlighting her favourite lines from articles she'd read. Energy was blooming through her eyes and her lips as she spoke, every word a divine symphony in that dulcet voice, every sentence a euphonious treble, her eyes gleaming with hints of nostalgia and bittersweet bliss as she told me why she adored her scrapbooks so much. I was paying heed to her words but soon lost focus in her voice and in her eyes that made the walls around me spin and all the other faces in the cafe dissolved in the backdrop. I could hear every word she uttered distinctly, but at the same time, they seemed so distant that I could not fathom out what she meant. I caught every time her eyes blinked and how she raised her eyebrows while accounting for why certain things in her scrapbook were the way they were, and she smiled every time she explained why she wrote a particular piece of broken poetry. And even as she spoke ever so normally, there was something spectacular in the way her lips moved to form words and how she gestured with her hands to explain certain things, that broken poetry was writing itself from the tips of my fingers to the roots of my brain, my memory subconsciously registering every action of hers as if she were a saint I'd write a biography about.

'So,' she said, closing her scrapbook and lifting her gaze from the table towards my face, 'What do you think?'

'I think you're beautiful. Your mind, your ideas, they're beautiful. And I think we might be onto something.' Quick save.

'Thanks!', she seemed to stutter, 'and, uh, what d'you have in mind?'

'I can see that your scrapbook is an amalgamation of so many different forms of expression: poetry, rants, rough sketching, newspaper cut-outs, and other things of significance that mean something to you, and although when put together, it may seem like a mess to an uncreative person, I think that it's a beautiful mess. It has an underlying meaning that cannot be sought by those seeking superficial happiness. Art is in itself a mess. We are all a mess, too. We have flaws, we have talents, we have realms where we excel and fields where we're but mediocre. We have days when we wish we never existed and days that we never want to end because they make us so unrealistically happy. We get hurt, we mourn, but we rise again. Sometimes, we cause hurt too, because that might be the need of the hour, and repent later. We have such different experiences but when we dig into the roots of it all, we realise that we feel the same things and ponder upon the same thoughts, despite living different lives decorated with different experiences and tales. And some of us find the commonality of being human so beautiful and extraordinary that we express ourselves in the form of *art.* We splash paints on canvases and blot papers with ink and overuse computer storage with uncountable words. We sketch, we draw, we write, we speak, we dance, we sing, we sculpt, we paint, because we want to be heard and feel that we are not alone in this journey of loving, hurting, repenting, learning and *living,* and we want to reach out to others who might be feeling like a pariah, and whisper to their shuddering souls, that they're not alone. We are artists and we show the world for what it is, and show to the world how much greater we can be. We are all trying to find love or running after the highest-paying job or chasing the most prestigious college or trying to heal our wounds or trying to undo our sins, and in this mess of running and scrambling, art unites us and makes us feel grounded. It makes us embrace the chaos within ourselves.'

Myra looked dumbfounded at the end of my tediously long speech, which was absolutely uncalled for to begin with. Her mouth was slightly open, mystified, and she tucked her ringlets behind her ears, as if trying to distract me from her lack of response, until she finally answered, 'Wow. Your mind is amazing. And although you said a dozen things in a very short span of time, I know exactly what you mean. We could have all forms of art, not merely writing and sketching, but everything. We could feature pictures of dancers, singers, sculptors, them and their art. It will be a beautiful mess.'

Yes, it would be a beautiful mess, just like *us.*

SEVEN

Crawling out of the Hiatus

On returning home, I was feeling different. I was neither focused nor dazed, neither blissful nor dejected, neither organised nor messy. But I was definitely feeling better than I was at the beginning of the day. Perhaps a good start after a failed week.

Artists express the world as it is. If I was an artist, and I was to express the world as it is, I could not keep running away from something which had no escape. I tossed my handbag away on my bed and rummaged through its contents, which weren't many, and picked out my phone. I first dialled Mom. It was two in the morning there and I had totally forgotten about the time difference until she spoke to me in a voice that was half-sleeping and still winding around in dreams. On realising that it was her daughter who seemed to lock herself up in a room-prison, her voice gained rigour and lucidity, and clearing her throat, she said, 'Alaina! Oh, my god! Beta, how've you been? Are you okay? What happened? Talk to me, darling.'

'Hi, Ma. I'm okay. I, umm, had diarrhoea,' I blurted out, understanding that diarrhoea would be less frowned upon than admitting to intoxication.

'Oh, no! Has Sparsh been looking after you? Should I ring up Dr. Patel and ask him to pay a visit home?'

'No, that won't be necessary.'

'Are you sure?'

'Yes, Mom. Don't worry about it. It was just a couple of, uh, loose motions. I've recovered now. How're you?' I was desperate to change the topic because my obnoxious imagination had already started picturing diarrhoea.

'Oh, we're good, Beta. Do you want to speak with Papa?'

‘Yes, sure.’

‘Hello?’, Dad’s voice was hoarse and unusually deep, but I was happy to hear it after a week.

‘Hey, Dad, how’s the trip going?’

‘It’s going amazing, dear, but how are—,’ I could hear Mom whispering beside him that there was no need to ask about that because the matter had been resolved. I felt at home after speaking to them, although technically, I was at home. It was pacifying. I had hardly entertained the thought of serendipity blessing me when my phone rang once again, an incoming call this time, from Sasha. I took a deep breath and straightened my back, attempting to prepare myself for some unwelcome news because she definitely would have something to talk about Alisha.

‘Hello?’

‘Hi, Sasha.’

‘Alaina! Where’ve you been? How are you? You literally vanished! I was scared that you might not even be alive!’

'I'm so sorry. I don't know what had gotten into me that day but I definitely went a tad bit bonkers. I came home and I was feeling dizzy all day, even after taking a four-hour long nap. In fact, I felt dizzy and out of place all week.'

'It's okay. It's not all your fault. You were drunk and some things might have triggered you. But you've been completely off the grid. I know you and Alisha have had past fights but you've never gone so long without reconciling. Is everything okay? Are you okay?'

'It's nothing.'

'No, you tell me what's up. No more hiding away.'

So, I told her what was up. From feeling overwhelmed with emotions to feeling underwhelmed with life, from questioning a friendship to possibly forming a new one with someone toward whom I had irrationally projected all of my mental chaos in the form of petty detestation, from existential crises to realising I'd soon be breaking a heart, I told her everything. And she listened. She listened without interjecting me. When I was done speaking, she answered, with no hint of judgement or control, that it'd be okay. She said that she couldn't even imagine going through a rollercoaster of multiple emotions at once and she understood that I was confused. She said, and I think it'll stay with me forever, 'Maybe if you stopped looking for the right direction, it would come and find you.' And I listened to her because I knew she was right. I cannot compel things to fall into place just the way I want. I cannot possibly have all that I desire. I can only hope but not expect because sometimes expectations hurl more harm at the expecting than those out of whom something is expected. We talked for an hour about our lives, about my brunch with Myra, about her and Kiara and how it was her first steady relationship although they still didn't have a label because it would make things complicated. And finally, when we had spoken enough for a day, I asked her what I probably should've asked while we were still on the topic of the events of the party. Perhaps I had expected her to manifest some concern toward the matter but I think that she didn't want to force anything until I was ready to face it. I took a deep breath in and let it out, and asked, 'How's Alisha?' A few seconds of silence followed. That I would voluntarily ask about Alisha was probably not anticipated by her. I heard her let out a sigh on the other end after which she started speaking once more.

She said that Alisha had been crestfallen for a few days but soon reclothed herself with charm. She has been putting on a smiling face but she is clearly, according to Sasha, still in low spirits internally. She has been coping with the situation by ranting about me to her minions and seemingly, she still wasn't ready to accept that she may have been in the wrong too.

'But she doesn't mean it, you must know that,' Sasha tried to reassure me.

I was not sure if I knew that anymore, so I answered vaguely, 'Hmm, so she won't apologise?'

'Would you?'

'I would if she had not started publicly bitching about me after a personal fight.'

'You're overthinking again, Alaina.'

'Am I?'

'Okay, how about this: take another week to collect your thoughts and focus now on your magazine work? We'll deal with this when time calls for it. I've to rush. Take care now, okay? Bye.'

'Buh-bye, love you.'

'Love you, too.'

I decided on taking Sasha's suggestion for the better and gave myself one more week to get my head straight. But then again, while I loved the idea of not dealing with anything presently, I was also beginning to feel increasingly conscious about the fact that I had already taken too much time from someone who was probably wondering what he'd done wrong, where he'd gone wrong. I wanted to go to him, pull him into a tight embrace, let him drench my blouse in tears of the sorrow that infects you when despite doing everything right, life still refuses to give you what you deserve. I wanted to console him and tell him that he'll be better off without me, that everything would be okay and we'd still be the same, goofy friends we were once upon a time, that he was actually not losing me but I him, knowing somewhere in the tips of my toes that'd curl up in anxiety and along the edges of my temple glossy with cold sweat, that even I didn't know with certainty if anything would be even remotely okay. But I was probably inflicting more anguish on him by treating him with silence than I would be if I were simply being honest. I opened text messages because I still hadn't marshalled enough courage to hear his voice lowering in disappointment, and he deserved better than ending things over a phone call. There were some seventy unread messages from him, including ten long essays. My stomach churned in anxiety. I didn't know how to deal with knowing that there was someone out there, caring and worried about me, hurting because I had been distant, hurting because I couldn't figure out my feelings. This was not fair. I did not want to hurt him more than he already was. *Why has this got to be so difficult? Why can I not love someone who unconditionally loved me?* I hated that I watched High School Musical and other similar rom-coms which made me believe that love would be easy, that being two attractive youngsters was enough to fall in love. I guess it was not all your path strewn with rose petals as your lover leads you to your date along the beach. They never told us about the thorns— the ones that sting you so deeply that in healing those wounds you'd find old ones that you'd ignored and eventually forgotten to cure, so they just sat there, like the dried bruises on your kneecaps, never to fade away, and to always remind you that you are not flawless.

By the time I had finished reading all of Arj's messages, there were black lines of mascara-laden tears dried up on my cheeks. This guy was in love with the idea of a girl that was definitely not me, and I realised that in following all the conventional norms of being the girl-next-door, I ended up checking all the boxes of the idea that I'd given him of me, understanding how childish and abominable it was of me to try to change myself to be exactly the girl a guy wants, so much so that I might end up losing my individuality in the process. After reading all seventy-five messages twice (I had counted by then), which took more than an hour, allowing myself to feel every word, there was one message that I knew would hit me for months:

'i know that i'm writing to you for the tenth time today and you're probably not going to read this anytime soon, considering you haven't read my previous fifty messages, but it's four in the morning and i'm laying in bed and i haven't slept more than four hours in the last four days. i can't get rid of thinking about you. i know now, after having asked sasha, because i was so worried about you, that you had a huge ass fight with alisha and you've been off the grid ever since. i hope you don't think that i invaded your privacy. i just needed to know if everything is okay. and i can see things have been different between us. i can feel it. you don't look at me the same way anymore. you don't smile at me with the same flushed cheeks anymore. you don't kiss me back the same anymore and i don't think you even like me kissing you. i'm not blaming you. i know we discussed before we got into all this that we'd take things slow and let life take us wherever it does. but maybe i did rush into things. And now i've messed everything up. idk if there's someone else and honestly, idc if there is. there's this weird thumping in my chest everytime i think of how it'd be without you and my neck dries up and my breathing accelerates when i think of losing you. and after having taken around forty buzzfeed quizzes, i've come to the conclusion that i'm uncontrollably, incandescently and madly in love with you. And yes, i did use those heavy words which i would never irl because i mean them. i'm in love with the way your lips curl in shyness when somebody compliments you and the way you tighten your ponytail when you get nervous before a test and the way you sigh at me in disappointment when i use the wrong grammar in a sentence and the way your eyes light up when somebody praises your poetry and the way you give your best effort into everything you undertake. and you have been putting your best effort into this relationship, to keep it alive, but i think it was dead a long time ago, when your kisses didn't have the same passion as the other times and when i'd hear your voice on the phone, sensing the lack of excitement as before. we were both in denial and i think we both came in with very different expectations. i do not care if i don't get to kiss you again or hug you again or hear your voice again or even see you again. i do not care if you leave me and never return. i just want you to read this, and you can leave me on read if that's what you want, and i want you to know and always remember that there was once this loser in high school who fell in love with the gorgeous, the beautiful, the talented and the kind, that is Alaina.'

I wanted to scream. I wanted to cry. I wanted to dig a hole and hide there forever, but most of all, I wanted to go back to the day when I started losing feelings for him and stop it from happening. But then again, it's a process and you can't pinpoint on a day when it started, because you yourself were unaware of it happening until it reached its kernel and then you're suddenly inches away from slipping from the verge. There was power in his words, the power of love that should be able to, as written in multiple books and displayed in several movies, defeat me. But it didn't. It didn't defeat my lack of love.

I wrote in response, 'Thursday. We need to meet. My house.' I don't know why I chose Thursday out of all other days of the week but my fingertips had typed out words before my brain could process what I was writing. I hated that I replied to over a thousand words of his in merely seven words but I didn't know what else to write either. I was about to keep my phone away when a new message popped up in the notifications, from Myra, that read, 'When should we meet/call next?', and once again, before my brain could form a response, my fingers had already typed spontaneously, 'Tomorrow, your house?', to which she replied within milliseconds, 'Okay <3'. I shut my phone off and started rummaging through my drawers in search of old journals where I had penned down free-verse poetry, so that I could select some for the magazine, all the while wondering why she had added a heart beside the 'okay'.

At dinner, Sparsh was smiling away at his phone, his right hand stuffing food in his mouth and his left hand rapidly texting someone. There was rajma and chawal for dinner, Sparsh's favourite. So, it was with some surprise that he had picked a human over his favourite combo, given that he never even chose Ira over rajma chawal.

'Ahem, ahem!', I cleared my throat teasingly.

He still didn't look up from his phone. So enchanted that he couldn't even hear me, I see. I cleared my throat once more, over the noise of chewing and typing and clattering of spoons and forks, more loudly and aggressively this time, 'AHEM, AHEM!'

He flinched and nearly dropped his phone on the floor, being taken by surprise. I couldn't help but laugh at the awkwardness that hung in the air, him holding a spoonful of rajma and chawal on one hand, and his other hand reaching down, hardly clutching onto his phone, raising himself slowly from under the table and looking at me in embarrassment.

'Stop it!'. The desperateness in his voice made me laugh harder.

'Lover-boy!', I teased, trying my best to subdue laughter, 'Who've you been texting all day?'

'Do I really need to tell you, though?'

'You promised!', I complained dramatically.

'Okay, okay, calm down, drama queen. His name is Aarav. I met him in an inter-school debating competition last year.'

'Own the Mic?'

'Yeah.'

'And?'

'And, uh, we had debated against each other and he had won. I had been jealous of him since then. I had nearly forgotten about him but he hit me on the gram six months ago and we've been talking since. In the beginning stages, I couldn't figure out if I wanted to *be him or be with him.* There was always this tension that I felt, but I didn't know if it was only on my end until he came out to me after talking for two months and then we started, you know, *talking* talking.'

'Oh my god! This had been going on for six months and I find out now, that too with you sneaking out early in the morning and not telling me voluntarily! I probably wouldn't have found out had I not awoken that early today.'

'Yeah, I heard your shower running and attempted to distract you with your favourite breakfast but it clearly wasn't enough.'

'I'm smarter than getting duped with food. Also, oatmeal is my ACTUAL favourite breakfast, but that's not the point. Why didn't you wanna tell me?'

'I wanted to be sure, you know, before telling anyone. Plus, he's still closeted and I don't think it was my place to even tell you. I haven't even told Ira yet.'

'Oh. Do you think it might be growing into something serious?'

'I hope so. I have never found someone who is so different from me yet so identical. I really like him.'

'I wish I had half the brain you have.'

'Not that I disagree, but why do you say that?'

'Oh, please. But on a serious note, I started dating Arj without being sure. In fact, I didn't even know what 'being sure' meant. I only felt lust and considered that enough for a relationship. I mean, it's about two hearts signing a consensus to share the most intimate parts of their souls, but I signed that consensus when I had no idea about my own feelings.'

'And so, you realised that now, which I'm guessing is at a place too far in the relationship, and now you're basically screwed?'

'Yep, basically.'

‘And is that why you locked yourself up and shut yourself away from all human contact in an attempt to run away from breaking someone’s heart?’

‘Yeah, and because I realised that one of my best friends is a big B.’

‘Alisha?’

‘Yep.’

‘I kind of saw it coming. Her aura never sat well with me.’

‘What do you mean by ‘aura’? She’s not like a repulsive person, okay?’

‘So are you not actually mad at her?’

‘I don’t know, Aarav! I just don’t know.’

‘I get it. I’m sorry if I pushed it too far.’

‘No, no, no, it’s completely okay. I appreciate you being here for me and talking to me. Sometimes I just really wish Mom and Dad were too strict with us about dating and alcohol. Ugh, none of this mess would've been created!'

'Firstly, trust me, you don't wish that. Secondly, do you ever think we'd actually adhere to those rules?'

'No, haha.'

'Sometimes it's just not the right person or the right time. You can't blame yourself for everything that's happening. You're not causing it all, although it may feel like that.'

'Thank you, Aaru. I really needed to hear that.'

*****

It was only ten o'clock and my eyes refused to stay open. Keeping my old, tattered copy of Pride and Prejudice on my bedside table, pulling the blanket to cover my head with the AC at 20 degrees, I shut off the lamp and drifted away, struggling not to ponder upon the six words Sparsh had uttered that were sure to disturb my conscience till I found their meaning, 'be him or be with him.'

Be her or be with her?

EIGHT

The Sky and Us

I had forgotten to pull down the drapes last night. Since I had imprisoned myself in my room for a week, I had also drained my room of any light and closed all openings that could let in any light. It was usually our house-help, Ram Dada, who'd pull up the drapes every day and I'd pull them down once the sun had set. But I was so busy with selecting poems for the magazine as well as composing some new ones that it had completely slipped out of my mind that the drapes weren't down. So, sunshine poured blazingly through the uncovered casements and kissed my skin 'good-morning,' mildly at first when the sun was still emerging from behind the clouds and then nearly burning me alive. The blanket was drenched in sweat, literally dripping wet. It was obnoxious. I jolted from bed the moment I felt the salty wetness against my lips and rushed to the bathroom to bathe.

It was the middle of June and the monsoons would flood the streets of the city soon. I liked the sun. I liked the positive vibes it radiated, only in the morning though. It was something about luminous objects that made me feel like they were telling me to look forward to things, to expect that things were looking up, to be hopeful and productive, to grow, heal and bloom. But I liked the rains better. They brought in peace and silence, the kind where soft sounds harmonised. Oh, to listen to puddles of water plinking on the road as hasty travellers plunged their wheels into the wet earth, the droplets rattling against roofs and murmuring against windows, making me wonder whether they were falling vertically or obliquely; to sip my cup of chai while composing imagined love stories in my diary; to philosophise with someone about the beguiling monster that was life— not the one we already lived but the one we wished for— and hope for the rains to clean out your soul just like it cleaned the earth.

Rain of my life. I kept thinking about what it'd mean to have the rain of my life. How long would I have to wait for someone to enter into my life and for once, not make it seem like it was not all about triumph and glory, that the mirthful masks of pride and class that people stick across their countenances were mere facades, and it was okay to sometimes feel desolate even when you're surrounded, to feel complete even when you're solitary, to have nights when you wonder if you'd be better off finding a place among the stars, to have days when you fail to fathom out the purpose of your existence? When would *my rain* wash out these searching questions and drain them to an ocean where *our* questions and contemplations would oscillate in phase like waves in quest of a shore that doesn't exist, but they still keep hoping that they'd find it, just as *we'd* still have hope to find answers to these questions. And even if we didn't find them, we wouldn't be disconsolate, for at least we did have each other— my *rain* and me— to ponder together upon the unsolved posers about the cosmos. But would it ever shower down? My rain? The bile that rises to my throat in anxiety, an upsurge of unrest in a high tide, would you make it recede? The trembling of my limbs and the shuddering of my fingertips against each other when I'm dreading, would you make them come to rest? The pounding headache devouring my consciousness and my heart fighting a battle against my ribcage, would you settle them? Would you find my soul, embrace it and console it in frail whispers that the sun would shine again? But if the sun did shine again, would *you* go away?

I had completed three assignments by the time it was ten and had also eaten breakfast. I had not realised until now about the amount of work you can get done in the morning and still have so many hours of the day left. You could literally squander the rest of the hours away and you'd still have something accomplished in the beginning.

I was sitting on the couch in our living room, chatting with Sasha on my phone whilst waiting for Myra's arrival. I had texted her this morning to be here by three but she took a step ahead and said she'd arrive by two sharply. We would be shortlisting our own poems today and also roughly selecting good submissions from the pool that Mrs. Whayton had flooded our mailboxes with. It was half-past two now and I had it almost confirmed that punctuality was not one of Myra's strengths. As I was frantically jumping from one application to another on my phone, in an attempt to dissipate my impatience, a notification popped up on my screen. Sasha had sent me a link. It directed me to Myra's profile on Instagram. Why had I not stalked her yet? That was new. The custom was to stalk the hell out of someone just after your first meeting. Her account was public and it had an aesthetically pleasing feed. Her pictures followed a Victorian theme in terms of the filters used, but she was as gen z as one could get. The girl that I had talked to yesterday didn't exactly align with the girl whose photos I was glaring at like a lunatic. Perhaps she was one of those who had a different internet personality to fit into the unrealistic boxes the world expected us to fit into.

With all the extra time, I couldn't help but think about what we'd do together. I imagined us sitting in my room and reading each other's poetry. But where? My desk had only one chair and perhaps she'd be uncomfortable to write on the bed. I could sit on the bed instead. But then we wouldn't be working *together*. We could sit at the dining table, next to each other. But there'd be forks and spoons and cups and plates around. There'd be a vase at the centre enfolded by a jar of water and a spoon and fork holder and Ram Dada would be sure to have a scowl on his face, eyeing me with disappointment. How long would she stay here for? Would we get bored? What would we do if we ran out of topics to talk about? The questions were endless.

I wondered what she'd wear today. She was looking so pretty in lavender yesterday. The images of her laughing while clapping her palms together and her eyes gleaming with passion when she spoke of her creative outlets, her hand tucking her ringlets behind her ears after being dumbfounded by my sudden leap into prolixity, and us asking for hot chocolate with whipped cream in unison, these pictures as if in a collage, would remain framed in my mind for a very long time. Suddenly, my mind revolted against the idea of entertaining thoughts about her. I couldn't understand why I simply could not get rid of her images in my head. Was some part of me beginning to develop warmth towards her? My heart fluttered at the thought but my mind groaned at it. But before I could debate any further, the doorbell rang(at 2:48 pm, finally!) and I jumped from my seat due to the abruptness by which the bell had taken me back. I hurried downstairs to unlock the door before Ram Dada's slow pace could make it. I opened the door ajar and there she stood, a few inches from the threshold on the other side, clothes dripping wet, hair completely washed down, looking disoriented. I stared at her for sonic moments, registering the sight in front of me. This was definitely not what I had pictured in my mind. When did it start raining? I was too engrossed in my phone. The sight in front of me was too hysterical not to laugh at, and despite trying to suppress my laughter for as long as I could, I eventually burst out, guffawing uncontrollably. Meanwhile, she looked abashed, head hung down to escape the gaze of shame and hands continually trying to soak the water out of her clothes. She was wearing a pink summer dress that would have been otherwise flowy but was now sticking against her body, hugging her curves ever so delicately. I beckoned her to come in after drying her feet on the doormat. As she struggled to wipe the mud off the soles of her sandals, I tried hard to dissipate my laughter. Couldn't offend a guest before she had even stepped in.

'You should've listened to me when I said 3 p.m. after all,' I teased, concurrently hinting at some ridicule at her impunctuality.

'I literally stay ten minutes away! So, I had estimated to arrive by 2:10 pm, which isn't so much different from sharp two, but before I knew it, it started raining cats and dogs. The roads were trafficked and I did not have an umbrella, nor were there any free bus stops for me to take shelter. So, I had to sign up for a wet journey, all the while on the lookout for a place where I could get an umbrella or something to cover my head with!'

'That sounds adventurous.'

'Right,' she replied, rolling her eyes.

'You had your handbag, though, to cover your head.'

'It has my laptop in it and it isn't waterproof,' she explained.

'It's okay. I promise that nobody shall know about this,' I said, still unable to fully stop laughing.

'Stop making fun of me!'

'I was just teasing, chill. Come on in, we'll get you dry and you can wear some of my clothes for the time being.'

After spending what seemed like an eternity in my bathroom, as I waited sitting on my bed, tapping my feet impatiently, she came out awkwardly, wearing my clothes. I lent her a pair of shorts and a tank top, hoping that would be comfortable enough for a rainy summer day. My clothes looked better on her than they did on me. The U-shaped tank top bordering the bridge of her breasts; her collar bones popping out in a sleek fashion; her arms hanging elegantly down from her shoulders; fingers fiddling with the towel with which she was attempting to dry her hair; her slim legs taking slow paces to make their way towards me.

'Are you still cold?', I asked, noticing that she might've been slightly shivering.

'Yes, a little.'

'Would you like some tea, or uh, coffee?'

'Coffee would be good.'

'Oh wait, I could make you hot chocolate with whipped cream!', I exclaimed, as if hitting an epiphany, in the tone of a child who'd get excited to show an adult his stick-figure drawing.

'Okay, if you say so,' she chuckled. She was smiling, finally. There was something about her smile that all other smiles I had looked at so far were devoid of. It was contagious, but in a way that it enraptured and bewitched you, as if inviting you to discover all its curves and edges, summoning you to run your hands along those lips which carved so leisurely across her olive skin that you felt relaxed, almost like your muscles slackened its furrows and contractions, dissolving into the mystery that was her. I knew so little, but at the same time, I knew enough to admire her. And despite how much I tried to fight it or deny it, maybe I was developing some warmth towards her.

It took me twenty minutes to prepare our favourite beverage, longer than usual. I wanted it to be as close to perfection as the ingredients available in my house would permit. I paid attention to every detail, adding cocoa powder, hot chocolate mix as well as chocolate syrup, which if word stood true, made the best combination for a sweet hot chocolate, as mentioned in an article I'd read when I'd searched up, 'How to make hot chocolate'. I then twirled the whipped cream over the steaming liquid, as if gifting the hot chocolate with a coronation ceremony. I lined a few choco chips along the slope of the conal cream to render it a fancy appearance. When I was entering the room once more, I noticed from a distance that she was sitting on the bed, a wet towel resting on her lap, eyes wandering around the room curiously, as if amused. Clearing my throat to catch hold of her attention, I walked in, the tray supporting the two cups almost trembling in my grip, not only because it was cumbersome but also because I was nervous. I had not given it a taste test. She turned her head around and smiled at me once more, extending a helping hand to hold the tray with me, and just for a moment, because eyeballs couldn't roll down under a tray, her hands went over mine, which she shifted to a more vacant region on the underside of the tray within seconds of the receipt of the stimulus of touch. The tinkling nervousness once more gushed from my toes right up to my thorax in microseconds and I was flushed. I lifted my eyes in a quick glance to catch that she had blushed too. I felt relieved that I was not the only one, and also somewhat beholden that she felt it too, whatever it was that we felt.

'So, you're rich,' she blurted out of context as we were sipping hot chocolate in peaceful silence. I was caught off-guard. I felt uncomfortable when people referred to my family's opulence.

'Yeah, umm, my parents are.'

‘I see,’ she said sardonically. I couldn’t figure out why she suddenly turned so cold. I was feeling uneasy and decided it would be best to change the theme of words, ‘Have you selected which of your compositions you want to contribute to the magazine?’

‘I’m still conflicted between some,’ she answered, taking a sip from her cup. In response, I kept looking toward her expectantly till she detached her mouth from the cup and cast a smile of relish, assuaging to calm the nervousness that had risen to my throat.

Within moments of the hot chocolate kicking in, we were engrossed in an erudite discussion about how the Renaissance was a watershed in the history of art, literature, and culture, trying to derive pointers from the movement that we could inculcate into the allotted theme. I had never before had a companion to engage in intellectual conversations with, the ones where there was no discomfiture in talking about abandoned topics like the uncertainty and inevitability of death, or how sex was actually a refutation of intimacy, how racism and misogyny were bootless mindsets of dogmatic individuals and how art was our only space to articulate our perspectives on such matters because the world was too noisy to hear voices like ours. By the end of two hours, we had prepared a framework for the sequence of the magazine and finalised the writings we'd contribute. We peer-reviewed each other's work in the process of doing so, which was not exactly plain sailing for me. I fell so much in love with every word she wrote that I couldn't reject anything. Unlike me, she happened to possess a mind capable of critiquing art. It was only after several rounds of her convincing me to read her writings like an emotionless person that I could bring myself to choose. We were yet to read through the other submissions but decided that that could be done tomorrow as well. Meanwhile, we didn't stop conversing. It was crazy how we simply didn't run out of topics to talk about and surprisingly, moments of awkward silence were negligible. I learned that she preferred mountains over beaches because it saddened her to look at the ocean choked with polythene and phosphorus, that she loved singing but was insecure about her voice, and when I suggested that she sing for me and I'd critique her like a professional, she shied away and hid her visage behind her hands. She also mentioned that she'd read some of my writings from past editions of the magazine and said how much she was flabbergasted by my compositions. I said that I was very gratified, blushing, and asked her to let me read some of her writings besides the ones for the magazine soon too.

It was six when she was shoving her clothes and notebooks into her bag, the same one as yesterday's, in a rush, muttering away in a jittery spirit that her mother would kill her if she did not reach home by seven because they had a movie night planned. All the while, I was trying to calm her down, saying that it was only six and she wouldn't need an hour to reach, offering a ride if she needed. She turned to me and said, 'A ride would be great' and at the very instant that those words left her mouth, I realised that the driver was on leave. She said it was okay but I fretted over her going alone at this time. She said it was only six and the sun was not down yet, but seeing that my eyebrows were furrowed in concern, she said I could walk her up to the point on the road that was two blocks away from her house.

The firmament was amber with splashes of pink scattered around. It was a cloudless firmament— all the humidity being showered down earlier— and a few isolated stars were twinkling gleefully at their own comfort. The moon shone in a beautiful crescent. It was neither dark nor bright, but it was the ideal amount of luminescence one desired to call it a day and dissolve into the natural pulchritude of twilight. We were walking along the footpath, our feet moving in sync, not speaking much because the silence spoke louder than words ever could during those moments. Our minds were conversing. I simply *knew* that they were. The roads were, as usual, throng with vehicles and an indistinct blend of innumerable honking sounds hung in the air. It was not so quiet, after all. But it was the silence hanging like a stretched string between our lips, tightening the tension, waiting for one to pipe up and loosen it.

'Do you like sunsets or sunrises better?', she asked, cutting the string.

'Both,' I said.

'You can't be diplomatic.'

'I'm not being diplomatic. It's very subjective to the situation. In general, I am in awe of the hues that the sky is painted with during dawn and dusk. I'd kill for pink and purple, especially.'

'But what's the criteria for the subjection?'

'For me, I pick favourites on the basis of what they make me feel. Not all sunsets are the same, nor are all sunrises. Some sunrises are hopeful while others make you question why you even have to wake up and live life. Some sunrises are serene; they make you feel at peace with yourself and occur sporadically, while others make you realise that you're another twenty-four hours closer to fate.'

'And sunsets?'

'As for sunsets, some are relieving to declare the end of a productive day, while others make you repent of having squandered another day full of opportunities. Some sunsets are meant to be enjoyed with your lover but the same ones can make you realise how forlorn you are in actuality. Some sunsets are contemplative and some sunrises make you question that same contemplation you had indulged in twelve hours ago. And there are myriad different forms that sunsets and sunrises can take.'

'Are they specific to their hues?'

'On some days they are.'

'Which days are those?'

'Those days when you've so much lost touch with your emotions that the sky must assist you in regaining the connection.'

'And which type of sunset is it today?'

'The relieving one,' I lied, knowing far too well that the sunset rendered an emotion too close to what you felt with a close companion or a lover.

'Oh!', she said, sounding disappointed.

'Did you have a different answer in mind?', I asked, hoping she would bring to words the thoughts I consciously kept shunning.

'Not really. I used to like sunsets better because I thought thcy wcrc prcttier, but I think now I might have a different perspective about sunsets and sunrises.'

We had arrived at the point which was two blocks away from her place. She thanked me for taking the effort to accompany her. I said that it was not a big deal. She then smiled for the umpteenth time that evening with her 'buh-bye' smile (by then, I concluded that she had different smiles for different occasions, much like sunsets and sunrises), and unalarmed, I was pulled into an embrace. Her cold fingers were against my bare back, sending electric waves to my chest. I was thanking myself for the decision to wear a cropped top. I had goosebumps on my arms as I wrapped them around her waist in response. She pulled me in closer, so close that I could hear her breathing near my hair and her heart beating against my chest. I don't know how long the hug lasted, but there was something about the way her hands draped around my waist and her fingers landed on my back, the way her head rested next to mine and how our heartbeats seemed to synchronize, that they resurrected to new life the defeated fire of passion that had been dormant in my soul for longer than I could recall.

NINE

The Heart is a Chaos

Thursday came sooner than I had anticipated and couldn't help but wish I had said Friday instead. The fret over how things would go had not once crossed my mind because I had been spending most of my time with Myra. I was beginning to feel guilty now, knowing that Arj deserved a better ending but also not knowing how I'd provide him with that. Remember how as children we adored playing with toys, be it dolls or balls or robots? We used to spend most of our time fiddling with them but as we matured, we outgrew them and didn't feel the need to play with them anymore. Nor did we have sufficient time to indulge in such leisurely games. And one day, just like that, we either flung them away with other items of household garbage or gave them away to artisans or to homeless children sitting hungry and downcast on the streets, or perhaps to the sons and daughters of our house-helpers. But days or weeks or months later, we felt the growing guilt emanate from the farthest corners of our souls, regretting that we let go of them, wishing that we could look at them properly one more time and brim our minds with thriving memories from the days long vanished when we felt untethered from the adversities of the world. This might be a fatuous metaphor to relate to the situation at hand but the feeling was not very different. We played with toys because everyone else did too, because that's what kids do. They play, laugh and enjoy the spring of life. Teenagers indulge in discovering life, often doing things that are tabooed or are not often spoken about or are forbidden. We are rebellious and often refuse to listen to what anybody else says. 'You only live once' is the motto that most of us follow. So did I. Because everybody else was doing it, I started a hunt for boyfriends when dating was all the buzz in the atmosphere. I didn't even know what it actually meant except the adolescent perception of physical attraction and posting pictures on social media to erupt a wave of envy among my peers. Arj was not a toy, but I realised today that I had been playing with his feelings for so long under the misconception that that was what dating implied. And now I'd be disposing of them, the feelings, with guilt creeping in, questioning: what if I could relive them?

In another two hours, he would be in front of me and we'd probably be bawling our eyes out. My train of thought of all the possible outcomes of this much-adjourned-yet-soon-arriving-confrontation was disrupted when my phone started ringing. It was Myra on the other line. We had decided to take a break from the magazine work for two days because I had a ton of college prep to do, and we didn't have much work remaining either. Just some finalising and refining were left. So, it was surprising that she was calling me only twent-four hours after we'd made that decision.

'Hello?', her voice said in the manner of asking a nervous question.

'I thought we weren't supposed to talk till tomorrow.'

'I know, but I had this brilliant idea out of the blue and I could not wait another day to tell you.'

'Go on.'

‘I stumbled upon a national magazine competition while scrolling through the internet, and apparently school magazine publications are also eligible for entries. The judgement is on the basis of creativity, content and presentation.’

‘But we’ll have to speak with Mrs. Whayton for that.’

‘We could do that tomorrow.’

‘But what’s the brilliant idea? Just entering into the contest or do you have a trick of guaranteeing a sure win?’

‘Well, according to my research, most submissions revolve around topics that have been followed by magazines for decades, such as fashion, sports, etc. However, the winners are the ones which uniquely represent their theme, especially when it’s a theme you wouldn’t conventionally expect a magazine to be based on. So, I was thinking that if, through the art we feature, we can tell a coming-of-age story, I think our chances of winning will be significantly higher.’

‘I have a picture in mind. I know what you mean.’

‘Isn’t it crazy how our brains cohere together?’

'It is. You come up with the innovations and I think of the perfect implementation.'

'I love how well we work together. We make amazing partners.' Her saying the words 'love' and 'partner' sent shivers gliding down my spine.

'Me too.'

We kept talking for about an hour till I told her I had other business to attend to and that I'd see her tomorrow. She sounded upset when I broke off suddenly because we were in the midst of a riveting discourse on Shakespeare's relevance in the 21st century. Our calls always end up traversing a course completely different from where it had started. Throughout the call, my heart was beating faster than usual and the tinkling nervousness had gotten the better of me again, only more intensely than before. I couldn't figure out my feelings. Was it longing? Or was I seeking the sense of belonging that I had lost, and was seeking for? Why did my limbs shudder timidly whenever I was less than twenty centimetres apart from her? Why did my lips crave to be touched on by hers? Why did my tongue curl up in shyness in imagining the taste of the skin on her cheeks or the backside of her hand? Why did the bridge of my nose desire to nudge not anyone else's but hers? Why did my fingers want to intertwine with not anyone else's but hers? Why did my eyes yearn for the sight of her smiling and blushing when I complimented her thoughts and her creativity? Why did I *yearn* for her?

I was at war with myself. This feeling of passion and longing, desperately wanting to hold on to her sight and trap her voice forever in my eardrums— they simply didn't feel right. They were like nothing I had ever felt before. What if Mom and Dad found out? *What would they think?* Would they think of me *differently*? Would my friends see me differently? Would I see myself the same again? Was it wrong to even entertain the thought that an attraction such as this might be felt, let alone feel it? The questions were winding around my head, creating an inescapable labyrinth. There would be no going back after this. Perhaps I was being paranoid. Maybe I had lost so much touch with feelings that I started picking up on any signs that I could to simply not miss out. Could it be a phase? I remember, the day of the argument with Alisha, I had uttered that I wanted to *explore my sexuality.* Perhaps I was still boozy then and may have blurted out whatever reached the tip of my tongue in the heat of the moment. But why did it reach the tip of my tongue in the first place? I know that there was nothing erroneous or sacrilegious in violating general social convention, nor was I a victim to the stringent shackles of religion and ancient belief. I admired seeing other people find love, regardless of gender constructs. But this was new. I had never acknowledged the possibility of diverging from the path of the social convention. Had I ever felt this way with a girl before? In trying to remember instances of attraction towards a girl, I realised that the kind of goosebumps and exhilaration that flared up through my nerves in her company was something new as a whole, something I had never felt with anyone before, girls or boys. There had been many crushes and a few cases of calf love, but perhaps I had never felt the fire of passion light up my heart before. This was my first. I couldn't fathom out how to acknowledge these feelings or accept them. I didn't know how to deal with this newfound identity. But was it newfound? Or had I been ignorant of it all these seventeen years?

I had been brooding over these questions, probing my individuality, till I was brought back to face the present with a ring on the doorbell. He was here. The time had arrived. There was no excitement in me like there had been for Myra to rush down the stairs and launch the door open. There was only malignant guilt and fear crawling into me from the tips of my toenails, devouring me gradually. I heard the doorknob being unlatched. Ram Dada had reached sooner than he would normally. Why did everything seem to be happening so fast-paced?

Moments later, he had come into the living room. We greeted each other 'Hi' and swung our arms into a friendly hug. It was our custom. I wonder how long it had been since we had been here together. Probably not more than three weeks ago, when, if my memory doesn't fail me, we were making out in the garage. I beckoned him to follow me to my room, and on entering, we sat ourselves down on my bed, next to each other, waiting for one to break the silence on the matter that had been pounding in our heads for over a week.

'How've you been?', he asked, realising that I didn't have courage enough to take the initiative of starting the conversation.

'I've been better.'

‘Since we last spoke?’

‘Since we last spoke.’

‘*Aunty and Uncle* haven’t returned yet?’

‘No, they’re returning next week.’

‘Oh, okay.’

‘Ya... what about you? How’ve you been?’ I hated that I was beating around the bush. *Come to the point, Alaina!* But I couldn’t so easily. If these were the last moments of civil conversation with him, then I must eke them.

‘I um... where do I begin?’

‘From wherever you like.’

‘I can’t. Not today. Will you say something today, Alaina, or will we be going around in circles for another eleven months?’

His words hit me like a ton of bricks.

Eleven months. It had been eleven months of us being together. In a few more weeks, it *could* turn into a year. How had those eleven months passed by? And why was it that I had hit the epiphany of the deceit of infatuation, which appeared beguiling at first but detrimental at the crux, after eleven months? Why had I feigned love? And love, why did you deceive me? Why did I say that I loved him at moments when I truly didn't? At that moment, I felt like I didn't know myself, the one who thought she was in love and thought everything in her life was perfectly stable and in sync with her 'routine'. I didn't know the girl who thought saying 'I love you' was as simple as how they'd shown it in High School Musical and who was fooling herself to have everything she could ever wish for only to distract herself from the broken edges of her soul. Because I now knew that I had way too many broken edges and I had barely begun to fix one, or to let it go. So, I finally mustered the guts to say what I had been putting off for the past several months, and spoke at length:

'I will. I will say it now or it won't happen ever. And it will get dragged on till heaven knows when and you will bleed to a point where the wounds will be incurable. Metaphorically, of course. The point is, I'm sorry. It's not you who's at fault. It's me. It's been me this whole time. And no, this isn't about somebody else or you not being good enough or faltering at some point. Gosh, you were more than enough. You were and still are so much greater than just *enough.* You are perfect. You are so kind, so generous, so loving, so caring, so amorous and so very charming that it's impossible not to fall in love with you. Yet I didn't. I didn't because it was not meant to be. You deserve so much better than a girl who has been following her best friend's footsteps and directions like a puppet, who mistook attraction for love, who failed to requite the immeasurable magnitude of love and care you gave to her. You taught me how to love and yet I failed to return it to you. I felt it, you know, every time you touched me or kissed me or hugged me or spoke to me. Even over the phone, I felt your love wavering towards me. And all that I could contribute in my kisses and hugs and words and touches were meaningless lust and flirtation. I failed you and our friendship. We shared such an amazing bond. You were the closest person I had to a male best friend and I lost that. I have lost that forever now, haven't I?'

At this point, I had started sobbing and I lost the ability to speak. He came closer to me, cupping my face in his hands, softer than ever, eyes lachrymose and despondent, with a look that said, 'It'll pass and we'll be fine,' and rubbed the tears off of my cheeks delicately. I returned him a look that answered, 'I don't think so,' and he planted a kiss on my forehead. We stayed like that for a few minutes, our foreheads touching each other and weeping uncontrollably. I think this was the first time I saw him sob, in person, with me. It stung a knife in my heart to see him so vulnerable because of me; to look at him hurting. I was willing to do anything to undo this moment. I looked up after some time and started speaking again, because I had so much more to say if this was the last time we talked, 'I don't know how I am going to ever face you again or face the reality of how much affliction I have inflicted upon you. I hate that you have to suffer due to my inability to figure out my feelings. I'm sorry, and I don't think apologising to you even a hundred times would suffice. The injury is too severe to be cured by apologies. But I need you to know that I still love you, I do, just not in the same way that you do. I love you but I'm not in love with you and trust me, I fucking wish I was. I wish I could control it. But emotions aren't felt out of compulsion. You can't force feelings and that is probably one of the harshest truths in life. I totally understand if you cannot forgive me or want to have no contact with me. Whatever helps you cope with this bomb that I dropped on you after eleven fucking months, you'll have my full support in it. But if you must know, they were the best eleven months that I have ever shared with someone in such tender intimacy, and they will always remain secured in a special room in my heart.'

I let out a deep breath as a weight that I'd been burdening myself with for nearly three weeks finally got off my shoulders. I waited patiently for his response, understanding that my words had a lot of content to register and he would need his time, concurrently tapping my feet on the floor as a method to fill the room with some sound that otherwise seemed deadly silent.

'Wow. I had known this was coming but I had imagined it to be some petty high school dumping scene that'd wrap up in like fifteen minutes. I never thought you'd make it so emotional and deep. You spoke about your feelings in such a raw manner and I'm thankful to you for that. Otherwise, we'd have developed needless bitter feelings towards each other. I don't know what happened in three weeks but you've grown. I can see that. You've matured. The Alaina I knew from eleven months ago could never speak of such profound things that even some adults try to run away from or struggle to express. Yes, I am in love with you and no, there is nothing I can do to make you fall in love with me. I accept your side of it. If I could, I'd kill you right now for making me fall head over heels for you and then dumping my ass. But you're not dumping me nor are you leaving me. I know that. You're prolly right. We're not meant for each other. But you too did teach me how to love and also gave me my first heartbreak. Thank you for two of the most important life lessons, Alaina Kaur.'

'Would it make this better if I said that it didn't kind of break my heart to break yours?', I asked nervously.

'No?', he answered, laughing.

And then we were both laughing, our voices ringing in euphony and our eyes bleared with tears, not worrying about what would happen next or what we would be to each other after he'd step out of my room, but simply allowing ourselves to forget everything around us and relishing this precious bittersweet moment. I looked at his brunette hair falling on his temples elegantly and his beaver eyes glistening softly in the glow of my bedside lamp. I wanted to savour this moment. The moment of two hearts realising that their beats indeed cannot dance in harmony because their sinews originated from different threads. He grabbed my face with his hand one last time, gliding down from my forehead, tracing the dip from my cheek to my chin and the bulge along my lower lip. I spotted the desire in his eyes, but he managed to keep a tight rein on his feelings and planted a kiss on my cheek instead, as if meaning to say 'goodbye'. And precipitously thinking that maybe I could undo what I had felt that day in the school corridors or the cafe or on the street when I had hugged *her,* thinking that maybe there was a slim possibility that this had all been but a disguised nightmare, thinking that maybe I could *force* myself to feel what I hadn't been feeling, I ran my fingers across his lips and allowed our lips to interlock. I realised what an irrationally stupid action I had committed right at the second when he kissed me back and I pulled away. He looked at me strangely. On the spur of the moment, I blurted out that I wanted to bid adieu to him with a final kiss to savour the moment. He said that he understood, hugged me once more, and left.

*****

The night was protracted and sleep seemed miles away. I was continuously flipping from one side of the bed to the other till I couldn't take it anymore. The anxiety, oblivion, and dilemma had invited a commotion in my head that seemed to be battling against my slumber. I could visualise a big jigsaw puzzle where none of the pieces were missing but all of them were mismatched. My life at present resonated with the jigsaw puzzle. I had so many questions but no clue from where I'd dig up answers. I should've been feeling relieved that I had finally ended things with Arj. It had been an action long overdue. Instead, I entertained this vague thought arising from some remote groove of my cerebrum that I had perhaps not done the right thing. What if Alisha was right? What if I had jumped to a baseless conclusion? What if my temptation towards Myra was but a phase? At the same time, I had not felt anything anywhere when I locked my lips with Arj a few hours ago, except for the taste of almonds and the moisture of saliva. But when I was with her, I could feel gooseflesh in my spirit. I could feel my heart leap in joy and my mind devoid of any worry.

The commotion could at any minute make me lose my senses. It was pounding. As though a godsend, I suddenly remembered the best person to talk to about this.

TEN

Finding Pieces, Slowly and Steadily

IT was on opening the door from my room and standing in the long corridor leading to the main living area of the house that I realised that it was two in the morning. I was glaring at the clock fixated on the wall facing me about twenty steps away, ticking away resoundingly in the silence of the early hours of dawn, and I couldn't help but think how quickly time passed while I was engrossed in thought. I went to bed at around ten.

There was complete darkness in my brother's room, or so I assumed on looking through the minuscule gap between the foot of his room's door and the marble floor. It was unearthly for him to be asleep so early. His days usually began at noon and no time before three in the morning marked bedtime. Occasionally, when I'd get out past midnight to refill my jug with water or satiate my stomach's cravings, the gap below the foot of the door would project a beam of yellow light onto the dark floor. I tiptoed the distance from my door to his, walking each step painstakingly so as to not awake him in case he was asleep, and not to grab any attention of my presence in case something suspicious was ongoing. When opposite, I pressed my ear excitedly against the door, resolutely trying to capture even a hushed whisper. I could hear indistinct chatter with intermittent pausing, as if in answers. Perhaps he was talking to his new swain. I did not want to barge in and give him a near heart attack, so I civilly knocked on the door thrice. There was no answer except for a sudden pause in his speech, and while he might've been trying to figure out who on earth would be knocking at his door at two in the morning. I then barged in. At least I had given him a warning priorly. It was pitch black and he was reaching to turn on the lamp on his bedside hurriedly, making a mess on the way and dropping a few things on the floor. Clunk, clunk, clunk. He turned around once the lamp was brightly radiating and fixed his gaze on me, blinking vigorously, as if to gain focus of his vision until he finally stopped and let out a sigh of relief.

'It's you, thank god.'

'Who else did you think it would be?'

'I don't know, a robber? A potential kidnapper? You tell me.'

'You think too much.'

'What are you doing here anyway?'

'I, uh, just wanted to have a conversation with my little brother.'

'And you want me to believe that bullshit?'

'Language, little brother!'

'As if you're a saint! I would have welcomed you for a conversation with open arms had it not been two in the morning. I know very well that you've developed a new habit of going to bed strangely early.'

'First of all, there's nothing strange about going to bed early. Maybe you should give it a try, it'll help with those terrifying eyebags, and secondly, it's a slightly serious matter.'

‘Should I be concerned?’

‘Maybe?’

‘Did you kill someone?!’, he shrieked, suddenly changing his tone from normal to panicked.

‘NO! What the fuck?’

‘Sorry, I’ve been watching too many mysterious murder documentaries on Aarav’s recommendation and the influence has been unhealthy, clearly.’

‘Oh shit! We were supposed to have a boy talk. I completely forgot!’

‘It’s okay.’

‘I never said I was sorry.’

‘I know you are though, a little at least.’

The deja vu started making sense when it lazily gave way to nostalgia. It was very much like that night when we had gotten lost in words and in the greatness of siblinghood, when the passing time was not perceived as misspent but every moment a gem that we'd store in our precious treasure trunk of memories. I looked at him with a flickering sense of pride as he spoke enthusiastically about the guy he might be falling for deeper than he'd imagined. He had grown up so much since that day two years ago when he was narrating to me his journey with his sexuality and how it was linked to his identity. Here he was now, looking happier than ever in the company of someone who showed that life was in fact not as difficult as we might think when you have the right person to remind you of your worth when you're too busy comparing yourself to others. They seemed to be each other's lights, he said, tagging along in each other's paths despite how separate or distanced the paths were, but never proclaiming sway over one another's paths. It wasn't easy to conceal the mirth that was taking over my countenance. He noticed that I was smiling and teased that I was in awe of his love story. I didn't deny it. The colloquy then gradually shifted its pivot to me. I had almost entirely engrossed my mind into what he was saying that I nearly forgot why I had come to his room. But the conversation proceeded so fluidly that we didn't even realise when we had gone from talking about his first kiss to my first heartbreak. Well, the first time I broke a heart if I were to word that precisely. He told me that he had never been the heartbreaker but he understood from where I was coming. We then spoke for several minutes about outgrowing people and losing interest in things you once used to find amusing because you realised that you enjoyed them solely on the premise that others did too, and he abruptly asked me, while we were still on the theme of friendships,

'Who is the new girl you've been hanging out with a lot lately?'

'Oh, just a new friend.'

'So, she isn't the same new girl you were hating on at school with your friends?'

'What?'

'Yeah, I've heard that there's some girl that you cannot stand.'

'Who even told you that?'

'Word spreads quickly when you're popular in high school. You should know that by now.'

'Well, she is the same girl and I don't detest her. Not anymore.'

'Not anymore?'

'Yeah, it was stupid jealousy.'

'And now?'

'Now we're friends.'

'Why do I sense that you are keeping something from me that you really wanna talk about but are hesitant?'

'How did you possibly figure that out?!', I asked in surprise.

'It's written all over your face.'

'Okay, fine. There's no point staying silent on this now. I think I was trying to delay when I'd say this to you because the moment I did, it would become so very real.'

'But how much longer are you going to keep running away from facing it, Di?'

'I don't know. But here goes nothing: I think that I might not be straight,' Sparsh gasped and squealed in ardour, nodding his head in a gesture of asking me to continue without interrupting me vocally, 'and I think that I might have a crush on her. The new girl, I mean. Her name is Myra. And the reason I'm sitting here talking to you at four in the morning is because I haven't been able to sleep for four hours. After all, my mind couldn't get rid of the thoughts of her and how I am feeling about her. I don't know. I'm failing to understand why I'm feeling the way I'm feeling. It's something that I've never felt with anyone before. I know that there is a physical attraction with certainty but I don't know if it's just my hormones raging in these adolescent years or some form of emotional attachment that's building up too. The intellectual relatability that I experience whenever we talk is out of this world. It's almost like there's more of myself in her than there is in me. She's just so perfect. She has a flawlessly eloquent way with her words. She's so smart that I sometimes question my education. She's beautiful, kind, sweet and she makes me want to do better and believe that there is so much more to life than unrealistic expectations we foist on ourselves. And god, she's so gorgeous and hot. But in thinking about her, something you'd said earlier resonated with me: do I want to *be her or be with her?* At the same time, while I am debating on whether this is a phase or not, I am also feeling like I am waging a war against my identity. I'm finding it difficult to forget who I was before her and convince myself of what I feel towards her as actually relevant and acceptable. Did you have these feelings too before you came out to yourself? Is that a thing? Coming out to yourself?'

Relief washed over me as I finally stomped on my thoughts and questions that had been haunting me for the past few days, releasing them once and for all. Sparsh looked reflective at the end of my confession, and after thinking for a few seconds, he said, with a solemn seriousness sitting on his face, 'I don't have an answer for whether you're straight or not. Everyone has different experiences and it just so happened that in my case I became sure of my identity after denying it for months because I could no longer turn a blind eye to it. I'm not the best person to consult for this matter but there are two things I can tell you for sure: one, considering you're not an obsessively creepy stalker, the way you described Myra sounds like you have a big fat crush on her, like a real one, and second, what you said about being confused— it's very similar to what I went through before coming out to myself.

And yes, coming out to yourself is a real thing. The confusion you're going through right now is being in denial. It's the internalised homophobia most of *us* go through.'

'But I am not homophobic!', I protested defensively, knowing well enough that I had not spent three hours that day when he'd come out to me to learn about homosexuality and gender fluidity only to be accused with homophobia one day.

'Towards others, you're not,' he explained.

'What do you mean?'

'You're not homophobic towards other members of the LGBTQ+ community but since you're feeling repulsive to the idea of yourself being gay, you're homophobic towards yourself. Basically, since our society has over the centuries hailed and glorified heterosexuality and declared it as the norm, we find ourselves disconcerted to feel or be something that is not upheld and approved by social convention.'

'Oh, wait. That makes so much sense. But didn't you ever have doubts about what others would think and how there was no going back after you've decided?'

'I did. Of course, I did. I still do, which is why I'm still closeted. But I can't decide. *You* can't decide or choose your sexuality either. It is an integral part of who you were, are, and will be from the very beginning. We just don't know it right from the beginning because we're barely out of the womb when they decide whether the cloth to wrap us with on the cradle will be blue or pink. And if you try to recall, Mum and Dad always used to warn *you* not to mess around with *boys* and *me* with *girls* because these stereotypical mindsets have been nailed onto them since their childhood days.'

There was pin-drop silence. Even the sound of cold air being blown out by the AC was heard distinctly. I took more than just a few minutes for his sentences to strike home and the truth to dawn on me. He was so blatantly right that I almost wanted to un-hear him. I almost wanted to dash back into my room, slam the door, jump into bed and pretend that I had only been dreaming. But he was right. There could be no more running away and in fact, I had neither the energy nor the intention in me to keep running away. It was time to turn around, trudge through the fraudulent wind that was antagonistic to my motion, promiscuous as ever in attempting to lead me back, summoning me not to surrender the path of illusion just yet. But resisting the wind and every other voice in my head, I will trudge through this time, and reach out to an old friend who was also my enemy. I must turn around now and shake hands with this fickle friend called life, even if it was unwillingly.

'Thank you,' I said and reached forward to hug him. It was a long-lasting hug and he patted my back to encourage me for this impending tussle with identity. 'Thank you so much!', I repeated with more emphasis this time as we broke off from the hug and I made my way out and into my room.

It was nearly five in the morning now and I found it futile to hunt down slumber now. I laid down on the bed and stared into the endless zilch of the ceiling. It was so plain and blank, looking nearly spotless, but despite how impeccable it looked from afar, I knew it had ridges and stains scattered here and there, nudging me in reminder once more that everyone is broken internally despite how stainless or invincible a facade might be protecting them on the exterior. Lost in the spiral of self-introspection, my mind travelled back to a particular sentence in John Green's TFIOS where he mentioned hamartia: a fatal flaw. Maybe I had found my hamartia, after all. *My fatal flaw*, I thought. Running away from life so far a distance that you end up stumbling upon fate. Running away from feelings so desperately that you end up welcoming numbness. In trying to compel myself to feel something for Arj, I had indeed encountered numbness. I also understood that I was giving myself more liberty to run away from my feelings in attempting to confute my identity. Sparsh was right. Every word from his mouth came out like a needle stinging me to the most hidden depths of my soul which I didn't hitherto know existed, persuading me to deviate from the path that was called 'normal' in popular terms and follow the path that felt normal to me. But what surprised me immensely was the profound maturity and intellect that he reflected through what he said. It was nearly impossible for me to buy that my fourteen-year-old brother had absorbed so much knowledge about human behaviour at a still tender age.

Sunlight drowsily penetrated through the windows and the curtains, indicating that dawn had dissolved into a stretch of daylight. I reached out with my hand to grab my phone on the other corner of the bed. It was six o'clock and I could hear mild showers pouring down peacefully. I saw that there was a new message from Myra. My heart skipped a beat. I opened the message and it read a question: 'Can we meet at Rosé Café?'. I answered that we could, but I couldn't help wondering if I'd done something to offend her or disappoint her when we were in my house. Her messages after I hung up that day became increasingly distant. I wanted to ask if everything was okay and if we were still the same, failing to defeat the fear slowly creeping in that I had not thought about how she felt. Perhaps she might not have the same feelings as me. Did I give away any sign to cause her discomfort? Drifting apart from her was the last thing I wanted. This was exactly what I had been dreading: losing people close to me because of my identity. When I said it out loud, it sounded preposterous. Somebody close to you should essentially accept you the way you are, encompassing your flaws and strengths alike.

*****

Feistily loud honking was summoning me from below the windows.

I was supposed to leave for the cafe at three in the afternoon but I was running late by thirty minutes. The driver seemed like he'd gone nuts. When Mom and Dad would return, he'd wear an innocent semblance of sincerity again. In hastily straightening my hair, I accidentally touched the heated iron and screamed like I had seen a ghost. I heard some movement behind me and figured it was Sparsh who had probably panicked once more due to his newfound murder mystery obsession. I'd put on some high waist jeans and a crop top, pairing them with sneakers and some light jewellery. I thought dressing up nicely could somehow distract her mind from the thought of any discomfort I'd caused her the other day (which remained a presupposition).

The city was looking ravishing. The rains had stopped and the afternoon sun was pushing its way through the clouds, beams of golden light piercing through every vacant space in the overcast firmament, touching the wet navy-blue roads delicately, glimmering in reflection and looking angelic. There was intense traffic on the road but I waited patiently for the cars to move. On the other hand, our driver— we called him Pranul Bhaiya— couldn't get rid of honking and aggressively shouting at every car enfolding us. I wanted to slide down my seat and hide below in embarrassment. The ride was uncomfortable and ignominious but I made it to the cafe finally. I was forty minutes late. As I carefully pushed open the door, I noticed from distant vision that Myra had already arrived and occupied the same seat we had on Monday. She was sitting with her back facing the door, so I could only see that her hair was up in a messy bun held together by a fluffy lilac scrunchie. I'd seen her wearing that scrunchie at school before. She was dressed in a blue-striped shirt with a thick collar surrounding her neck and the same handbag resting on the floor in her company. As I reached our table from behind, I cleared my throat in an attempt to capture her attention which seemed to be indulged in a magazine of sorts, or so I could notice as I looked over her head. She turned around with an initial confusion quickly evaporating into excitement, like the one that lights you up when your favourite festival you've been waiting for all year finally arrives. She smiled and said 'Hi' accompanied by a friendly wave of the hand. I returned the welcoming gesture with a smile and sat myself down opposite her.

'I'm sorry for being late,' I said quickly before she could frame any comments on my unpunctuality.

'It's not a big deal! I've kept you waiting for me for an aggregate of no less than three hours, if my mathematical brain is functioning. Compared to that, forty minutes is as tiny as an amoeba.'

'What a nerdy analogy! Anyway, won't you ask me why I am late?'

'Looking at how pretty you look today, I'm sure it was time that struggled to keep up with your styling habits.'

I was blushing immediately. Was she only being sweet or was she sprinkling a hint of flirtation? I felt so new to this that I couldn't tell the difference. Moreover, she was a saccharine person intrinsically. It would invite disaster if I had been too quick to read the signs erroneously.

'So, umm, what are we doing today?'

'I should be asking you that. Did you speak with Mrs. Whayton?'

'Yeah, I've spoken to her and coordinated with her about the framework with all the sections to be there in the magazine. The design samples have been emailed to her as well.'

'And the submissions?'

'Yes, I've forwarded to her all the selected submissions too.'

'And about the competition?'

'Yep, told her about that. She said that she's glad we did so much in-depth research, which I did mention to her that mainly you did, and yeah, she'll take care of it.'

' "Take care of it" meaning?'

'Meaning that she'll be the one who'll enter our magazine as a participant of the competition and handle other formalities.'

'Oh, okay.'

'You sound disappointed.'

'Well, it sounds like we're actually done with our work ahead of time so I guess we don't have to work together anymore.'

I didn't know how to answer that. She sounded slightly crestfallen but simultaneously added a hint of sardonicism in her sentence. For the first time, I couldn't read her. Silence hung in the air for about a minute till it was beginning to get uncomfortable. I couldn't stand the tension anymore. It was not the same tension that had built up the day I was walking her home or the day she was in my room, wearing my clothes.

'So, I am taking it that you want to go home?'

'I never said that,' she replied with coldness once more.

'What's wrong, Myra?' Saying her name intensified the tension and I spotted, by the skill of expeditious observation, that she was somewhat subdued.

'You must be happy that you're finally not obligated to hang out with me,' she blurted out.

That dropped as an unanticipated bomb. Of all the responses that I had imagined in my mind that one could possibly imagine within a span of three seconds, this one wasn't on the list.

'Why would you say that?', I asked in a tone that screamed that I was offended, and perhaps my voice had raised slightly for I had managed to turn a few eyes to look at us.

'Um, why don't you take a wild guess?' The sardonicism in her voice was growing increasingly unbearable.

'I literally don't know what you're talking about!', I exclaimed, throwing my hands dramatically in the air.

'Oh, how much longer are you planning to pretend for? I know that you *dislike* me.'

'Who on earth told you that?'

'Everyone at school, in my grade and in yours. According to them, you cannot stand me. I wonder how you coped with me for the past week. I mean, you could've just been honest about it instead of pretentiously making me hot chocolates or offering me escort walks back home!'

'Woah! Dislike you? DISLIKE YOU? Myra, if I began telling you how much I like you, I wouldn't be able to stop today. Or tomorrow, or ever,' I realised right in time that being too expressive of how I *actually* felt about her might scare her away until I knew if she felt the same way, so I smoothly dissolved my words into those with an amiable aura, continuing, 'you're the most talented junior I know and you're one of the closest friends I have right now whom I can actually trust. Don't believe in hearsay. I love hanging out with you.'

'Really?'

'No, I just said that to kiss your ass.' We both burst out laughing, heartily at first and quickly growing into an uncontrollable chortle seconds after, our eyes blurred with tears and our hands on our tummies. To a third person looking at us, we would appear to be mirroring each other. That only further added to my previous thought: *she had more of me than I had of myself.*

After wiping the joyful tears off of our cheeks and finding stability of position again, we realised that we hadn't ordered anything. The waiter had been eyeing us, with peripheral vision from the counter, suspiciously and angrily, as if at any moment he'd march to our table and force us to get out. Then again, it was not like a hundred customers were struggling to find vacant tables. He didn't really have a strong argument to kick us out, except that, of course, we had not paid for anything.

'Wait so, if those rumours are incorrect, then why would someone start it? That too, including me? I'm like the least popular person in this school.'

'Please, I'm sure you're not. You must have already awed people with your artistic abilities! As for the rumours, in short, I kinda had a fallout with Alisha, my best friend, or ex-best friend, I guess? And you know, she's pretty popular and loves to create gossip. I'm assuming she did it this time too.'

'Wow, I could only imagine having so much drama in my life. Actually, no, I can't even imagine.'

I chuckled lightly at her comment, and asked, 'Do you wanna get out of here?'

'I thought you'd never ask.'

ELEVEN

Apprehension

'What do you think?', I asked her with eyes full of agog.

'About the beach?'

'No, about this spot at the beach.'

'It's the most serene place I've ever been to.'

After leaving the cafe, we hopped into our car and I brought her to my favourite place in the city, the Juhu beach, but at a particular spot which I had discovered during one of my adrift ambles here back when I was little. It was a rare spot from where not only did you have a nearly quixotic view of the sunset but you could also evade the crowding of the heavy populace of the city. We were sitting on the sand, unbothered about our clothes getting dirty, glaring at the prodigiousness of the Arabian Sea. The waves were dancing rhythmically, ascending with vigour and descending with grace, touching the shell-paved shore seductively, as if asking us to go there and dip our feet in the water, allowing columns of sand to swish into the spaces between our toenails. We sat beside each other in tranquillity, brisk sea breeze rustling through our hair and the smell of salty sea air infiltrating our nostrils. We didn't speak for a long time but this silence was comforting, unlike the one in the cafe. Even in silence, we knew that we were speaking to the waves. We were telling them about our deepest regrets and biggest dreams, about the times when we'd smiled the widest and cried the loudest.

I loved the sea. It was not merely about how exquisitely the sun set into its blue waters or how the waves glimmered in amber at the break of day. The waves told me about the nature of life, about the impermanence of everything in life. Everything is ephemeral, be it victory, failure, euphoria, melancholy, faith, desperation, love or loathing. They keep coming and going, just like the rise and retreat of the waves. They are fickle, making entries and exits from our lives every now and then, until they would vanish one day with ourselves, just like the wind would stop blowing one day and the waves would cease dancing.

It had been around thirty minutes of us residing in silence. Neither of us felt awkward, but the tension mushrooming between us was undeniable. Without warning, she sidled up right next to me, making the distance between us nearly zero. Our shoulders delicately rubbed against each other. She rested her head on my shoulder and placed her right hand on my left one, casually intertwining our fingers and my feet slightly twitched in excitement, hopefully unnoticeably. I still couldn't fathom out if it was a friendly gesture or something beyond that; whether this was her way of thanking me for the compliments I had bombarded her with earlier or if she was trying to tell me that her heart raced and her cheeks flushed when she thought of me too. She held my hand up, supported by hers, silhouetting against the vermillion sun that was subsiding into the endless horizon from where the waves seemed to originate, and said, in a voice so low and hoarse that it struck chords in my nerves, rendering irrepressible titillation, 'Your fingers are so pretty.' I had not a clue of what response I should give. A 'thank you' simply wouldn't suffice.

Her words were heavenly to me. Every artery in my body was flooding with blood because my heart was throbbing at such a pace that it was impossible to maintain stability of thought. My mind was lost in a mesh of ideas of what I could say. Every cell in my body wanted to scream, shriek, just say out loud, so that even if she missed my words by chance, they'd echo back from the sea. I wanted to tell her at that very moment that I was incandescently falling for her, that there was something way more intimate than friendship that I felt for her, that although I myself failed comprehend whether it was lust or love that I felt for her— because the flame of desire was inextinguishable— I would rather talk to her for uncountable hours than have any physical contact if that's she wanted. But I was scared. Her hand now left the company of mine and placed itself on my thigh. I instantly regretted having worn jeans. I imagined the touch of her skin against my skin. The goosebumps that would be produced by the sparks that would light up simply by how her skin would feel against mine. Perhaps I had been longing to feel her, every inch of her, in its entirety, for so long that even if a piece of cloth was still separating my thigh from her hand, the denim seemed to dissolve away and every nerve in me was dancing in glee. Her hand then reached up to my neck and slowly glided up to my cheek, cupping my face and pulling me closer. So close. I could hear her breathing against mine. I had read about this in novels but never did I believe in them until today. Whatever would happen now would change everything. Was she actually this close to me? Were our lips really parted by barely a centimetre? Or was this another daydream? Like the many I had whenever I thought of her? I had imagined us in such a position many times in my head before, but never had I thought that it would be so near to perfection. The sun was setting gloriously in front of us and light zephyrs were striking against our skin. I looked at her eyes. They seemed to stretch to an extent larger than the vast sea we were sitting by. For the first time, I didn't look away from her. Instead, I let her pupils talk to me. I felt like they were asking me to find something. What could it be? My mind was travelling back to all intimate instances of friendship I had experienced. I needed to be sure. Had I ever been so physically close to Sasha or Alisha? We hugged, kissed each other on the cheeks and maybe even had a friendly peck or two when we were drunk beyond consciousness. But did I ever feel the heat of passion with them? I didn't. Nor were Myra and I drunk. What did it mean? What if she wasn't sure of her feelings and was still exploring? Had I not also just begun exploring?...

Usually, every hour I spent with her in conversation seemed to disappear within seconds. But there was something about today. It was different. Every second seemed painstakingly long as I held her gaze and leisurely got intoxicated by it. At any moment her gaze could pulverise every iota of me and I would surrender myself completely to her without revolt. But the dread couldn't be boycotted anymore. Her fingers were now touching my lips, circling from my upper lip to my nether, inching closer every second. And now the tips of our noses were touching each other and I could feel her soft eyelids stroking mine. It could happen at any moment now. Was I ready for it?

And was she?

'Home' I blurted out suddenly, cutting the string of tension, extinguishing the flame of desire, and completely ruining the moment. She started in her place and shifted away from me by quick intuition.

‘What?’, she asked with a tone of embarrassment and disappointment, her voice not the low, hoarse one as before.

‘It’s six!’, I answered, pointing at her wrist, ‘You have a curfew of six thirty.’

‘Oh. We should probably head home, then.’

I regretted my lack of self-confidence instantly. She looked so abashed and disappointed that it made me want to cry. Could I just not have things go how they were going? She was taking the initiative of something which I couldn't even imagine doing in my wildest dreams. She was leading. Could I not have just simply followed and let her lips dance against mine, kiss every part of my body she desired? What was I afraid of? Maybe at the moment, I was not ready for it. Maybe she had not been longing to taste my lips as much as I had longed for hers. Maybe she wouldn’t have liked it. Or maybe I wouldn’t have? Was desire not enough for a kiss to be exceptional? Perhaps everything would collapse if I did not like *it.* But I couldn’t presume without trying, could I? The opportunity had come to me with open arms, looking so tantalising, making me desperately want to grab it. But I shied away. The opportunity would probably never return. I had missed it, failing myself once more. Or maybe I had failed her?

I was dropping her at her place and the awkwardness that enfolded us throughout the ride was unbearable. This was no more the comforting silence where our souls seemed to be conversing with each other. This was an excruciating silence where our souls were at war with each other. One was disappointed and the other was repenting. Neither of us knew what would follow. Was this the end of it? Of whatever we felt? Even if it lasted for merely a week, she had made me feel things I had not my whole life. She had taught me the greatness of intellectual discourse, the intimacy that words could create without the need for touch. She had taught me that despite longing for someone most desperately, you'd still be alright in being apart from them, as long as you knew they were happy. She taught me that despite desiring someone from every ounce of the auricles and ventricles of your heart, you were still okay if you didn't mean as much to them as they did to you. Her smile brought me relief and bliss but her tears would make me want to not have met her at all, not have caused her any pain at all. And although I had never seen her cry, her sitting away from me at the opposite end of the car seat, several inches away, glaring out of the window and not speaking to me, was worse than if she'd just spoken bitterly to me. Our silences made everything else seem irrelevant, whether they were the desirable ones or the undesirable ones. If this— *we*— were to end today, would I be okay? No, of course, I wouldn't. I would've ruined another magnificent thing in my life and crawled into bed, crying myself to sleep for several nights, all the while trying to find excuses of how I wasn't at fault. But I knew that this time I was. I turned towards her, looking at the frizzy curls that her scrunchie couldn't hold all together and her hands sitting on her lap, fidgeting in nervousness; the same hand which had minutes ago been on my face, and I could feel the dejection flickering out from her heart and pierce mine. We eventually arrived at her place and she got down the car, without saying a word to me, not even a 'goodbye'. Perhaps we had spoken so much in silence that even the final adieu needed to be silenced too, *if* it was final. She kept walking without looking back and my heart was breaking in a staggering fashion until she stopped in her tracks, turned her head around, and looked straight at me. She was many metres away and I could not make out what her eyes were trying to communicate to me through the glass window. But I sensed some hope. Before I could say anything or perhaps get down and bid her adieu, even if in awkwardness, she turned back once more and continued walking. She didn't look back this time.

Pranul Bhaiya was driving slower than a walking elephant. Maybe he had sensed the low spirits in me. While my mind was spinning with all possibilities of what would happen when we see each other again, whether soon or not, my eyes fell on something a little over twelve centimetres away from my feet resting on the floor of the car. I nearly jumped from my seat in fear of what could possibly be standing near me in darkness. On inching closer, I saw that it was Myra's bag. She had forgotten to take it. This appeared to be a godsend. I could see her tomorrow again on the pretext of returning the bag. But she never once let her bag be separated from her hand or shoulder. Even while sitting in the cafe, she would intermittently keep clutching onto its strap. It seemed to be her chamber of secrets, something she'd carry if ever her apartment was on fire. Even at the beach, while she had one hand on me, the other was engaged in keeping the bag as close to her as she could. I couldn't help but wonder: what if she had deliberately left it behind?

TWELVE: The Unexpected Return

The first thing that caught my attention on reaching to ring the doorbell was the noises of people chattering ardently inside. I was completely distracted from my spiralling thoughts of the events that had happened hardly an hour ago, from which I had still not recovered. I pressed one ear against the door to make head or tail of the voices, trying to discern their words and recognize their sources. There was a female speaking squeakily, as if bursting with elation, and another male voice, loud and deep, a sense of monotony in the way he was speaking. Sparsh usually didn't have people over without priorly informing me, especially not adults. The voices were an awful lot similar to those of my parents. But they were not supposed to return home until Monday.

When I finally gave up on my attempt to solve the mystery behind the voices and rang the bell, silence fell as quickly as a car running at full speed came to an abrupt halt on spotting a creature in front of it. Ram Bhaiya opened the door and I espied the folks inside. As it turned out, Mom and Dad had arrived early. They looked at me and were instantly in raptures. Mom rushed towards me and gave me a welcoming hug. I hugged her tighter, realising I should be the one welcoming her. I shot the initial 'Hello!', 'How was your flight?', 'How was your trip?' and other kindred phrases one asks when a traveller returns. Then we came to why they had returned early. They said that their business there was over and they had kept a day extra for looking around the city. However, they had already seen enough of the city to retain images of the most popular spots distinctly in their minds. So, missing us too much, they decided to prepone their flight. Sparsh looked at me from across the room, rolling his eyes at this adversity, with a look that said, 'Ugh, why?'

We sat for dinner with an uncomfortable deprivation of talk. The only sounds that mildly attenuated the discomfort, but truly only added to the awkwardness, were the clattering of spoons and forks, the slurping of beverages, and the unnecessarily loud chewing. It had always been like this here. Our parents thought that buying us expensive gifts, taking us to their elite parties, planning exquisite annual trips, and rewarding us with other materialistic privileges of life were enough to keep us content. They thought happiness could be bought. Well, to some extent, yes. But I cannot recall an instance where we conversed about how we were feeling, how our days went, and other normal topics of conversation that flowed in most families, or so I expected. It would always be about stocks and shares— stuff that my brother and I never really comprehended and so when our turns came for speaking, it could mostly be about school, plans for the future, and other lifeless themes. It sucked. In many of our past conversations, Sasha would tell Alisha and me about how supportive her parents were about her sexuality, how she gushed over girls with her mother, how she discussed bad days with her parents and how they'd advise her to stay strong and get through those days. Naturally, I felt envious of the relationship she had with her parents but more than envy, it was a sense of missing out that distressed me. Several thoughts raced through my mind. *Was it in any way my fault that I didn't open up much to my parents? Was it wrong of me to keep waiting for the day when they'd approach me and ask me how my day was? Should it be me instead who'd go to them and ask them how they were?* Then again, I would most likely not receive the response I would be expecting. Their answers were always brief. Sometimes it felt like speaking to robots because I had become so familiar with the kind of topics they'd talk about that I could almost, every time, precisely predict their replies. I know that they do care about Sparsh and me and always want the best for us. They've worked so hard to guarantee us the pleasures of a comfortable lifestyle. But their mindsets don't align with ours. I understand that we are generations apart from them and so they are not supportive of matters like high school relationships, drinking, and if you even so much as utter the word homosexuality, they would look appalled, as if their ideals have been vandalised. I don't wish to change who my parents are or how they think. I don't even know if it's right for me to entertain this strife in my mind because Mom and Dad have given me so much. There is guilt in me but there is also fear that they would never be acquiescent to accept my identity.

A silent dinner was followed by a noisy unboxing of gifts that Mom and Dad had bought for us. Sparsh looked extremely excited and hurriedly started opening his packets. His excitement brought a smile to my face. If this were happening a month ago, I would've too been as excited, or perhaps more excited than Sparsh to open my gifts. I would've been tearing packets left and right, impatient to find out what items of luxury my parents had gotten me, and simultaneously sketch situations in my head of where and how I could boast them. But now, I felt like I was far beyond materialism. There was unrest brewing in my chest. A rushed exhilaration interlaced with writhing nervousness. I could tell, from my peripheral vision, that my parents were looking at me with surprise, wondering what had happened to me in a span of only two weeks of their absence. I lifted the packets from the floor and told them that I was too exhausted and simply wanted to go to bed, promising that I would open the packets first thing the following morning.

As I was making my way to my room, I pictured the list of things that the packets I was carrying could contain. There were certainly going to be clothes, shoes, and jewellery from posh brands. Expensive chocolates could be there too but before they were leaving, I had told my parents that I was on a diet for summer parties. The day that they were leaving now seemed like an eternity ago. So much had happened, so much had changed and yet somehow everything felt the same. Two people that I had considered to be indispensable parts of my life now proved to be dispensable after all. Their absence didn't mean the end of the world for me as I had once believed. Ironically, I felt free, like life had only begun. I felt like my wings had been unclipped, even if not completely. It was a start.

At the moment that I entered my room, my eyes fell upon her bag. Ram Bhaiya had probably brought it here. I dropped the packets on the floor and kept looking at her bag sitting on my bed for several minutes. The desire to open it and rummage through its contents with the hope to find out something was unquenchable, something mystifying, something that would tell me more about her, something that would probably be the key to the mystery that lay beyond her cryptic eyes, those eyes which seemed to be summoning me every time I looked into them, as if to find something out, to figure something out— what could it be? At the same time, it felt so wrong, almost to the extent of the commission of a crime, to violate someone's privacy and compulsively invade into a world that she perhaps still wasn't ready to show me. But I couldn't also deny the existence of the possibility that she might've intentionally left the bag behind. What more could there have been to hide? In a week, I had learned more about a girl who had hitherto been a stranger than I had known about anyone else, despite being in their company for several years. No doubt that I knew of multiple aspects of my friends' lives. I knew almost every detail of their daily activities, especially when it came to Alisha and Sasha, and Arj to a considerable extent. But I never felt like I knew them. I knew what they did but *who they were* still remained a question shrouded in enigma. But with Myra, we discovered each other together. We explored parts of each other together. We found bits and pieces of ourselves that we'd thought we were devoid of in each other. Beyond amatory desires which might've developed over time, we had an unshakeable foundation of friendship. For the first time, I felt like I understood her, and she understood me. Perhaps, it is natural for romance to bloom when two souls are so intimately intertwined with each other that every emotion felt by one seems to be shared by the other, even from a distance.

At this point, it seemed like the bag was glaring at me instead of me at it. I spotted the edge of a tattered page peeking out of it. Maybe I could quickly take it out entirely and see what it contained. How much harm would it do? I realised that if I kept questioning this too much, I would only end up confusing myself to an extent that I'd probably spend the rest of the night standing stationary beside my bed, plucking away rose petals of whether or not I should take the sheet out. Impulsively, I hopped onto my bed and dashed the partially torn piece of paper out of the bag. It was now in my hands. Adrenaline sprinted from my kidneys, vivifying every nerve in my body. I saw that it was a poem that she had composed in that paper. Her handwriting looked rushed yet beautiful. It was titled, 'Could it be me instead?' I began reading it.

Could it be me instead?

I. On the green, under a firmament washed with amber, pink, and magenta all the same.

II. Brisk zephyrs rustling through the mesh of your waves, carving elegantly about your neck.

III. I shift my hand towards yours across the blades of grass until all I can feel is skin. Soft, delicate skin.

IV. Your fingers entangle with mine, welcoming me to your cosmos.

V. It was more than a mere touch. It was electric sparks bursting from the tips of my fingers to parts of my body I didn't know existed.

VI. You run your hand through my chaotic curls and I cup your countenance in my palm.

VII. You smile. I smile. We flush into redness more intense than the collapsing sun.

VIII. My heartbeats quicken in pace till they're pounding against my chest, knocking at my ribs to break through them, and catch your heart.

IX. You come closer. I flinch in anticipation but you pull me back in.

X. Your lips over mine. Mine over yours. Together, caressing and loving each other. My heart starts beating faster.

XI. Our lips detach. You glare into my eyes with a look that reads, in my mind, 'I know it feels new, but it feels safe.'

XII. I reach out to hold your hand again but you dissipate into the dust.

XIII. No grass, no firmament. The sun has sunk, and hope is lost. You are home but home dwells in my head.

XIV. You must be sniffing into his shirt now. He's fortunate to have your contagious laugh ring in his ears, while here on my bed, as the clock strikes midnight, I can only hope it'd be me instead.

- **Myra.**

The paper was shaking in my grip. I felt so many things at once. I felt reunited with the ocean as waves of exhilaration ascended through me. I felt a zephyr of relief sweep past me. While curiosity emerged from my toes, regret twisted around my neck and gagged my chest. She wrote about running her fingers through wavy hair. I had wavy hair. But just to be sure, I took a quick glance into the mirror to confirm that I did. 'Puff!', I sighed in relief. She wrote about the sunset and we had an explicit discussion on sunsets not long ago. She thought that my laugh was contagious. The image of her smiling from my laughter made me blush. She also mentioned a guy. Who was she hinting at? I had never brought up my social life as a major topic of conversation. How did she know about Arj? Did she think that I was with him? And why did we never discuss each other's social lives? I tossed the questions away before my mind entered into a spiral of endless interrogation. The important takeaway was that this wasn't one-sided. She felt it too. All this time that I had been trying to deny the development of intimate feelings towards her, trying to refrain myself from imagining us together on the presumption that it would never happen, she had been developing similar feelings towards me too. I felt a sense of relief, a much-needed one after the disaster that had happened today. I didn't want to be sure about my feelings until I had hers confirmed because I didn't wish to fall into the whirlpool of unrequited love. Nor did I want to feel exploited, or exploit her, while still battling to understand what I actually wanted. I knew that having her lips on mine would've been a blessing rather than an exploit. But in the state of uncertainty, she could've just been feeling adventurous and may not have had her emotions in place. Or, it could've been the other way round. I just wanted it to be perfect, without any doubts attached, and at the moment, pulling away had seemed like the right thing to do. Whilst struggling to formulate reasons(excuses) for why I took flight from a kiss I had been dreaming of for days, I couldn't repress the regret flooding over me. I felt like I had wasted time. Maybe we would've been in a different place now. Maybe a nervous kiss would've escalated to a heated session of making out. Instead, I chose to 'be sure'. I was frowning upon the kind of decisions I make. No wonder my emotions are always all over the place. But one thing was certain now: Myra and I had unfinished business and there was no way in hell I was not going to complete it.

THIRTEEN

We are but Metaphors

Two paces forward and nothing would be the same after.

It was a sultry summer afternoon. I took all morning to muster enough courage to come to Myra's place and for some reason, I thought that three in the afternoon, when the sun was blazing with its full potential and not a sound could be heard, not even the honking of cars and shouting of rash drivers, would be the perfect time to pay her an unexpected visit. The streets were unusually empty today, with a few travellers scattered here and there. There was the occasional cawing of parched crows in complaint of the excessive heat.

Besides that, not a sound could be heard. Her bag was hanging from my shoulder and I was standing in front of the door to their flat. I had found the whereabouts of her residence from the security guard who had been snoring with his head leaning on his table, sitting languorously on his chair. I had to scream thrice into obnoxiously sweaty ears to break his slumber. By now, I had been waiting like a frozen soul in front of her door for twenty minutes, thinking that whatever would happen after I stepped in would be irreversible. Shutting my eyelids and taking a deep breath in, defeating the anxiety revolving around my mind with the sword of impulse, I clicked on the doorbell and it rang. It rang resonantly in the silence of the sultry afternoon, sounding like it could be heard clearly from even a mile away.

I heard clicks and clocks as the door was being unlocked from the inside, and as it opened, the angle widening, I descried *her* standing, looking inquisitively at the uninvited guest, wondering which lunatic decided to come at such an odd hour. When she had recognised the uninvited guest as me, she looked slightly baffled.

'Hi!', I greeted warmly.

'Hey!', she answered with an air of confusion.

'So, umm, you left your bag in the car yesterday. I just came to return it.'

'Oh, thank you! I was worried if I had left it back at the beach and somebody had stolen it.'

At her mention of the beach, an atmosphere of awkwardness surrounded us once more. Somehow battling against the uneasiness, I forwarded the bag to her, saying, 'Here.'

'Thank you!', she said and was about to close the door when I interjected the action right in time, 'Wait! There's something you should know. I mean, I want to talk to you about something.'

She stared at me for a few moments, confused, then replied, 'Come inside?'

'Yes, please.'

I followed her to the living space and we sat down on the sofa. She looked at me in a rapid glance and got up, as if realizing something, headed towards the kitchen and returned with a glass of water. I gulped down all the water at once, not realising how thirsty I had been till the first drop of water reached my parched throat.

'So, what is it that you want to say to me?', she asked me with a tone of formality that one uses in conversation with strangers, after I kept down the emptied glass.

'I just wanted to say that.... that I'm sorry. I shouldn't have tried to invade your privacy but I... read your poem about me. Well, I'm assuming it's about me.'

'Oh...,' there was a pause which I wasn't very fond of, but she soon continued, 'Which one?'

My heart jumped to my neck. There were more? I was flattered and surprised concurrently. But I was still beating around the bush and understood that it would probably be best to get to the point instead of whiling away more precious time we could spend together.

'The one where we were sitting on the grass and the scene was set during sunset. But what I came here to say is that I'm sorry for running away yesterday. Or rather, shying away. I was scared, you know. This is all so new to me. I hope you know what I mean.' Why couldn't I just utter the word? Feelings, attraction, crush. I simply couldn't say anything directly. It felt so weird and uneasy but it shouldn't have. It was probably because it was something so unconventional that a part of me still thought that it was something wrong. Heterosexuality had been screwed into our brains as the only acceptable norm before we even understood what emotions meant.

'I get it. This is so new to me too. And when you pulled away like that yesterday, all of a sudden, I thought maybe I had misread the signs and taken a leap too far. I thought that I had almost violated you.'

'And all this while I was wondering if it was one-sided.'

'It's okay.'

'What's okay?'

'You said you're sorry so I said that it's okay. I mean that I forgive you. It's not your fault. It's the world's fault. They've built us in a way that although we know it's not wrong, we still think that it is.' She had just read my mind. Another instance of how brilliant she was and another reason for my ever-amplifying attraction towards her.

‘I know. It sucks, doesn’t it?

‘It really does.’

‘Did we waste time?’

‘I don’t think we did. If anything, I wasted all my life before meeting you. I think in the past week I've discovered more of myself than I have in fifteen years.’

‘Me too.’

‘Every moment that I have spent with you will always find a special, reserved room in my heart, whether it was in the oblivion of each other’s feelings or in the knowledge of them, whether it was in denial of our identities or acknowledgement of them.’

I was blushing and was completely bereft of any words. How can someone sound intellectual and romantic simultaneously?

‘I wanna take you someplace, come on.’ she said. She held my hand, entangling our fingers and I followed her footsteps.

We were at the terrace. She had first collected a tiny picnic box from her room before heading here. We spread a blanket on the burning floor and placed a small plastic table in the middle. She had also brought a copy of 'Pride and Prejudice' and one of 'Call Me By Your Name' from our stuffed bookshelf which she placed on the table. We sat ourselves down on the blanket comfortably, which had already heated up. Instead of sitting on opposite sides of the table, I decided to sit right next to her, facing her at the same time. She slid closer to me, so close that I could feel her breath more than mine. Was I voluntarily trying to align my breathing rhythm to hers? Or were my thoughts so muddled up that I could not dictate my actions anymore? I couldn't tell the difference.

'You are so beautiful.', I said. My face had turned fully crimson and I couldn't maintain eye contact with her.

'You are just talking, no actions,' she answered in a voice that was roaring with desire.

She shifted a step yet closer to me. I gasped, quietly. I was surprised, yes, because this was all so new to me. It was new to her too, but someone had to take the first step, right? On the inside, I was relieved that she barred me from making the first move once again. I couldn't muster enough courage to do it. *Just talking, no actions.* Perhaps she was right. But when her hand slid under my top and grabbed my waist, abruptly at first, then dissolving into mild caresses, I felt all the commotion ebb out of my body. My mind relieved itself from all the confusion and questioning. I felt tranquil. The kind of tranquillity you feel when you're floating silently on the surface of the ocean, isolated. No noise, no intruders. No voices to ridicule you or point guns at your insecurities. My heart was simultaneously beating with sparks and the goosebumps on my hands intensified. It was a feeling difficult to put to words; something like driving on a curvaceous road. There's a sudden rush of exhilaration and uncertainty tingling through your body when the car bends towards the curve, but all of that dissipates, even for a millisecond, into a strange calmness, during the transition as the car moves towards the curve on the other side. Just like the car, I was meandering through my emotions. Highs and lows. Highs of bliss and euphoria, and lows of peace and calm, but nothing of doubts this time. Nor any fear.

Unalarmed, she grasped the other side of my waist with her empty hand and pulled me closer, only our breaths separating us now. *Was this actually happening? Was this really her first time with a girl?* Because she seemed to be so good at this. So good at keeping me nervously waiting for her next move while still wanting her previous one to last. Tinkling nervousness once more reverberated through every vein in me. Breaking my bubble of nervousness, I ran my hand through her chaotic curls while she cupped my jaw in her palm. She smiled, mischievously yet lovingly. I reciprocated the smile. Her hand glided up my waist and landed on my cheek, stroking it softly with her thumb. I flinched in anticipation but before I could pull away, her lips were over mine. Mine over hers. Dancing over each other in light strokes until eventually, they detached themselves from each other. I used to wonder while watching couples on the screen about how every kiss was perfectly timed. Was that possible in reality? What if their rhythms didn't match? What if one goes too fast while the other wants some gentle strokes and it ends up being a disaster? When do you stop? How do you realise when the time is right to stop? But at that moment, I knew. I knew that it only takes the right person to nail it all and achieve that perfect, dreamy, ecstatic kissing that 'rocks your world', which seems so fabricated on screens. At that moment, all the tension in my muscles relaxed into zilch. I felt so many emotions: anxiety, excitement, desperateness, mirth, cheer, passion and the desire to know what would come next, yet I felt complete desolation. More desolate than a glass vessel that's never held even a drop of liquid in it. More desolate than a starless firmament. A void of nothingness which seemed to be brimmed with passion.

Was this wrong?

I couldn't fathom out my emotions. Well, it's not like I excel in that realm anyway but the confusion after the *act* left me more dubious than the pre-*act* confusion. But everything did feel so right; so *different.* I had never felt this way before. Maybe we disappeared into a different dimension for the few moments that it lasted, for it was no earthly or familiar feeling that kindled in me. Everything did feel right yet here I was questioning it. Why couldn't I ever make up my mind?

She gradually proceeded to plant soft kisses on my neck. I was over the moon. No more did the question of whether it was right or wrong hover in my mind. There was no way something so pleasing and exciting could be wrong. The feel of her soft, damp lips against my skin ebbed out all the stress from my body. It was like every muscle in me relaxed all at once and my mind no longer felt clenched with dilemma. I felt as if I were levitating from all the woes of the world. My surroundings were spinning and I could hear nothing but bliss screaming itself out from my chest. She gradually broke contact from my neck and looked me straight in the eyes. We both burst out in laughter, blushing all the while in a deep magenta. We didn't say anything for many minutes but our harmonising laughter spoke enough. I knew that we were both thinking: *we finally did it.* I crossed my arms over my stomach to catch my breath, because the laughter was imperishable and our shyness only increased. With much effort, our laughs finally receded into suppressed giggles, eventually dissolving into silence.

'I thought you were a bitch at first, not going to lie,' I said, thinking that if anything was blooming between us, she deserved to know everything first.

'Why so?'

'Well, I was an insecure loser with relationship and friendship problems. At home, Mom and Dad have always created a competitive environment. I literally get insecure about everything in competing to be the best, and only end up passing for good enough, but, writing was my safe space in this rat race. It still is. It's the only realm where I excelled without competition and when you came in, being complimented by Mrs. Whayton on your very first day, I was crazily jealous. But now that I've read one of your poems, I get what all the gush is about. And over time, I found out how amazingly talented you are and I began comparing myself to you, feeling envious all the time. To be honest, I don't even know what the detestation was about.'

'But you later realised that the envy was actually love in disguise!', she teased gleefully.

'Well, don't satisfy yourself too much. I got to know you better and I realised that more than wanting to be you, I wanted to be with you. Well, I definitely wouldn't have been here today without my brother's assistance, I must admit.'

'Sparsh? Isn't he like fourteen?'

'Yeah, how do you know?'

‘Maybe you are yet to unearth the brilliant stalking skills I possess.’

‘I cannot wait.’

‘But, let me get this straight: Sparsh is fourteen years old, and HE gave YOU, a seventeen-year-old, relationship advice?’

‘He’s more experienced in this field than I am.’

‘What do you mean?’

‘He just *is.*’

‘Okay,’ she answered with an air of perplexion. I knew that if I told her, she would understand. But it wasn’t my place to tell her. I wouldn’t be able to carry the constant guilt of trespassing the private boundaries of my brother. I thought for a while about how I could divert the theme of conversation or not make it too obvious, then spoke, ‘I know what you’re thinking. I may be the one with a higher count of relationships but I’ve never been emotionally attached to someone, until now.’

‘Oh, is that so?’, she said playfully, then flowing into a more serious tone, ‘Since you’re being honest, you must know that I wasn’t fond of you either in the beginning. I was new and when Mrs. Whayton introduced you to me on the first day, I was really hoping to find a friend because I felt so out of place among all the in-house kids. But you seemed so disinterested in even saying ‘hello’ to me. And eventually, I got to hear that you’re one of those popular girls in school so I drew a picture of you as a spoiled girl squandering mommy and daddy’s money.’

‘Woah! I wasn’t expecting so intense a bullet of attack, but I’ll take it, and surrender to you!’

‘Come on, I was being serious. But later as I got to know you, I realised there was so much more to you than a pretty face and big bank.’

‘I would take that as a compliment and say thank you! And I wasn’t being myself ever, you know. I was following the dictation of a popular life— having a boyfriend, attending crazy teenage parties, having a famous and wide friend circle even if I didn’t feel like I ever belonged there. I was ignoring how misplaced I felt in this fixed life which might superficially seem to be very eventful but in reality, was more distasteful than bitter melon juice.'

'I love how you combine humour and irony to drop truth bombs. But I've been meaning to ask, what happened though? I heard rumours in our class that you and your so-called best friend, Alisha, had a big cat fight. And all her fans from our grade were, umm, gossiping about you. And yeah, that's how the whole news of you not liking me reached my ears.'

'Yeah, it was the most pathetic week of my life. I just wish that it had been publicized, but then again, that's an unrealistic wish to have when the fight literally included Alisha Kumar. The fight had completely turned my life upside down. But it also helped me reach the epiphany that I had been trying to reach someone else's standards all this time. I mean, I wasn't even ever in love with my boyfriend of eleven months!'

'Oh. So, you weren't together with him when we were hanging out?'

'Not exactly.'

'What do you mean?'

'We're not together anymore. It's not like I'm cheating on him or anything. So, we're good, if that's what you wanted to hear.'

'Yes, that's all I needed to hear. But are you okay now?'

'Not completely, but you made it a lot better,' I said with puppy eyes.

'Now I can't deny that puppy face,' she said in defeat, inching closer to me and pecking me sweetly.

The remainder of the afternoon passed by in reading the novels that we'd brought from her room earlier and kissing every now and then. She lay down on her back on the blanket, with her head resting on my lap, while I took turns to read out loud our favourite chapters from the two books. I had never felt so intimate with anyone before. I could feel a connection with her on a spiritual level. In the absence of vocal words, our eyes would send messages to each other. And sometimes when I'd stop after reading a paragraph to absorb each sentence that I'd read in its entirety and to picture the visuals of the author's words in my mind, she didn't complain. In fact, the unannounced pauses in between weren't awkward, for she would be doing the same.

' "*I fell in love with him the way you fall asleep, slowly and then all at once*".', I said while quoting Hazel in John Green's bestseller.

'I don't know about Hazel, but I fell for you the way one wakes up.' she said as I closed the book and put it down.

'And that would be?'

'Hesitantly at first, then slowly getting myself to embrace the sunshine hugging the exposed areas of my skin, and finally ending the stage of trying to procrastinate further once I realise how much more the sunshine has to offer me than illusive dreams,' she said, lifting her dreamy eyes up to look at me.

'Am I your sunshine, then?', I asked, running my fingers through her long curls.

'Yes, am I yours?'

'No, you are my rain.'

FOURTEEN

Unlocking all Doors

Never had I been so happy in my life before. It had only been a week since the day on the terrace and I was beginning to foster faith in the popular belief that once you find the right person, everything would fall into place. Nothing could possibly go wrong. I felt at peace with myself and with life. Things were normal at home, with lesser awkward silences and formal table talk than before. I was spending most of my time outside anyway, going to the park, the beach, the Rosé Café, vintage shops, bookstores, all with Myra. Sometimes we'd set out from our houses to just roam around the city, somehow saving ourselves from the lethal traffic, in search of something that we were both unaware of. I felt so intoxicated by her company that it didn't matter where we went or who surrounded us. As long as her hand was linked to mine and her dulcet voice echoed in my ear, I needed nothing else. Everywhere that I went to turned into an isolated island when I was with her. All the voices around would silence into distant susurration of waves. The world around me would become an ocean with our little island mounted above it, with nobody to dictate my actions, nobody to direct me around and nobody to keep pointing out my flaws. I felt free. I did not care if there were folks glaring at us, wondering what two young girls with eyes drunk in love might be up to. I did not care what Mom and Dad thought of the frequency of Myra's visits to our house or mine to hers. Perhaps Mom had assumed that I had found a new best friend and Dad never really exhibited much interest in my social life. After much pampering, Sparsh agreed to stop teasing me on how I went from loathing a person to falling head over heels for her.

The other day we had gone to that spot on the beach where we had almost kissed. This time we came with better preparations to ensure that our clothes, hair, and footwear didn't have sand particles wrapped around them and render us a most irritating itch. We spread a blanket on the sand with food, diaries, pens, and books. We then flung ourselves down on it, which was already heated up with not a minute of being in contact with the sand. She had suggested that we should try to re-enact the events of our failed kiss. I was hesitant at first, feeling abashed to be made to go through my folly. She said that to save me the embarrassment and guilt, she would grant some mercy and play my character and I hers. I couldn't reject the idea of being her, even if it was in a jocular manner and that too, for a very short period. It was no longer about me comparing myself to her or desperately trying to demean my abilities. It was just that she was so good, with a greatness of soul and a profundity of wisdom unmatched, that I, in many ways, looked up to her. I admired her, revered her, drew inspiration from her and loved her all the same. I had not confessed to her yet that I loved her. But I did not deem it necessary. In some ways, I wasn't ready to say it yet either. Whatever it be, I didn't think not saying it didn't imply that I didn't. We relished being in the company of each other's souls, even for endless hours, without getting bored or exasperated. There was no place for jealousy or envy or insecurity to reign over our bond. It was purer than refined gold and more beautiful than golden sunflowers blooming on a balmy day. And these were the kinds of absurd similes we'd come up with when we'd have our pens and diaries with us.

And so, she became me and I her. The act was full of interruptions with our laughter and awkward fits, and we couldn't recreate the tension that had been built up that day. In between giggles and pointing out how terrible the other was at acting, we eventually reached the point where our lips were once more separated by hardly a centimetre, and imitating my abrupt rush of panic, she pulled away and started laughing. I grabbed her arm and brought her closer to me once more, saying in a whisper, 'Only if this had been a movie, you'd have pulled me back again like this', pulling her so close that our lips were then touching each other but still stationary, and said with a voice so full of desire, 'and done this.' And I kissed her like it was my very first time.

She told me one day that she wanted to show me a different side of Mumbai. I was confused initially because having lived here for seventeen years, which was basically all my life, it was difficult to believe that there was a part of the city that I was ignorant of. But I didn't wish to miss any chance of being with her and so agreed upon going on a trip to meet this 'different side' of the city. As it turned out, she was right. After travelling past several buildings, houses, malls, shops, pedestrians, hawkers, cars, bicycles and all other elements of the urbanized world, she brought us to a place far away from the noisy lanes and congested roads. It was verdant all around, as if we were in some viridescent valley. There were trees, tall and short, grasses of various sorts, with the croonings of sparrows and chirping of cuckoos dancing harmoniously in the air. The smell of wet soil added to the tranquilising aura. Puddles of placid water were scattered on the ground, glimmering in the light of the first sun rays after an unabating downpour. We were standing in front of what seemed to be an unending hiking trail and I was already exhausted from the sight of it. It was winding, with a mystic tenebrosity adding to its surroundings the farther you looked, appearing as if it got narrower as one went ahead. She had perhaps read the look on my face and said that she had been here before and there was nothing to worry about. No snakes that would come crawling to inject their venoms into my leg and no birds on flight that could potentially land their droppings on my freshly washed hair. To offer further reassurance, she said that she would hold my hands and lead the way throughout. I trusted her experience and my instinct, which prompted me to overcome the doubts revolving around the mysteries of the wilderness that lay ahead and simply have faith in my partner. Were we still partners? In a work way, maybe not anymore since the matter of the magazine had been sealed a long time ago. But we were still partners, I guess. Just in a different way.

And so, we walked along the winding path, with me nearly plodding. I couldn't help but expect the path to lead to a grove guarded by blood-thirsty dragons any second. While dread pulsated all across my chest, I couldn't help but be mesmerised by the sights as we progressed. I espied some of the most exquisite elements of nature during our hike. The path was wet, radiating a fresh aroma of monsoons, with some muddy spots here and there which Myra warned me about beforehand as we proceeded. I hardly managed not to dip my sneakers into one. As if in whispers, we could hear brown crickets chirping and green grasshoppers clicking, fading away in sound as we sailed forward. Among multifarious varieties, I could identify a few mahoganies bordering the trail, as well as the gnarled roots of some mangrove-like trees encroaching upon much of our already-narrow walking space. Our conversation while hiking on this winding path was limited but not dead. At about one-third of the total journey, we came to a halt because I was panting like the air was devoid of oxygen. As we stood in the middle of nowhere, enveloped by the green, she told me that this region was an extension of the Western Ghats and received one of the heaviest rains in the country, hence the wetness and moisture. I told her that I was amazed at her local geographical knowledge. As we started moving ahead after a few minutes, we mostly dwelled in silence because 1. There were too many hurdles and dried sticks on the ground that we needed to avoid and our brains couldn't handle talking alongside (at least mine couldn't), and, 2. The beauty of the place had left me speechless. I had been to so many places all around the world but nothing had brought me as much bliss, awe and peace as this. There was something about being in the lap of nature that could not be matched by any of the ostentatious luxuries of the human-built world. Yes, the Eiffel Tower or the Burj Khalifa soaring high up into the face of heaven with its sleek edges and gorgeous architecture was a sight to behold, but it was nowhere near the beauty of towering trees with their curves and green boughs creating a breathtaking contrast against the blue sky. For the first time, I preferred the mild chirping of birds and the fluttering of leaves and all of the sounds made by insects— which I would've earlier claimed as weird— over loud music bursting out of speakers in parties that a lot of people attended only to find a sense of belonging in a social life when they knew very well on the inside they'd only come crawling back home to discover more bruises in their broken souls. I know I did. I realised that day how selfish people were and that I was indubitably one among them. Whatever we do, we always have an ulterior motive. So, what if you started an award-winning company? So, what if you created a non-profit helping those in hunger? So, what if your childhood best friend turned out to be the love of your life? Did you do it without putting up a story on Instagram or bragging about it in your friend group or tweeting about how many people you helped? The problem is, most of us always feel the need to show. We fear dwelling in mediocrity or lagging behind everyone else. Everyone must know how great we are or *they'll* disgrace us as talentless or aimless. And if everyone were to believe that your existence is in fact futile to the progress of humanity, would the world around you actually collapse? No, it wouldn't. But as Shakespeare said, the world's a stage and we've all painted facades over ourselves to evade from who we are and what our end is. But nature, on the other hand, is altruistic. It persists to live without bothering to flaunt, it persists to be magnanimous without protesting against us for not returning its selfless love, and in this stage full of artists constantly feigning their identities to become someone who everybody will like, it is the only bona fide element grounding us to reality. But sometimes, I don't want to be grounded. I want to remain high on superficial social standards. I want to be a people-pleaser because I'm part of a system whose fuel is external validation. However, on that day, with my feet united with the muddy soil and my head feeling lighter than a feather as it roamed in the humid air, I wanted to be grounded and let go of all the superficial standards I had been struggling to meet all these years. And just for a moment, I let go of her hands and absorbed the surroundings around me, inhaling every atom of the moist air, listening to every fluttering leave, every whooshing zephyr and very chirping cricket, trying to dissolve my limbs, that felt weightless, into the peace of the ethereal being that was nature. Seeing that I had detached my hand from hers, Myra turned around and looked at me with a worrisome look, asking if I was okay. 'Haven't felt more okay in days,' I answered. We eventually reached the cease of the path which had once seemed endless. And she wasn't wrong. It truly was a different side of the city. We were mounted on what seemed to be a plateau. Below, you could view the city in its entirety, unfiltered and unadulterated. The blue roofs of

Dharavi popped out vibrantly amidst the monochromatic modern skyscrapers. I realized that I had never truly appreciated the beauty of the place where I was born. The world seemed so tiny from that altitude. I could hardly spot any people but the few that I did looked like puppets running on paper-made roads. It was hysterical in a way. How insignificant my problems seemed when I saw the world from an eye that knew nothing about the desires and wants of the human mind!

She asked me if I liked the view. I said that I loved it. She asked if I was sure, as we were standing nearly on the verge of the cliff beside each other, facing the city expanding like a wide stream from a waterfall. I turned her towards me and cupped her face in my hands and said, 'If you must hear it, it was worth walking around ten thousand steps. And I have seen nobody more beautiful than you in this heavenly place.' And we kissed there with every sign of affection, not caring that a steep slope was not five inches from us, thinking that if by chance we slipped, we would desire no better ending. At that moment, I also realised that we had shared our most intimate parts with each other. The spot at the beach was my safe spot. I didn't go there only to wander around. I would go there when the unrest rising in my throat needed to be unshackled and let out into the void of the ocean in early morning hours, when my twitching toes needed to feel the touch of the dry sand to stop twitching, when my chest heated with fear and my head riddled with despair needed the salty sea zephyrs to rustle through the tangled strands of my hair and wash away the overweight pulling my shoulders down. Nobody knew about that place before her. It was my haven when everything and everyone seemed unfamiliar. And I understood, then, that more than the spot and its ideal distance from people, it was about me reuniting with nature when the world around me became too human. And this extension of a plateau, which at first had seemed like a death trail disguised as a winsome valley, was her safe place. She told me that the long duration of the hike would help her shift her focus from fights with her mother or how she didn't feel much welcome at one of her friend's parties that day. It helped her find herself and realise she was much more than how she was perceived and treated by others, even if they may be her loved ones. She said that this place made her realise that she was so much more than a nerdy-looking spectacled girl with frizzy hair whose nose was mostly buried within books or whose fingers were constantly tangoing with ink and words. And she was right. There was much beyond what one could just see her to be. And I realised how blessed I was to know her true self, even if in parts, because she was her own kind.

The Rosé Café had easily become our most visited place. I was sure that, at this point, it gained most of its sales from us. In fact, we didn't even have to order. Within fifteen minutes of us sitting and chattering at our table, steaming hot chocolate with whipped cream would come running to us, and then we'd have either burgers or pizzas, or, if we were feeling too special on some days, we'd order mac and cheese. We usually tried to go there during the afternoons when the place was practically empty. We'd eat, drink, crack stupid jokes, laugh and talk. While sometimes we talked about our favourite animals, on other days we'd reflect upon how absurd it was to think that the cosmos would still be in its womb state after the cease of our planet. On the other hand, we didn't talk at all at times. It wasn't because we were mad at each other. Nor did we run out of topics. We were simply just not bold enough yet to vocalise some thoughts that were still too intimate and had not been fully comprehended by ourselves either. I wasn't ready yet to say to her the kind of things I wanted to explore with her, besides just talking and writing and roaming. There was so much more I wanted to do and I could tell her from the glint of desire in her pupils that she wanted to as well. But we simply weren't at that stage of confidence yet. Parts of us still doubted if this was what we really wanted; if this is who we truly were. If this was even *right*. The thing about doing something unconventional is that till you find a source of validation for yourself, you'd never be confident enough to have complete faith in yourself. Although it was easy for me to forget everything else when I was with her and I was aware that I was the happiest when with her, it was also easy for dubious questions to invade my mind any second. Sometimes when we would be chatting together, whether on the phone or in person, on topics nowhere related to the fear of revealing our identities to others, there would fall abrupt silences of several minutes and we would both know what the other would be thinking about. It was like dreaming. Despite however enchanting it might be, despite how firmly you may believe that it is real, somewhere in the back of your mind you know that you're dreaming and you'll soon have to burst the bubble and encounter reality once more. We were living in a reality that was true only for the two of us. For my parents, I was just enjoying the summer with a newfound friendship. For my friends except Sasha, I was a bitch who had demeaned the queen bee, Alisha's dignity. I don't think they would identify as friends anymore. I don't even recall the last time I'd spoken to them. For Arj, I was a lost stranger who had broken his heart and vanished like the rains in the Thar. It was during these silences that I questioned if I had alienated myself from everyone else in finding love in someone.

The beach was incontestably our favourite place to hang out at. There was life amidst the undulating waves, lapping at our feet as their foamy ends kissed the shore. We'd sit by the area where the water was vibrant enough to rise till our knees. But in our visits to the beach, the scene was quite different, especially when we weren't in the spot. From my spot, you could only find the peace of vacancy and catch sight of the most gorgeous view of the sun, the waters, the shore, and people dancing away in the celebratory aura of nature. But you couldn't feel the sea in its entirety there, you couldn't feel the water rise through your body and soothe every twitching artery. So, we would go to the spot either to seek solace or when we failed to keep our hands off of each other. But right by sea, there were people around. And we were still scared.

No matter how much we tried to mask the dread of being outed, it screamed itself out loudly when we would be sitting two feet apart, our shoulders no longer touching each other, our fingertips desperately trying to reach the other's but curling away in fear, our hearts wanting to listen to the other's beating but abstaining themselves, and when our words took shape of friendly conversational exchange instead of how we otherwise spoke to each other. Despite pride flags flaming in some parts of the city and the revolutionary movement for gay rights sowing its first seeds in the country, we were scared. Neither of us was brave enough to admit that we had become to prey to homophobic predator of society. We were scared to be seen, to be heard, or to even arouse the slightest inch of doubt in someone. It was during these moments when we'd pretend to be nothing more than friends for the outside world not to budge an inch from the belief that we weren't, that would provoke feelings of dubiety in me: was this truly a blessing or a curse in disguise? Sometimes I failed to be certain of her feelings. It was mostly when she would not kiss me back when I'd plant a peck on her lips or when she didn't hug me as tightly as I did her or when her voice echoed with disinterest during colloquy. It sucked because I did not want to doubt her, especially after having seen how crestfallen she had gotten the day I dodged away from our possible first kiss. Was that why she perhaps didn't like the beach? Because it resonated memories of failed endeavours with her? In those moments, I wished that I had the superhuman power of reading others' minds. In fact, I didn't even bother about other people's minds except hers. I wanted to know if just like me, her mouth dried up at the thought of my lips. I wanted to know if just like me, she could hear her heart squeal gleefully at the thought of my smile. I wanted to know if just like me, tinkling nervousness tap danced around her thorax. The inquisitiveness was unquenchable but I had to deal with the fact that I would never find the answers to my searching questions.

FIFTEEN

Sleepovers and Unspoken Feelings

Myra was coming over to stay at my place tonight. It was a big thing to me. This was the first time ever that I would formally introduce her to my parents as the amazing person she was. And although I'd hold up the pretence of us being merely companions, I couldn't help but hope that they would in some way approve of her. I didn't really believe in seeking approval of something or someone that I deeply and truly love. And so, I found it difficult to fathom out the origin of this need for approval. But I realised that in a way, I was seeking their approval of myself. Myra was in several ways my own reflection, but in several ways not, too. She was my reflection on the sea. It was distorted and constantly fluctuating along with the swaying waves, but it was still me. Some parts of me were several inches apart from the remaining whole, and some so clustered together that they formed an entirely new image. And so she was my distorted reflection, whose segregated pieces when put together orderly, rendered meaning to my individuality. And what was this individuality? Well, from what I have learnt in the past month, it was a dynamic. It was transposing itself from one thought to another, one person to another, one emotion to another, one musing to another, one inference to another, one liking to another, constantly. Yet it retained some parts perpetually, those which were quintessentially me, which had my name inscribed all over them. Presently, that dynamic had arrived at a seventeen-year-old girl at the cusp of adulthood, who was still exploring her tastes, still discovering new things about herself day in and day out, who was beginning to comprehend the implication of heavy words like love, hate, and betrayal slowly but steadily, while also currently finding herself trapped in a labyrinth of love, friendship and betrayal that seemed inescapable. And the source of light fortifying me not to give up and stay afloat, to keep following it and have faith that there will be a way out, was Myra. So, it was important to me that they approved of her, which in a way would be an approval of the chaos I was.

At around eight in the evening she had arrived at our door, with her right shoulder strained with the load of her bag looking more rotund than usual, being brimmed with clothes. Her vacant hand reached out to embrace me from the side and I requited, while greeting her inside. We went into my room and kept her stuff in place. I shut the door and clicked the lock close, then pulled her towards me while she was trying to lay out her nightwear on the bed. I attacked her with kisses on her forehead, neck, cheeks, the back of her hands, the tip of her nose, just not her lips. She started giggling instantly and tried to get out of my hold, as if trying to plead to let go of her because someone might come in and catch us. I revolted against her revolt till we were fighting like little children who tried to wrestle in a jocular fashion, not realising that we had reached every corner of the room in our minuscule wrestle till the back of my legs were leaning against the edge of the mattress on the bed. Losing my balance over the floor, I tumbled on the bed and she fell along with me. We were cackling our lungs out. As our cackles gradually receded and we regained the normal pace of breathing, she turned towards me, her face a few centimetres away from mine. Our legs were entangled together, the heat of desire rising from our toes and infiltrating our hearts. She ran her fingers through my dishevelled wavy strands. I just got out of the shower when she had arrived, depriving me of the opportunity to comb my knots out. With her fingers, she untangled the meshes and straightened them out ever so gently. I felt embarrassed and hid in the safety of her bosom. She laughed unobtrusively, as if I had done something silly or petty. She carefully raised my head from hiding and caressed my flushed visage with her soft palms.

'These little things about yourself that you consider shameful and abashing, I love them all. I love them as much as I love your gems. There is nothing to conceal,' she said in a way that only magnified the love and reverence I had for her.

'Are you sure?', I asked, still not quite able to believe that I was so admirable that even my flaws could be loved.

She did not answer, but slid her hand down to my chin, and grabbing hold of it, pulled my face closer to hers till there was no space between our lips, our noses colliding with each other. As I parted my lips, I could smell roses in every breath she took. I traced her lips with my tongue and she welcomed the invasion with acquiescence. There was raw emotion in the way her fingers were caressing my head and my back while our tongues tangoed delightfully. My toes curled up and my knees felt weak as they bent into the empty space between her thighs. The tension rippled out of my forehead and my arms as all my senses unfurled into how soft her lips felt against mine. We turned over and suddenly, I was on top of her. I parted with her lips and proceeded to her neck. After lingering on her neck for a while, as she sighed in delectation, I slid down to her chest and stayed there for a while. I looked up at her in apprehension till she nodded a desperate 'yes, please'. She lifted her back from the bed so I could take off her top. Surprisingly, her hands slid inside my blouse, the feel of her warm fingers radiating with heat against my cold back, sending waves of hypnotic passion to all my senses, and she started unhooking my bra. I was startled a little to see that she was proceeding fast, but I was not complaining. Things seemed to be escalating rapidly after we undressed each other, all the while kissing in an attempt of not disrupting the tension. But I couldn't help but entertain the invasion of doubtful worries: what would this lead to? What if she wouldn't like it? Was *it* really happening? Her lips were on the edge of my clavicle when a vigorous knocking made us jump from our places, and came in Mom's voice in a chord of hospitality, 'Girls, dinner's ready. Come soon or the food will get cold!'. Her words were like a delaying barrier to the after-shame, but as soon as she stopped, her words dissipating into the quiet air and her footsteps growing distant, a lump of awkwardness collected in both of our throats. While I was completely flushed from head to toe, she kept looking around the room as if trying to find something interesting, all the while refraining from catching my eyes. I hurriedly grabbed my bra and blouse and put them back on, and she replicated, keeping her eyes fixated on the curtains. We jumped out of bed and proceeded to the door with quick paces. On reaching the door, we both forwarded our arms to turn the knob and they clashed. Could this get any more awkward? My arms retreated from the reach of the knob, but she did the same thing, and it only got all the more awkward. I quickly reached forward with my hand once more and unlocked the knob at last, before she could reach out again. Clashing with each other's shoulders, we left the room, each looking straight ahead and trying hard not to exchange glances or words.

The seating arrangement at the dinner table was a saviour. Myra and I were seated next to each other which saved us from any optical encounters. Opposite us were seated Dad and Sparsh while Mom was busy serving us food, introducing the history and recipe of each dish as she proceeded from one hot case to another. None of us displayed any interest or investment in Mom's words except Myra. She really was making an effort to instil a favourable impression on my family. She kept smiling and nodding to Mom's words. It looked like Myra was the teacher's pet and Mom the overly-enthusiastic teacher, and the remaining three of us bored students who were tired of the buttering and flattering. Once she was done, Mom sat down on one of the vertical ends of the table, the seat which we usually refer to as the winner's seat. Our family had started a tradition two years ago to reserve that seat for special occasions. It would be occupied on a special day by someone among the four of us who had accomplished something commendable. On other days, we just sat along the horizontal dimensions of the table. Exceptions were made when we invited guests over. So when Mom sat down on the winner's seat, she had a triumphant smile carved across her countenance, eyes looking teasingly at Dad, to which he responded by an eye-roll of vexation. Although Sparsh and I may not have the best relationship with our parents, the kind of youthful friendship they had with each other was one source of perpetual delight in our household. I could only wish I found a partner like that. Individually, my parents were amazing people with cool personalities, and together, they mingled as an exemplary couple because their disparities and similarities aligned so perfectly with each other that they seemed to balance each other out by just the ideal amount.

For the first few minutes, there was a complete absence of words as we all were engrossed in eating. There were occasional moans from Sparsh and Dad in expression of how scrumptious the food was, interspersed with a chef's kiss or two from Dad. The dishes were not my favourite, but they were Myra's favourites. Nevertheless, I relished each bite. I had especially instructed Mom to cook the majority of the food items she liked. From my peripheral vision, I espied Myra relishing the flavour of Mom's cooking too. That she was a silent eater I had known for a long time. But I never thought she smiled while chewing away her favourite dishes. Perhaps those smiles of satisfaction and relish had got concealed behind the huge cups in which restaurants mostly served hot chocolates. As we neared towards clearing our plates and the sounds of chewing, nibbling, drinking, gulping and swallowing could no longer compensate for the lack of conversation, Dad cleared his throat and directing his words at Myra, he asked, 'So, *Meera*, am I right? You study with Alaina, I hear.'

'Yes, Uncle, it's actually *Myra*,' she answered with a warm and welcoming smile, emphasizing on the pronunciation of 'y' in her name, and continued, 'and Alaina and I study in the same school, yes. I study a grade lower than hers.'

'Oh,' said Mom in a realising tone, 'that's new. Alaina's always befriended people of her age or elder. Great to see you being more open-minded, beta.' I wanted to get up from the table and run away at this point. My skin had turned crimson in embarrassment. There was also an undeniable tone of sarcasm in Mom's voice and I couldn't help but feel the urge to reply sardonically too, but I maintained my cool and simply rolled my eyes instead. Both Myra and Mom chuckled lightly at this.

‘So how is it that you both met?’ Either Mom had a diploma in ‘How-to-lengthen-small-talk’ or she was suspiciously curious about our friendship.

‘Through the Literary Club,’ I cut in before Myra could slip out kinder words and eke out this conversation unnecessarily. ‘Mrs. Whayton assigned us to work together for the annual magazine.’

‘Oh wow, she’s a writer too!', Dad exclaimed abruptly. Perhaps I had praised her so much to make my parents hold her image in high esteem that on meeting her, they could hardly believe that person could be so great and talented at such a young age. That, or Dad genuinely thought that the world was running short of writers. I honestly couldn’t tell.

‘Mrs. Kaur, the food was really delicious! Thank you so much. I was taken with surprise to see all of my favourite dishes assembled on one plate.’

‘Always a delight, dear! Besides, all credits must go to Alaina for strictly instructing me to cook all your favourites.’ At this, we all rose from our seats gently and proceeded to the kitchen to deposit our plates, bowls, spoons, forks and glasses near the sink. Dad insisted that there was no need because Ram Bhaiya would do it eventually anyway, but we countered that it would be magnanimous of us to reduce some of his burden.

While returning to my room, I was walking in front and Myra behind me. The awkwardness between us had dwindled since we had set out for dinner, but it hadn't vanished altogether. As we entered, she shut the door behind us and whispered in my ear, with a voice as melodious as ever, 'Thank you.' I stopped in my tracks as every crest and trough of those two words rested on my ears, as if echoing inside my body and sending goosebumps down my hand. I realised that I might have been looking strange standing there like a frozen ghost, so I turned and sat down on the bed. She came and sat beside me, her fingers sheltering themselves, fidgeting now and then, resting on her lap. Not a word. It was as if her lips had been taped to silence. We remained quiet for several seconds till I realised it was her who had spoken last, so technically, it was my turn to speak. Had we both been expecting the other to respond and so the silence stretched out longer than it should have?

‘This won’t be very different from you sleeping in your home if we don’t talk for the rest of the night,’ I said in an attempt to lighten up the heavy air of awkwardness roofing over us. The attempt was met with triumph. She began chortling heartily, and the contagion of her chortle was so strong that I was roaring with laughter not long after.

‘Arrogant of you not to reply decently to my thanking you’, she teased.

‘But on what premise are you beholden to me, my lady?’

‘On the premise that you remembered all of my favourite dishes even if I mentioned them randomly one day during a casual conversation. Also, for telling your mother to cook them. She really has a magical hand.’

‘Now I can’t tell whether you’re complimenting my mother or me, but welcome and thank you anyway.’

‘I love how naturally we got over the awkwardness,’ she said, scooting over close to me.

‘Yes, very naturally,’ I mocked.

‘I mean, an hour’s not so bad.’

‘And what now?’

‘I say we bring some sprinkles of that awkwardness back’, she said and started kissing my collarbone again, exactly where we had left off. All my senses were afloat on a dreamy cloud once again. After leaving a trail of kisses around my neck, her lips found mine. Her breath destabilized my own rhythm of breaths, but was inviting at the same time. I almost dissolved into how divine her lips felt against mine and how her thumb was gently stroking my cheek till I realised that the door was not locked. Unwillingly and abruptly, I broke off from the kiss with panic-riddled eyes. Myra looked puzzled with hints of worry conquering her eyes. I sat there frozen for a while, forgetting that I had stopped to rush to the door and lock it.

‘Did I do something wrong?’, she asked fretfully, her face looking pale.

‘I can’t do this,’ I blurted in anxiety that someone might have heard or seen us.

‘What? Why?’

'I meant, the door was unlocked and it's best for us to control our hormones till everyone else is asleep.'

Fortunately, the colour returned to her face and she smiled with the company of mellow giggle. I continued, 'Besides, we can smooch any day. I have other fun stuff planned for us tonight.'

'Uwuu, what's that?'

'First, I want us to put on face masks and lip scrubs.'

'Okay?', she said, sounding confused.

'So, the idea is to have a "glow-up" of sorts, if you know what I mean. We'll wear these relaxing masks, lay down on the bed and chill watching a movie or something for an hour. Then we help each other dress up, like what we see in American teen shows.'

'So, like a slumber party?'

Those two words triggered me down a memory spiral I was not wishing to revisit for a long time. She took notice of how I had zoned out of the present, and realising that the words had a different implication for me, she quickly diverted from the topic and said, 'Take out the masks already!'. It was conspicuous that she had said that to cover up and prevent me from getting triggered any further, but it worked. Plus, I did not want to waste my energy in remembering a time when I was more chaotic than now. I went to my dressing table and took out two packets of sheet masks and lip scrubs respectively, while she sauntered towards the entrance and locked the door.

We put the masks and the lips scrubs on each other, the translucent masks unable to conceal how magenta our cheeks had turned from all the blushing. Not over a few months back, I was labelling these things as 'cringe' as I sat in the cafeteria with Alisha, Sasha, and others whose faces were now blurred sketches in the back of my head. But to be actually experiencing it felt so good, to say the least. My heart fluttered at every touch of her hand on my body, feeling new every time, despite having gotten used to it. We lay down on the bed with our backs upright in order to watch the television in a comfortable position, but the occasional drippings from the sheet on our clothes kept the embrace of comfort miles away from us. Tucking pillows behind us and pulling the blanket till where our thighs transitioned into hips, we tried to make ourselves as comfortable as possible, although the mask feeling moist and chill against our skin really hindered us from focusing on anything else, especially relaxation. We turned on the television to watch some random movie we weren't really paying heed to. Fifteen minutes into the movie, we had already surrendered on adhering to the convenience of the mask. Slowly but noticeably, we both kept sliding down from the pillow till our backs were no longer sitting upright against the head of the bed. The pillows dropped down to a horizontal position in the absence of our backs holding them vertically and under the influence of gravity, of course. Eventually, our heads were resting on the pillows, our eyes nearly shutting and our exhausted brains dissolving into the tender comfort of the cotton. There was probably something in the material of sheet masks or the hydrant they contained that made my eyelids involuntarily canopy over my pupils. While it was refreshing, it made me feel extremely drowsy. Looking to my left, I understood that I was not the only one and Myra was beginning to feel sleepy too. I glided over to the left to get closer to her and she welcomed my arrival into her space amorously. She swung her arm around me and with a little bit of shifting and adjusting, we were cuddling. She dug her fingers under my blouse once more, only this time devoid of any desire or lust or passion, but brimmed with compassion and care. She began drawing circles around my belly with her fingers. I suddenly felt a rush of insecurity tide through my body and attempted to evade her grasp, but she seemed to comprehend without any speech the pessimistic sentiment that had overtaken me, so she pulled me closer before I could barely move an inch, and whispered into my ears with such affection as I had never felt from anyone before, 'You're beautiful.' She then started drawing triangles, rectangles, hexagons and other random geometrical shapes. I almost dozed off in the calm environment, her sweet caresses, the movie playing as background music, dim lights, us tucked away in blankets comfortably. I kept my eyes close not only because the mask was creating hurdles in keeping my vision in focus but also because I wanted to allow myself to fully dissolve into the peace, realising that this too, like all other things in life, was ephemeral, and instead of worrying about what could've been or what will be in the days unborn, I could engross myself into the beauty of this moment unadulteratedly. Misconstruing my infantile attempt at meditation for sleeping, she suddenly stopped drawing shapes and switched over to letters. I could not help but feel solicitous about her wrist and fingers starting to ache already, but simultaneously, I was curious to learn what letters would she trace across my skin. As always, my curiosity ruled over any other emotion and pretended to be asleep, although not actually pretending because meditating while lying down visually resembled sleeping itself. I failed to guess most of the words because of how fast she switched from one word to another, but one time, she traced the letters leisurely and lazily. I could discern several lines forming angles, a straight line, a right angle, an egg out of nowhere, an acute angle, three lines, and more angles and eggs. She wrote them slowly and after ending the sentence she didn't write anything over it. She stopped drawing completely and simply reposed her palm on my belly, straightening her fingers from all the twisting and curling. It took me several minutes to fathom out what she had written. And I felt stupid for taking so long to discern it. I tried to keep myself composed while my heart was squealing in unimaginable raptures. I wanted to hug her, kiss her, dance with her, jump up and down and just twirl in excitement. I felt impatient but I also felt somewhat relaxed to know that we were on the same page, that the emotions were mutual. To think that someone who had been a stranger to me a month ago, to a deeply-loathed and envied person in my knowledge a few weeks ago to someone who meant so much to me, if not family, then literally just next to family in rank of priority, it sounded like a beautifully crafted storyline from a novel, the one that made you plant faith in the idea of love and hope that you would find something so pure and intimate like Bennet had found in Darcy, like Dante had found in Beatrice, like Elio had found in Oliver, like Heathcliff had found in Catherine. I could name dozens of love tales, recite every line of Romeo and Juliet, but I will never find among those words one thing to pinpoint at that she gave me. Because she gave me all of it. I felt love. I felt lust. I felt passion. I felt desire. I felt intimacy. I felt affection. I felt care, compassion, companionship, and reverence. I felt all of them at the same time— each time I looked into her eyes. For me, her soul was hallowed, even with the flaws that she frowned upon, even with the insecurities that she wailed about during solemn nights, even with her troublesome hurricanes and her tranquil waves. It was at that moment when she had carved those eight magical letters across my stomach, that I understood what love was. By confessing to me, she actually brought to life an emotion so strong that I was not quite ready yet to face it. And it was not that I would love her only if she loved me back. For love was nothing about that. It was about your soul finding a haven. It was about your voice finding ears that would never get exhausted or irked by it. It was about your ears finding a voice, that regardless of how repeatedly they listened to it, never sensed monotony. It was about your mind finding another mind so much like yours that it was impossible to believe that they were two different minds whatsoever, and so your mind could bring to words uncanny or conventionally condemned thoughts that you unwillingly suppressed for so many years thinking nobody would understand. But now someone did. Someone did comprehend the labyrinth that you metaphorized life as. Someone did embrace the chaos brewing in your head rather than disdaining it. Someone did understand how smart and dumb you could concurrently be. Someone did not only accept but also adore your so-called insecurities and flaws. And if you'd ask me what love was, it was talking to a stranger till night awoke into dawn, not feeling the need to put a filter on yourself. Love was learning not to hate some bits and pieces of yourself, or even all of yourself. Love was finding such safety and comfort in another soul, or place, or thought, that you wouldn't mind if love didn't find love in you back. All you wanted was to hold on to love, whether in memories or in the moment, and for once feel that you can be everything you want without the dread of being degraded.

Suddenly the timer blew off and all tranquillity was interjected within seconds. I had set the timer for an hour. But for some reason, it felt like it was merely seconds ago that we had put on the masks and laid down on bed. At the sound of the timer, we both started at our places. Her arms disconnected from me and we were both sitting upright on the bed, taken by surprise. We looked at each other, hands resting on our chests and breathing heavily, smiling at each other because the adrenaline had erupted too vigorously for our vocal cords to find any laughter. I shut the timer off and we got up from the bed, making our way to the bathroom. After taking off the masks from our faces, we dabbed the material into our skin, a refreshing moisture sinking in. I then pulled open a drawer brimmed with make-up products. Myra gasped at the sight of the hoard. I tittered at the confounded expression on her face. 'I don't use most of them.', I said, trying to assuage her bewilderment with some modesty. I picked out some products and we went back into the room. We sat down on the bed, spreading the products on the bed. I asked her to show me the dress she had brought (I had already informed her that an occasion demanding glamour might arise). She looked at me nervously, sliding her hand slowly towards her bag and bringing it closer, her mouth trying to form words but too hesitant to say them.

'Tell me?', I said, understanding that something was bringing her discomfort.

'Huh?', she said, as if she wasn't expecting me to detect her uneasiness.

'I know you want to tell me something.'

'Yeah, um, it's nothing.' But I knew it was not nothing.

'Myra,' I said, with a mildly stern tone, then transitioned into comforting assurance, 'you know I don't judge, especially not with you. Is there a problem?'

'Look,' she finally admitted, taking off the facade, 'I know you have an iconic fashion sense and I totally dig it. But I am not the most knowledgeable person in the field of fashion, so, like, the dress might not be *the best* but it is *my best*. Also, I don't know how to put on like party make-up.'

I couldn't help but smile at her innocence. 'Of course, honey. That's not something you need to tell me. I will appreciate you in rags too. Clothing is just an exterior bearing. You are so much more than that. And if by mentioning your ignorance in the realm of make-up, you are suggesting that I do it for you, my brushes and blushes would be honoured to touch your skin.'

'You're so sweet, Alaina.'

'Why, thank you very much.'

'But the last line was just not it.'

'Yeah, I agree. I instantly cringed. But that doesn't harm my sweetness, does it?'

'Absolutely not!', she exclaimed.

'Then, what are you waiting for? Show me the dress already!'

She pulled out a silver glimmering short dress with a halter neck and a slight back-cut. 'Wow,' I exclaimed, 'it's beautiful.' She asked me if I was complimenting only for the sake of it and I answered that had I been feigning it, it wouldn't have been uttered instantly. To that, she smiled at me with a sense of agreement. I then got up to open my closet and let her choose for me. She chose a satin pink gown with a deep neck V-cut and a long cut till the things on the right side. Its back had a twisted network of threads. I was both relieved and surprised at her choice. As I grabbed the dress from her hand and started undressing, she interrupted, 'Wait! Let me wear your dress and you wear mine.' She caught hold of my wrist and pulled me close enough to her so that she could undress me. I knew exactly what she meant by her proposal and there was no need for further elucidation. Wearing each other's clothes thus became another language of our love. It was one of the ways we could become each other. It made our bodies feel united and our souls common, as if each and every atom that formed ourselves truly originated from the same mother, whatever that would be.

SIXTEEN

Voicing Silences

It was nearly half past midnight. We were laying on a white furry carpet on the floor which was long enough to save our heads from getting flattened by the floor, but not long enough to keep our legs fully relieved of the worry of ants and cockroaches scurrying up our toes. How had three hours passed with such ease, I could not tell. Conversation came naturally to us and every hour would pass by way quicker than it usually seemed to. It always bemused me how we could talk about anything and it'd still end up becoming interesting. To think that a conversation can propagate for longer than an hour in the absence of any gossip or gushing over other people's lives was not quite believable to me. Today, we started from complimenting how good the other looked in the opposite's clothes to uncontrollable flirtation to laughter so unquenchable that we could hardly breathe. As the laughter died, we listened to the silence of the night until she asked me where I usually bought my dresses from, which eventually grew into a chat around fashion. We clicked a ton of polaroid pictures of which she took five prints, saying that she would superglue it to the walls of her heart. From fashion, winding through different themes, we finally landed on creating our own sequel to the Harry Potter series. And we were laying down on the fur, toes twirled around each other, her head resting on my chest, her hands hugging my waist, and my hand caressing her head while also occasionally playing with her curls.

For a few moments, we didn't speak. We simply let ourselves dissolve into the beauty of the moment and much like other times, our minds communicated louder than our voices ever could. I also realised then, that one day after twenty years, perhaps when I would be at different crossroads of life where this night, this peace and this fluttering feeling swirling in my tummy and soothing my senses will seem strange and unfamiliar, when these hands which now played with her curls would forget the touch of her soft messy hair on them, when these lips now dying to dance with hers would not remember her taste, when she and I, *us,* will be a magical tale trapped in a time hole unknown, then on that day, this furry carpet and the soft bed and the walls surrounding us will throng with memories of a youthful love. The sands of the Juhu beach, the waves dribbling over the shore, the chairs by the window of the Rosé Café, the viridescent valley concealed in a part of this city unearthed, they will all recall times when two young girls had invaded them and learnt to love without fear. And maybe in twenty years, wherever I would be, perhaps with a new lover or without any whatsoever, because god knows that the most beautiful things in life are most ephemeral, then I would search for the same sense of meaning in their gaze and in their kisses as I had found in hers. It still could've been a mere amalgam of infatuation and crushing, but sometimes, I didn't want to overthink it. For the first time, I did not want to question anything. I did not bother wasting thought on whether our relationship would last or be sustainable in the long term. All that mattered was that we were here, at this moment, with such unimaginable mirth and tranquillity that even if it would vanish in the near future, we would have this moment to hold on. *I* would have this moment to hold on to— on days that tasted of bittersweet nostalgia and on nights that would feel too deafeningly desolate to survive through.

I was beginning to get the impression that Myra could doze off at any moment, so I shook her awake. She looked at me a little confused at first, then raised her eyebrows in a way of asking why had I beckoned her to wake up.

'I have something planned for us,' I said excitedly.

'What?! At this hour?', she asked, with surprise and ardor vibrating in her words.

'Of course, I had to wait till everyone was soundly drifting away in the arms of Morpheus.'

'Ahh, your fancy phrases have no end.'

'You already know it!'

'So, what's this surprise you have in mind?'

'I'm too smart to fall for that trick.'

‘Okay, then! Show me!’, she exclaimed with irrepressible impatience.

I took out a handkerchief from my closet and wrapped it around her eyes to block her vision. Then, holding her hand, I led her towards the surprise. It had been in my mind for several days. About two years ago, I had seen on Pinterest an aesthetic picture of a fort built with blankets, pillows, and sticks. In the picture, the blankets were forming a pyramidal tent with fairy lights lining their margins and edges. There was a mattress kept inside it, garnished with pillows, food, books, chocolates and all sorts of decoration that made the picture look too dreamy to be real. A random idea had invaded my brain on stumbling upon that picture. I thought that I would try to recreate that someday for someone who would reserve a special place in my soul. Myra and I did not exactly do couply acts. Yeah, we would hang out a lot, talk for more hours a day than humans normally do, have moments of physical affection, but we never talked about what became of us after we kissed for the first time on her terrace. We never labelled our bond as a romantic relationship, or never called ourselves a couple. In all honesty, I was still scared of pursuing something against the long-held social convention. It was normal but it was not common. And people, mostly, feel the need to follow the generic path, to jump in with the multitudes, to ensure that they're not the only ones doing something, because we all fear judgement and social spurn. No matter how much conviction someone may have that they are not judgemental, it is human nature for a thought or a comment to pop up in your head when you see something new or different or unheard of in the popular world. We simply cannot control it. So, even if we weren't a "couple" in the public eye, I just wanted to do something that would feel more couply, and I wanted for us to create a memory that would forever be locked in our hearts. I never thought at the time when I had looked at the photo that I would find someone with whom I could share a fort and stargaze through the night, but now felt like the right time. Maybe it was not the right time, after all. But the person felt right and I would not want to look back on today twenty years from now with regret, pondering upon what could've happened.

We walked outside the room and proceeded towards the rooftop, me leading her by the hand, taking our steps slowly by the count, almost dragging our bare feet across the marble so as to not produce any sound of our feet lifting and landing on the ground, all the while pressing our lips tightly in prayers that we wouldn't wake anyone up. We eventually made it to the terrace successfully. When we reached a few centimetres away from the spot where I had set up the tent, I unwound the knot of the handkerchief and liberated her pupils to unfasten and hold sight of what stood in front. I returned her specs to her, and adjusting her vision, she digested the view. I nearly thought that she despised the idea until she gasped and put her hands over her mouth in surprise. I was looking at her face sideways anxiously, waiting for her to confirm that the gasp implied surprise and not shock.

'You made this?', she asked in disbelief.

'Yes,' I answered nervously.

'For us?' The sound of 'us' coming from her mouth, in that dulcet voice I could keep listening to till the end of time, made me feel wanted.

While I was deeply inspired by the photo I had seen two years back, I did not completely replicate it. Combining some elements of it with some ideas of my own, I took a white blanket and balanced it on umbrella stands that we used on our annual picnics. There were only three of them, so they formed a triangle mounted on a rectangle that eventually slanted so much that it ended up looking like a pentagon. It was fully open on one side which formed the entrance and I designed the margins of the cloth with whatever leftover fairy lights I could find from last year's Diwali decorations. Using a spare mattress from the storeroom, I lay it down on the floor with a few fluffy cushions to render us comfort. Instead of scattering things on the mattress, I placed a small foldable table beside the mattress with cookies, muffins, sheets of paper, and pens. I kept the pillow on the end of the mattress that faced the entrance so that we could stare at the sky if we desired. The result was not as elegant or gorgeous as the sketch I had drawn in my mind, but considering that it was the efforts of one hour (I remembered about the photo out of blue precisely an hour before her designated time of arrival), it was not so unsightly.

'Yes, for us,' I answered with a smile, spotting the growing joy in her eyes.

She flung her arms in the air and rushed into a hug. It was a really tight one, one that screamed, 'I cannot tell you how happy I am!'. We did not break away from the embrace for about five minutes. It was a fulfilling hug, very different from our first one when I was dropping her off at her place. There was no tinkling nervousness or excitement of the unknown this time. I could feel the warmth from her heart penetrate my body and spread through my vessels. I felt safe and protected, in a way that I was certain about being myself without any facade or pretence. I understood then that she was perhaps the only person, besides maybe Sparsh, that I could be entirely open to and not have to dread giving too much of myself away. I had become so engrossed in a race to please everyone, to do things others would like or do things like everyone else did that hardly did I realise that I was beginning to lose myself in the same race. In all honesty, I still haven't found myself. There is so much more to oneself than one might believe. Every day, I discover new feelings and explore new aspects of myself. Every day, I unearth a new element about my identity. At times, I strike such epiphanies about my individuality that it becomes difficult to believe that I had existed without that discovery hitherto. But every day, I am a step closer than I was yesterday.

I found parts of me in her whose existence I could've probably not imagined about had we not met. And in that hug, in the warmth of her heart beating against mind and in her tranquilising breaths soothing the edge of my ear, I knew that I would not have to fear that being myself would disgruntle her.

*****

'What are you writing about?', she asked, scooting over to my corner of the mattress.

'Nothing,' I said, shying away.

'Is it about me?', she asked with an evil smile.

'Maybe?'

'Oh! Come on, let me read! You've also read so much that I've written about you.'

'No, I've written it for a special occasion,' I answered, not surrendering just yet.

'Which occasion?'

'You'll know when the time comes,' I said with a satisfied smile.

I tucked the paper away below the mattress with one hand and with the other, I grabbed her face and pulled her closer. She planted a tender kiss on my forehead. I snuggled into the cosy space enfolded by her arms and rested my head partially on her collar and partially on her chest. We were laying on the mattress with our legs inwards and heads poking out of the entrance of the tent, glaring into the seemingly endless profundity of the firmament. It was particularly starry that night. Or morning? I was pretty sure it was around two in the morning by then. When we had arrived here about an hour ago, the sky was swathed in shredded clouds, but they seemed to have wandered miles away from us, perhaps somewhere near what looked like the horizon in our view but was only a wide stretch of black and grey canvas for someone else. I had never quite understood the craze behind star gazing till I finally got to experience it. And although it was not stargazing in the real sense of it, it was out worldly nonetheless. That there could be something even more elegant and exquisite than this was difficult to imagine. The sky had always rendered a liberating sensation to me. It made me regain faith on days that desperation got the better of me. It motivated me to seek purpose when my surroundings felt meaningless. It made me want to become greater, consoling my wailing heart on days that it felt minuscule and irrelevant because it was in itself a proof of greatness. And on most days, it ignited in me an inextinguishable curiosity to learn more about myself and to keep sailing on the quest for identity, because just like the horizon was only a deception of the firmament's cease, every failure or triumph was only a deception of the loss or gain of all impetus, and every action had so much more to it than what we may perceive at first glance. As cliche and boring as it may sound, you can always get yourself up after a downfall and you can soar higher even when you think you've reached the maximum attainable altitude. But the ephemeral fashion of rise and fall is rogue; it's easy to dwell in excessive bliss or despair. Superfluity and fluctuating between extremes have never been desirable. So, to evade dwelling in the deception engendered by superfluity, I have, on many days, learnt from the sky, even if it may be uncountable kilometres above me, how to ground myself. But today, the sky emanated a different emotion altogether. It captivated me. The stars glistening and twinkling hundreds of light years away from me were a constant reminder that we were all so insignificant and small, yet we choose to glorify ourselves, our lives, our problems, and our stories as if they are the most crucial things to be made known if the planet were to meet its demise tomorrow. As I brooded over this philosophy of the futility of our existence, wondering all the while if Myra, as she patted my head, was also introspecting on questions that we couldn't answer ourselves, some distant sound crawled their way into my ears. I disengaged myself from her embrace and got out of the tent in search of the source of sound. After a few seconds of looking around, I spotted a tall building with light flashing through a window at a floor high up, and figured it must've been a late night party. It was strange that people began a party at two which was generally a time when parties came to an end or wear nearing their ends. For some reason, I felt a scramble of enthusiasm jingle through me. I turned around to see Myra sitting up partially and looking at me with perplexion. I rushed towards her and pulled her upright by her arm. She closed her eyes and indicated with her eyebrows that she was too lazy and tired to do anything at this hour. I cast an imploring look at her—the swelling tears in my eyes from exhaust really adding to the whole pleading expression—and she rolled her eyes and finally gave in. I placed one hand on her shoulder and draped another around her waist. She recreated the posture with the opposite hands and we started slow dancing. The music, in whatever fragments it reached us, was loud, banging Bollywood music. But we were too fatigued to even lift our arms or jog at our positions. Our foreheads were resting against each other. Both my arms were now around her neck and hers around my waist. We were pendulating about the same spot on the floor. The starry firmament extended like a deep navy, almost blue canvas, canopying us with sparkles of glitter spread all over. Music was twirling around us in peaceful silence. It was a moment possible only in a sketch or in writing; so brimmed with perfection. I detached my head from hers, and going around her neck, whispered into her ear, 'I love you too.' As the words left my lips, there was not a sliver of regret. It felt relieving. I had kept these three words locked away in a demure corner of my soul, and until yesterday, I was almost sure, if not completely sure, that I would never be courageous enough to voice them out. The fear was not so much about not hearing them back as much as it was about being vulnerable in its entirety.

No shackles were separating our souls now. She knew me, every part of me. Never could I have thought about submitting myself so willingly to someone that I would even combat the dread of losing myself. Yes, maybe she wasn't aware of the number of guys I had hooked up with or the details of the past gossip I had partaken in at school. Because none of those things encompassed who I was. I was a girl who for seventeen years had lost her identity in trying to become someone else, in trying to meet others' expectations, in trying to win over everyone's affection. I had created an image of myself as a partially-popular, little spoiled, gossiping pretty face who had a long history of boy business and performed decently at school. But I was none of that. The hands that have touched my body did not define me. The gossip and rumours that have floated around me did not define me. The friend groups that I had compelled my way into under peer pressure did not define me. But nobody hitherto was ready to look beyond them and comprehend that there was so much more to me than superficial veneers. Nobody till I met Myra. She took me to utopia and I will always remember that. And at that moment, in such tranquillity that even our breaths mingled with the fading sound to generate music, I simply knew that it was time she knew. Had she not traced the words across my belly earlier, I would have still confessed how much she meant to me. She deserved to know.

Once those words rose from the demure corner of my soul I had thought would be never disclosed to anyone, and finally found meaning in a drowsy whisper, I came face to face to look at her. She looked slightly taken by surprise. I noticed that her cheeks, in the flickering gleam of the white fairy lights running down on battery, had flushed a deep magenta. Suddenly she seemed to flood with all the energy of the universe and dissolved her lazy embrace into a tight hug, pulling me in. We kept hugging for longer than we could keep count of, glee emanating from us all around. We eventually broke off once we began feeling beads of sweat break out on our armpits and our necks.

There was so much more to say. There were so many things that I still wanted to confess to her because those three words simply did not encompass all the things she meant to be. But we were too tired to talk any further. And perhaps certain things must be left unspoken for them to be felt in their entirety.

We dragged our feet towards the tent and flung ourselves down, not caring if it was our feet or our head that landed on the cushion. Sleep came to me quickly today. As my eyelids dropped down slowly, I could spot the first mild blues of dawn lightening the sky.

And then it was all black.

SEVENTEEN

Ahead

There was an uncanny damp substance forming a film over my lips and sliding into my mouth through crevices which my lips had failed to close in the state of slumber. It was when drops of water sprinkled over my eyelids that I realised that it was drizzling. I got up in alarm and shook Myra's shoulders vigorously to wake her up. It took her several minutes to realise that I was screaming, 'It's raining!' in real life and not in her dreams. She jolted from bed, blabbering some words that made no sense, and took some more time to completely teleport from dreams to reality. Once she looked up at our tent drenched in water, she understood what was happening and instantly got up. We hurriedly took the tent down, and turn by turn, brought all the things under the shade of the roof. Then, we proceeded downstairs and into my room, our clothes dripping water on the floor as we scrambled inside. It was half-past six when we reached my room, dropped all the things to the floor, and looked at each other exhaustedly, knowing on the inside that it was a terrible idea to stay up so late but neither admitting it. I dumped the wet canvas into the bathroom along with our partly wet dresses. We changed into the comfortable clothes we had been wearing before deciding to glam up and crawled into bed. Myra began snoring within milliseconds of getting into bed. I understood that she was a heavy sleeper. Having had previous experience of running on three to four hours of sleep, I did not really feel sleepy anymore. But I was feeling horribly fatigued. My eyes were hurting so much that I kept them shut, but sleep didn't come to me for a second time. I felt extremely exhausted and disoriented. This was the first disruption in the healthy sleep schedule I had started following two weeks ago.

At eight sharply, the alarm stormed off. As it turned out, I eventually dozed off because somebody cannot possibly not fall asleep if their eyes are fastened. Only after hitting the 'SNOOZE' button eight times did I get out of bed. Myra was still fast asleep. She was a heavy sleeper, indeed.

I entered the bathroom to meet with the sight of a disarray of wet clothes dumped atop one another to form a tiny hill. I sighed and somehow made it to the basin without tripping on the wet canvas and washed my eyes awake. While I was brushing, Myra also seemed to have awoken. I heard her footsteps approaching the bathroom. Giving me a weary smile, she started brushing her teeth.

For breakfast, Dad had cooked for us two cups of steaming hot coffee and French toast. The coffee was enlivening. As the caffeine travelled through my oesophagus and hit the pit of my stomach, I immediately felt awake as the warmth of the coffee spread across my chest and down my arms. Dad was not particularly a skilled chef but he could produce magic with French toast, and today was no exception. He said that if we wanted more, we could take it from the kitchen. Planting a quick peck on my forehead, he waved adieu to us and said, 'Enjoy your meal, girls!' and left for work in a hurry. I was quite baffled to see his strange affection in the morning but concluded that he perhaps wanted to look like a good father in front of my friends. The toast was probably not Myra's favorite meal in the world but she seemed to enjoy it, or so pronounced the blissful smile that her lips had curled into. Once we heard the click of the door indicating that we were out of Dad's earshot, I began speaking:

'I'm really sorry for making you stay up yesterday. You look so tired and drained. I feel so guilty right now.'

She turned towards me, her under-eyes sunken due to the lack of rest, and answered, 'Don't be. I won't say that I'm not tired and that this will not mess up my entire sleeping routine. But would I have preferred sleeping to the most magical night ever? Definitely not.'

'You're just saying that not to dishearten me.'

'Your heart is now mine and I have vowed to myself to take care of it.'

'You and your clingy sentences.'

'Don't pretend like you're not a craver for them.'

With such exchanges of flirtatious (and obnoxiously cheesy) chat, we passed the morning. She left at around ten o' clock because summer break would be over in a week and she had several assignments due on Friday that she needed to complete. I wished that she could have stayed longer but I understood her concern and bid adieu to her. We went all the way back into my room under the excuse of getting her clothes out of the dryer (I had placed all the wet clothes into the dryer after morning refreshments), but we truly only intended to steal a kiss without anybody's observance. As I shut the door after she left, I turned around to meet the gaze of Sparsh. He was standing behind me. It appeared as if he had been waiting for me. I nearly jumped at the unexpected sight. It took me a couple of minutes to regain track of my breath.

'What are you doing here?', I asked, still struck with some aghast.

'I was heading out.'

'Where to?'

'To Nikunj's place for completing a group project.'

‘Okay. Were you here listening to everything we talked about?’

‘No, I came when you were hugging and then she left and you closed the door.’

‘Right.’ In truth, Myra and I had not talked about anything so confidential that the human ear must be forbidden to hear it. She had only whispered into my ear that she loved me while we were embracing, and I said it back quite audibly. I shifted towards the side to clear out the entrance to provide Sparsh with enough space to leave. I wanted to ask him something but found it difficult to raise the words from the pit of my stomach to the edge of my throat. Eventually I did, but it remained stuck in a lump in my throat for numerous seconds and when his feet finally crossed the threshold, I spontaneously got rid of the nervousness and said, ‘Sparsh, what do you think of her?’

‘Huh?’

‘What do you think about my *girlfriend*?’

‘I think she’s amazing,’ he said, with a bright smile on his visage. The anxiety instantly receded.

‘It feels good, doesn’t it?’, he asked.

‘What does?’

‘To utter the word without discomfort.’

‘Girlfriend?’

‘Yeah.’

‘Yes, it does,’ I answered with a shy smile, and shutting the door closed once more, I walked towards my room with a sense of validation.

At two in the afternoon, while I was entirely engrossed in writing my Economics paper, my phone began vibrating aggressively on my bedside table. I was already cursing whoever had disrupted the concentration that I had rebuilt after losing it for many days until I saw that the name on the screen read, ‘Sasha’ and felt immediate regret lash down over me. Just after the kiss on the terrace, I had promised Sasha that I would call her because I had something amazing to tell her but eventually forgot about spending all my time with Myra and also ended up ignoring her messages. Releasing a heavy breath of guilt, I clicked on the receiving button and mumbled nervously, 'Hello?'

'WHERE HAVE YOU BEEN?'

'I am so sorry, Sash! Really, so sorry. It literally slipped out of my mind and you know that I've been MIA for a long time now. Please hear me out before getting mad at me.'

'FIRST OF ALL, I AM ALREADY MAD AT YOU! SECOND OF ALL, YOU BETTER HAVE A GOOD EXCUSE ELSE YOU'RE DOOMED!'

'Okay, can we please not scream? You're intimidating me.'

'Fine, go on,' she answered in a milder tone.

'So, umm, I don't even know where to start.'

'Maybe you could start by confessing what *amazing* shit you've been up to that has wiped me out of your memory,' she remarked snarkily.

'You remember how I had mentioned that day that I wanted to explore my sexuality?'

'Which da— oh yes, I do remember.'

'So, I did.'

'BITCH WHAT? ELABORATE, PLEASE!'

'So, I have arrived at the conclusion that I am in fact not straight.'

'You're talking in a roundabout manner. Be specific! Give me deets! What have you been up to?' All the wrath in her voice was slowly dissolving into increasing excitement.

And so, I told her about everything. From wanting to be her to wanting to be with her. From realising that my envy was in fact attraction in disguise. I told her about how our partnership for a school project grew into an amicable companionship only for us to eventually come to terms with the fact that it was a lot more than friendship, after all. I told her about the internalised homophobia that I had been dealing with for the past few weeks and although I was getting rid of it gradually, it still crept into my head at times. I also told her about the numerous adventures I had embarked upon with Myra and the wonderful places we had explored, both in ourselves and in the world around us. I did not give away too intimate details, though. I wanted a few things to remain known and shared only between Myra and me. She asked me to describe my experience of kissing a girl for the first time and I answered that I had never felt my senses unfurl into nothing but bliss before this. And as I spoke, with my voice swarming with excitement and nervousness alike, she listened. She listened with every bit of attention that I desired from a best friend, without interrupting, and once I finally stopped talking and let out a heavy breath, she realised that this was not another short pause and finally broke her silence, 'I am so happy for you!'

'You are?'

'Yes, of course. I cannot imagine how it must have been for you to go through all of this by yourself. I'm glad that you found someone who makes you so happy. You have grown more in the past few weeks than you have all your life.'

'Shut up!', I complained, embarrassed.

'You know it's true. And you must know that had you opened up to me before, I would have never judged you. But I get it. It's really scary to open up to someone about things like this, especially when homosexuality largely remains a forbidden topic in our society. And perhaps had you reached out to me before, maybe things wouldn't have played out the way they did. You're happy and I am happy that you are. At least you're not in a mental ruckus anymore.'

'Haha, that's right. You were right. I had to stop looking for the right direction and wait till it found me.'

'I'm always right.'

'Says the girl who thought she was straight for twelve years of her life!'

'Can we please not bring up my dark past where I thought I liked men?'

'If you insist! Speaking of men, I'm still not quite sure of what I would identify as.'

‘So, are you bisexual or?’

‘I don’t know! Why do we need to put a label on it? All these terms make me so confused.’

‘You don’t have to, hon. Keep exploring till you land upon a discovery. There’s no rush.’

‘Yeah, I agree. Also, I just realised that all my life, I think I only was crushing on girls which I had mistaken for jealousy.’

‘How many girls would that be?’

‘Around ten?’

‘Alaina! Oh my god, you’re nasty!’

‘Okay, stop teasing me now! Are you still mad?’

‘After you’ve struck me with such beautiful news, how could I be?’

‘That’s right.’

‘I had to ask you something, by the way’, she said matter-of-factly, suddenly shifting to seriousness from playful chit-chat.

‘Go on.’ I answered, inquisitive about what possibly she could ask me with such solemnity

‘I know that your friendship with Alisha has probably hit an iceberg, but in case you forgot, it’s her birthday in three days. She’s throwing a huge party. Maybe you could come? She would be really happy to see her childhood best friend on her eighteenth.’

That took me by surprise, not because her birthday had slipped out of my mind (I did remember it) but because I couldn’t sense our conversation heading that direction. In fact, during the past few days, I was frantically trying to engage myself in anything that could distract from the thought of her birthday that crept into my mind periodically. I remember three years ago when we were at Sasha’s place celebrating her fifteenth. Sasha doesn’t like throwing big parties and thought that birthdays are really not that big a deal. So, it would usually only be the three of us having a shit ton of fun. We were talking, laughing and eating at her balcony when Alisha suggested an idea that on each of our eighteenth birthdays, we would go absolutely bonkers. We would strike off three things from our bucket lists that our parents would never allow us to do. One was a two-day road trip all by ourselves, another was throwing a humongous party loaded with all the alcohol in the world and inviting almost the entire school, and third was going to a strip club. Instinctively, Alisha had picked the second one. We had even decided that we would plan all three of them unanimously. And all these days after the slumber party of not speaking to each other and clutching on tightly to our egos, a part of me was still hoping that she would ring me up someday to respect and execute a promise we had made three years ago.

'Did Alisha tell you to convey this to me?'

'Not exactly, but—'

'So, she still doesn't want to see me?'

'Look, you can't blame her, Alaina. We both know she has an ego vaster than the Pacific Ocean and you really did utter some harsh things to her.'

'I am not blaming her, but didn't it ever occur to you that she always wants everything to go according to her?'

'If you're asking me whether or not I perceive her as controlling, I do.'

'And you still call her your best friend.'

'Oh please, just because your friendship broke off like three weeks ago doesn't make you any different than me.'

'So, were we both in denial, then?'

'Maybe. We are all flawed in some way or another, are we not? But we can always try to make amends, or, in cliché terms, "be the bigger person". For instance, the whole dramatic gossip that she had started around you only lasted for a week. She hasn't uttered anything negative about you ever since.'

'Fine, I'll take your word for it. I'll come to the party.'

'Yes, yes, yes, thank you! She'll be very happy, trust me, she will! And so will you! I love you! And I'll see you there!'

'Love you, too.'

'And you still call her your best friend.'

'Oh please, just because your friendship broke off like three weeks ago doesn't make you any different than me.'

'So, were we both in denial, then?'

'Maybe. We are all flawed in some way or another, are we not? But we can always try to make amends, or, in cliché terms, "be the bigger person". For instance, the whole dramatic gossip that she had started around you only lasted for a week. She hasn't uttered anything negative about you ever since.'

'Fine, I'll take your word for it. I'll come to the party.'

'Yes, yes, yes, thank you! She'll be very happy, trust me, she will! And so will you! I love you! And I'll see you there!'

'Love you, too.'

EIGHTEEN

Braver with Every Breath

I woke up gasping for air. For several moments, I couldn't detach my eyelids from one another. With much strain, I opened my eyes and looked around in search of light. But it was nowhere. Dense darkness all around. I almost thought that I was still subconsciously dreaming till I realised that I had woken up from a nightmare a few hours before dawn. I was breathing heavily and my fingers were strangely trembling. I couldn't control it. But they eventually became stationary. I couldn't remember exactly what was so morbid that I had seen to be in such an appalled state, but the fragments that I could recall told me that there was a pool of blood. As I regained my composure, I slowly drifted back down on the bed, my eyelids closing over the blinding darkness and falling asleep again.

The second time I woke up, it was around ten in the morning. I had forgotten to set the alarm and ended up oversleeping.

Today was going to be a busy day with a ton of work awaiting me and waking up two hours later than usual was not the start I was looking forward to. I got out of bed, already demotivated, feeling like I had lost two precious hours of the morning, not realising that I still had the rest of the day in hand. It was when I sat down at my desk with my Math textbook open and clicking the pen in my hand aimlessly that I realised how screwed I was. I was staring at the numbers, symbols and text in front of me for a solid minute till I finally began making sense out of them. Midterm exams were going to start in a month and I was far from prepared. The past few days had mostly been spent in the company of Myra. I didn't realise until now how quickly time had passed by. We usually ended up spending a lot of hours together whenever we met. And although we engaged in intellectual conversations, it was never related to coursework, but other themes that actually *mattered.* I calmed myself down and encouraged myself with the idea that I still had a month and a week in hand. I could use the day to complete the pending projects and assignments, three in total, and start preparing for midterms from tomorrow.

Majority of the day was spent writing two thousand-worded essays and completing thirty Math questions till my brain literally felt like it was shrinking into a clenched fist, hurting excruciatingly if I tried to focus on any sum. The calculus in front of me was definitely wrecking my brain rather than sharpening it. I got up from the chair at the study table and lay on the bed. I did not realise that I had been sitting there for over six hours till my butt muscles relaxed into the soft mattress. I glared at the emptiness of the ceiling above me and thought about Alisha's birthday party which was going to be held in a little more than twenty-four hours. The thought of deafening loud music, wild and relentless teenagers swaying their bodies and deteriorating their livers with alcohol, champagne being sprinkled on clothes and multi-colored lights blinking to the beat of the music, made me nauseous. I couldn't even imagine how strange I would feel actually being enveloped by that dynamic if the picture of it already made me want to throw up.

Conversation between Myra and I had been minimal in the past two days, if not zero. We had a mutual understanding that we had perhaps whiled away some time, if not all, although neither of us wanted to admit it in fear of disappointing each other, and ourselves. She had a bunch of school work to complete and I had midterms to study for. We would exchange a few words along the lines of 'how are you', 'how's studying going', 'how's that assignment coming through', but despite trying our utmost to mitigate the feeling of *difference,* the distance was palpable. And it was growing.

As I stared at the ceiling, hardly fighting the urge to shut my eyelids and fall asleep, I wondered what it meant to be squandering time away. One part of my mind was barking at me to get up and sit back at the desk, aggravated that I had already wasted a lot of time and was running against the clock now. Another part prompted me to forget about studies or school and have all the fun I possibly could because life's too short and you don't want to end up in your forties having no cool anecdotes or tales of shenanigans to recite to your children, nieces, and nephews. And you definitely don't wish to be laying on your deathbed, pondering if only you had done things differently or picked different priorities, maybe you wouldn't be dying with mournful memories. But the world is a stage and we must all play a part. We are all running a rat race in the quest of being known, being rich, being found or being happy. Being anything but ourselves. But if the final destination shall be the same for us, why must we play a part at all? Why can't we just be ourselves and do whatever we want instead of doing things which are but a superficial illusion of success and happiness? Some people will tell you to live in the moment and others, to work hard and enjoy later. And while my mind was spiralling around this dilemma, I realised that I had zoned out, got back up again and trudged back to my desk, succumbing myself to the world's demands.

As I clicked on 'submit' for my final assignment for the summer, relief flooded all over me, despite the fact that I would have to start cramming from the very next day. I just wanted to relish this moment as the stress and tension ebbed out of my body. When I was about to crawl into bed after changing into my pjs, a knock at the door startled me. I guessed it was probably Mom who wanted to check if I was doing okay. She had looked pale as a dead body in the afternoon when she saw me sitting at the desk in the same position since morning. How do you tell your very Indian Mom that you spent all summer romancing a girl and once the lovey-dovey fever was beginning to wear off, you suddenly realised that you were screwed?

Dragging my feet unwillingly towards the door, I flung it open. It wasn't Mom. It was Sparsh looking at me with a sorrowful expression hung on his visage, eyes swollen with tears and skin drained of any colour. He appeared to be trembling. I felt a lump of bile rise up to my throat. I had never seen him in this state. He looked shattered. Without uttering anything, partly because I didn't know anything empathetic enough to console him and partly because my voice was stuck in my throat in an excruciating muteness, I pulled him into an embrace. He sobbed into my bare shoulder and I wondered if he might have deposited some snot there too. But as his weeping grew increasingly painful than complaining, I understood that something serious was going on. I didn't let go until he beckoned me to. We walked towards the bed and sat down there. I suddenly realised that it would be kind of me to give him some water, so I walked towards the table beside the bean bag which contained a whole lot of food supplies for midnight hunger, and picking up the bottle, walked back toward him. He gulped down the water like the thirsty crow that couldn't get its beak into the pot but when the pebbles raised the water level eventually, drank it like it was the first time it had tasted water. He emptied nearly half the bottle and gave it back to me. I shut the lid and placed it on the floor. Then turning towards him, I asked in a frail voice, 'What happened?' I was not sure if I sounded sympathetic or pitiful or condescending, because my intention was only to add glints of console but he didn't respond for several seconds. He was looking down at his fingers, fidgeting nervously, till he finally raised his head, and staring directly at the blank wall in front of him, answered, 'We broke up.'

The soreness in his voice was undeniable. He was definitely referring to Aarav who had been madly falling in love during the past few months. Although he hadn't spoken very much about his relationship with him, and perhaps I had not shown much interest to know every nook and corner about it, I comprehended that he truly was feeling something as never before for this guy. Whenever he referred to him, his eyes would sparkle up and I could practically feel the warmth radiate from his heart.

‘Oh,’ I said after thinking about a suitable response for a while. Clearly, I didn’t function well under pressure.

‘It was perfect, you know,’ he continued, ‘it was too perfect to be true, and I guess that’s why it ended. He ended it. His parents found out. Yesterday. They found out yesterday. They snuck a peek into his phone one day when it was unlocked and managed to read our texts. They couldn’t decipher most of the gen z terms we use,’ he laughed a little, ‘but it doesn’t take Einstein to figure out that I wasn't merely a friend. They are very conservative, his parents. They’ve grounded him for two weeks. And they’re keeping his phone in their custody. He managed to text me somehow. He wrote this long ass para about how he couldn’t do this with me anymore, how his parents made him realise that his grades were more important and I was a mere distraction for him that stuck along for too long, that everyone goes through this *phase* and he would soon get over it, and how he needs to focus on other things now. He said he needed me to vanish from his life. I tried texting him back, thinking maybe somehow we could make it work, or maybe our goodbye didn't have to be so abrupt and harsh, only to realise that he'd already blocked me.

'He said I was a distraction! Can you believe it? "Just a distraction" were his exact words! I can't believe it. He was not even quoting his parents! He directly said it to me! I was here all this while thinking that the feelings were mutual, that we were both falling into the spiral of love equally. What did he mean by "you stuck along for too long"? Is it like a small-time *dhanda* that he runs? Have flings with guys when you're bored and once you've had enough of them, find new ones?! I dunno if his parents actually found out or it was an excuse to get rid of me. And was he also playing with someone's else's feelings while playing with mine? What the fuck do I do now? I feel like shit. I feel like a useless piece of shit that's been played with and dumped. I feel like shit, shit, shit, shit,' and gradually the loop of shits dissipated into sobs.

I took a deep breath, thinking my sentences over to make sure that I wouldn't utter something that would further trigger him. Letting out a sigh, I said, 'No, don't you dare say that. You are not fucking shit. You are not useless. Don't ever say that again. You are the kindest person I know. You know what makes you a thousand times better and greater and more powerful than him? It's that you loved him. Yes, you heard that right. Love is not for the weak and vulnerable. It's for the brave and invincible. You are invincible. Loving someone is the biggest risk that you can take in life, and the irony is, it isn't even a risk that you decide to take on voluntarily or get to evaluate before deciding. It happens so naturally. Maybe he was lying all this while or maybe he was not. Maybe he is a little wrecked inside and got manipulated by his parents into believing that he had committed something erroneous. Maybe he put all the blame on you to free himself of any guilt, to convince himself and his parents that he wasn't wrong, because god do we not crave for validation from others! There are so many maybe's, so many possibilities. But one thing is certain: you are not a useless piece of shit. You are brave. Look into the mirror to your right,' I placed my palm on his shoulder and squeezed it tightly as a gesture to encourage him, 'and say that you are brave. In fact, we are brave. We are the warriors on the frontline of life. We love not knowing if we will receive it back. We love not knowing if the fruit shall be bitter loathing from the beloved. We love not knowing what repercussions await us. We love without fear of getting hurt although we very well know that in the end, one will. We love while the rest of the world dwells in envy, loathing, ruthlessness, and hatred. Let's look in the mirror and chant that we are brave.'

We looked into the mirror, fixing our gazes directly at our own pupils, at the ceaseless cosmos that seemed to hide behind them, and recited in unison, 'We are brave.' I smiled at his reflection in the looking glass, and his reflection smiled at my reflection back. 'Hey listen, do you maybe wanna go to Alisha's grand eighteenth birthday tomorrow? It'll definitely be a good distraction.'

'I'm sorry, did I hear Alisha?', he said, poking his index finger into his ear as if trying to remove any hindrances to his hearing. My cheeks flushed in embarrassment.

'You did. Trust me, I'm surprised too. I wasn't planning on going though, if you must know. Hell, I haven't even been formally invited. But Sash convinced me beyond saying nay. She suggested that I could try to be the bigger person and make amendments if I could. So yeah, I'll go. And I doubt I'll actually have anyone to hang out with because I'm sure Sash will be busy with Kiara and I haven't spoken to anyone else from that social group whatsoever all summer. You'd be a great company.'

'She posted a public invitation on Instagram for the entire school, so I don't think it would do any harm if I went.'

'Oh, she did? I don't think I've been following her account regularly, but that sounds like her.'

'Yeah. You could bring Myra along if you want. Anyway, if most of the school, if not all, is coming, I'm sure she'll dissolve in well without drawing much attention to your relationship.'

'I guess so. You know, we never put a label on it? Like we never had an official, written or spoken, consensus that we were girlfriend and girlfriend.'

'I think it's better not to put a label on it. It only creates space for unrequired commitment issues and unrealistic expectations.'

'But doesn't it also indicate that you might have the other's permission to have flings with other people too?'

'Are you doubting her loyalty?'

'Not exactly.'

'Are you doubting yours?'

'No! Of course not! I would never do that to her.'

'Then the best you can do is believe that she wouldn't either.'

We chatted for another thirty minutes about what images of the party we had imagined in our heads. Although I didn't feel as excited for it as I would've maybe a year ago, nor as affectionate towards the host herself, I couldn't help but think that this would be the last ever big party of my high school experience. In fact, the only *big* high school party. I had always dreamt of what it'd be like to be the IT girl, to be the face that everyone's wandering eyes were searching for, and to be the centre of attention at the party. But I grew to realise how meaningless a source of satisfaction that actually was. It turned out that Sparsh and I indeed had very similar pictures in our minds, both of which had elements picked up from those popular coming-of-age Hollywood movies that we all secretly craved for being the protagonists in. As he left, I noticed that although his face was not pale and sobby anymore, his eyes were still glazed over with pain, and I suddenly felt deja vu snake around my mind. Eventually the deja vu cleared into nostalgia as I remembered the similar scene I had encountered a few weeks ago, and a twinge of guilt tightened around my chest.

I didn't know what heartbreak felt like but I sure as hell could see what kind of a calamity I had inflicted upon someone else.

NINETEEN

Losing Grip

As we stepped out of the car, Sparsh and I could hear the loud, banging DJ music reverberating in our ears more intensely than ever. We had detected faint party music right from when we were thirty minutes away, and throughout the car ride, I kept dreading the moment when I would actually step down and let the deafening sound impair my eardrums. The party was stationed in the backyard. Alisha's family resided in an ostentatious three-storeyed mansion, four-storeyed if their flamboyant rooftop with a swimming pool and a hot tub side by side was included. Apart from the gorgeous garden and lawn that rolled out as entrance to their mansion, they also had a backyard that could accommodate a thousand heads with ease and was the perfect location to throw a lavish party. Alisha's parents had specifically instructed their architect to design a particularly dimensioned backyard that would suit their materialistic exploits. I could see jets of disco lights being flashed above us towards the sky every other second. There were a few people hanging out in the front lawn which was strewn with emptied beer bottles. The appointed time for the party was eight in the evening and it was around nine when we arrived. It was unusual for people to show up on time. Then again, considering she had invited all high school kids, some might've stuck to the core Indian principle of punctuality. The faces in the front lawn were known but not familiar. I could spot only two guys from our grade conversing in a corner while periodically sipping beer from their bottles. Besides them, everyone else seemed to be juniors who weren't habituated with such loud, noisy music and sought a quieter place for their chatter. Sparsh told me that he found some of his friends so he would go and mingle with the crowd and invited me to tag along if I wished. I decently refused, saying that I would wait for Myra's arrival. It was odd to be the only person standing outside the gate while everybody else was giggling and drinking on the other side of the gate, and by texting Myra, I understood that she was going to be here in sooner than fifteen minutes. I possibly could not stand stationary with four-inch pencil heels on the same spot, so I walked in. I thought I would make my way to the backyard without anyone's notice, but the clicking of my heels produced too loud an abrupt disturbance to the harmonious music playing in the background— a mix of old Bollywood and pop Hollywood songs— for people not to take notice. Most were unbothered and turned back to their friends and acquaintances, but some checked me out from head to toe. I felt distinctly uncomfortable. The last time I was exposed to so many pupils at a public gathering was probably the pool party Alisha had thrown half a year or so back. I guess nobody in our school lived in as ginormous a residential complex as Alisha, so all the big parties naturally fell to her organisation. I was wearing a black leather dress, body-tight, hugging my breasts, waist, and hips, two straps of cloth from the shoulders sliding into a deep cut, flashing out my cleavage ever so teasingly. My beachy waves were curled to give them a bouncier and in-place appearance. My lips were tinted with deep maroon and silver hoops hung down my earlobes. I didn't feel like putting on much make-up so a pink cat eyeliner was the only other colour on my body besides black, maroon, and silver. The dress was hardly two inches below my waist and I wasn't prepared for so much of my body to be caught by the human eye, given that my long arms and not-so-slim back were already inviting a peek, so black knee-length boots were the perfect match I resorted to. Sparsh nicknamed me 'leather girl' as we were on our way. Sounded kind of feisty, but of course, I wouldn't admit that to him. Having spent a lot of time on Pinterest in the past few weeks, because I still needed to use some app on my phone if not the obvious socialising platforms, I had grown fond of e-girl fashion. Drawing inspiration from one of the pictures I had seen there, I also wrapped a silver chain around my neck.

The smell of sodium infiltrated my nostrils as soon as I stepped onto the threshold segregating the backyard from the main house floor. There were more people than the aperture of both my eyes could catch into sight at once. Most of them were dancing. I saw a girl grinding next to the DJ. Needless to say, it was Arshiyaa, Alisha's favorite minion who could run to any extent in contesting for attention. There was a small bar at the back with two bartenders, one male, and another female. Around twelve teenagers were swarming around the counters. The ones right in the front were gulping down shots like the world was ending and it was the only available liquid to quench the dryness from their throats, and the ones at the back appeared to be protesting for a chance. There was also a food counter where I spotted my saviours, Sasha and Kiara, hanging out, eating, chucking, and talking. Clumsily making my way through sweaty bodies that were flinging their arms, swaying their hips, and bobbing their heads in all available space and directions, hardly preventing myself from touching any of them, I finally made it to the food counter.

'HIIIIII ALAINAAA!!', Sasha squealed in the most drunken voice possible. Kiara was giggling aimlessly.

'Hey, Sash! I can see that you're really drunk.'

'YESSSSS!!', she answered almost proudly, emphasizing so much on the 's' sound that she almost sounded like a hissing python.

'That's why we're dumping so much food into our mouths!', Kiara explained, still giggling, 'So that the smell of alcohol cannot be detected! Or else Sasha's parents are gonna kllllll herrr!'. I wanted to say that chewing gum would probably make the job easier, but neither did the two of them stop giggling to give me a chance to speak, nor were they in a state conscious enough to listen to my words seriously. Plus, it looked like they strongly believed that their trick would work so I did not want to dishearten them. I picked up a french fry from the plate which the two of them were hardly holding with their shaky hands. It was strange to look at drunk people. They would be laughing and smiling for no reason, mumbling random gibberish from time to time. They ended up looking very foolish to the sober eye. Some would even bawl out in the worst possible breakdown, sometimes crying at the stupidest things. I wondered how I behaved under the influence and how imbecile I must appear to someone sober or not as drunk.

'ALAINA!!! Why do you look so solemn? Come on, loosen up! Have a drink!', Sasha said as she shoved a beer bottle in front of my face. I grabbed it and started drinking at my own pace.

'Oh, come one!', Kiara groaned, 'CHUG IT DOWN, BITCH!!!!' I reluctantly finished all the beer as fast as I could and my mouth seemed to explode with pops and sparkles. As soon as the beer glided down my throat and jumped to my tummy, I could feel the old party animal in me kick back in.

'Where's Alisha?', I asked out of genuine curiosity. The effect of alcohol was resonantly beginning to vibrate in my voice.

'Oh, Alisha? She is inside.', Kiara answered in a comparatively less giggly tone, and Sasha continued, 'There are strippers, both male and female! She and some guys are inside. I think they're having a group makeout!'. While I had anticipated the presence of strippers, I had not firmly believed that Alisha would *actually* book them. A group makeout sounded even more horrendous.

'ISN'T THAT YOUR GIRLFRIEND?', Sasha nearly announced to all the guests as she looked over my head at the figure of Myra walking towards us from a distance, while I was still in the process of registering the wildness of stripping and multiple people smooching. Although I wasn't particularly religious, I whispered 'Thank god' under my breath for there being around fifteen loudspeakers mounted on different spots in the yard, dissolving Alisha's words into nothing but indistinct chatter amidst the wilderness of disco music. I turned around to see Myra enrobed in a satin white one-piece gently embracing her body, neither too tightly to reveal all her bewitching curves and edges nor too loosely to become ill-fitting, falling till her knees with a sharp cut extending till her thigh on the right side, gorgeously revealing her sleek leg. It was sleeveless and seemed to have a medium back-cut by the front looks of it. Her lips, full and plumpy as ever, were tainted with a matt pink lipstick and her hair was straightened, which had transformed her mien tremendously. Although I loved her messy curls and the childish innocence they added to her visage, I couldn't help but grow on the matured look that the straight hair bore. She was wearing silver-coloured wedges. It had only been a few days of us being apart and she already looked like a completely new person. While it took me a good minute to register the transformation, I could feel my heart racing rapidly against my chest as I realised how much I had missed her. With a shiny white purse clutched in her left hand, she marched confidently toward us. I had never seen her like this before: charming, carrying an enchanting beauty in the glimmer in her eyes, oozing with confidence, taking each step so poshly as if she wanted to be seen and taken observance of, as if she wanted mouths to gape in mystification and lustful eyes to wistfully desire her. I was absolutely smitten.

'Hiii!', she greeted gleefully as she came to halt. We hugged. The tinkling nervousness had possessed me once more and I attempted to gulp it down. My mouth felt dry.

Kiara and Sasha briefly introduced themselves to her in their drunken voices, not without my assistance, and vice-versa. They pleasantly greeted each other and I managed to include a disclaimer that since Myra and I weren't official and preferred to keep it that way, it would be best if Kiara and Sasha would remain silent in our regard. After a few rounds of small talk, they said that their bodies by now had enough alcohol to join the dancers and made their way to the main area of the party. 'You look so fucking gorgeous!', I blurted as soon as we were out of Sasha and Kiara's earshot. I simply couldn't get over her straight-hair look. It was hypnotising.

'Wanna go someplace else?', she whispered in response. There was lust quivering in her voice and something about it made it impossible to resist. Out of the blue, she licked my earlobe and I moaned silently in reflex. I could feel her saliva slightly stinging into my skin. 'Are you drunk?', I asked fretfully. I didn't know Myra to be a drinker.

‘Well, I thought a little booze wouldn’t harm!’, she answered in the same drunken, libidinous voice.

‘Looks like I missed out on a lot in the past few days,’ I remarked.

‘Maybe,’ she giggled.

‘Wait, why don’t we meet your friends first? I just realised that I don’t know any of them while you know of every nook and corner of nearly non-existent my social life! I wanna meet them!’

‘Why are you killing the mood?’, she groaned.

‘Come on, this would be the perfect occasion. You could just introduce me as a friend.’

‘Oh please, I don’t think you would need an introduction.’

‘So are you not comfortable with introducing me as your friend because of my past?’

‘No!’, she squeaked with a shrug, ‘Come on, *babe.* Let’s please not ruin this moment!’, she once more whispered into my ears in a voice I had never heard before.

It was undeniably a shock to encounter a drunk Myra, but the way she led me inside, pulling me by a hand pulsating with desire, I was too enchanted to overthink this. On the way, I gulped down a shot of tequila out of instinct and as soon as the intoxication kicked in, everything around me was blurry. I felt like people were talking to me and looking at me, but I could neither see them nor hear them. Muffled voices and hazy figures spiralled around me. The only person in focus was her. She turned her head behind to look at me once we had headed inside the house, looking at me with longing and passion so intense that I could almost collapse. I heard a lot of shouting and exhilarated screaming once inside and caught some figures that did appear to be strippers from my peripheral vision. There were several people inside, although not as abundant as in the backyard. I caught a glimpse of Alisha as Myra led me up a spiral staircase. She was seated on the couch with strippers grooving and stripping on the table close to her. A host of boys from our grade surrounded her, looking back and forth from her to the table, as if unsure which sight was more worthwhile to fix their gazes at. Due to distance and alcoholic haziness of vision, I could hardly fathom out what she was wearing or how she was looking, but all I could perceive was more skin than cloth. Suddenly, Myra stopped in her tracks in front of me and tilting her head, asked, 'Is that Alisha?', pointing her finger vaguely at the crowd gathering around the couch. 'Yes,' I answered, not quite sure if I heard her question correctly.

'Hey, I don't know where to go,' she admitted.

'I'll take you from here,' I answered with a smirk.

I had been to this house enough times to know where the guest room was and how it was the *room* your friends were referring to when they would groan, 'get a room!'. Before I knew it, we were in the bathroom of the guest room and we double-checked if it was securely locked. By surprise, she pinned me against the cold marble wall and attacked me with passionate kisses on my lips. Her one hand was clasped onto my hip dominantly while the other was fiddling with my dress, trying to open it and slide her fingers in. I draped one arm around her waist and used another to glide up her leg through the slit in her dress. Distant music reverberated within the four walls but all I could hear was the sound of our heated breaths. We had been making out vehemently for a good five minutes until gradually, the music got replaced by a unanimous chanting. We stopped and looked at each other in confusion. The noise seemed to originate from below us. There were shouts and gasps of numerous voices. They didn't sound cheerful. We sensed something serious had occurred. Myra let go of me and we both rushed outside without saying anything to each other. The air smelled of alarm and uncertainty. I didn't know what was happening. The world around me was spinning at the speed of sound and as I sped up through the flight of stairs, the shouting and gasping voices only got all the more distinct and rang in my ears like the nefarious chant of a cult. My heart was at my throat, beating away vigorously. Every contraction was an appalling dread into my arteries. Something about the screams told me that they portended something dangerous; something morbid. By the time we reached the ground floor, the screams were dissolving. A sullen and ominous silence was slowly diffusing into the air, accompanied by a few raised eyebrows in confusion from visitors who had arrived there just now like me. Everyone was crowded at the front near the main gate, gushing and whispering in disarray. Squeezing my way through the noisy crowd, hitting against myriad sweaty shoulders and restless heads, I finally made my way to the front and saw him. There he lay, frozen like a statue bathing in a pool of blood. Scarlet red blood. Eyes glaring lifelessly into the endless void of the firmament.

I froze.

My limbs felt numb and a strange chilling wind rustled from the top of my head to the tip of my toes. I couldn't feel my skin. I couldn't feel the physical presence of my body. My heart collapsed from my throat and hid somewhere untraceable. It was an uncanny coldness that overwhelmed me till I abruptly let out a smoke of breath and panted heavily for air. I had forgotten to breathe.

As I stared numbly at the sight, my mind raced with so many thoughts. *No, that cannot be. That cannot be him. Must be someone else.* To my right, I turned to see Alisha, eyes riddled with shock and mouth gape at a loss of words. She was hurrying from someplace else and struggled to make her way to the front to behold the dreadful sight. Myra was lost somewhere in the crowd behind me. But I was not bothered about her, or anyone else around me for that matter. A chill shiver ran down my spine as I was beginning to decode the implication of what lay in front of my sight. I flung down on the stone-cold floor and extended my shuddering hands towards his unconscious body bathed in a pool of blood. The crimson blood felt disgustingly cold against my warm fingers. The precariousness of what had occurred just hit me.

Then came the tears, running down my cheek like a fierce waterfall.

The world around me was spinning and my voice dropped down to the pit of my stomach. For a few moments, I couldn't feel my heart beating until the churning of my stomach turned into a heartbeat of its own. Before I knew it, I was screaming, panting, and wailing at the sight of my little brother lying lifelessly on the ground. *No!* A part of my mind shrieked. *He cannot be dead! It cannot be! There must be more time, God, please there be more time.* There was a clamour ruling over my head. I simply couldn't comprehend it— the idea of never seeing him again, never listening to him again, never sitting with him late into the night and talking about things that made voyaging through this journey easier. Would I have to journey through life alone now? Would I sit in his room and cling on to the last memories of laughter and tears that had once reverberated within its grey walls? Would I remember him at the sound or sight of anyone who was called by his name? Would I forget what he looked like, sounded like, talked like, laughed like, danced like, sang like, and *been* like someday?

I felt two arms drape around my chest and console me into a pitiful hug. It was Alisha. 'He'll be okay,' she said calmly while she was on the phone with her parents, summoning them to help resolve this calamity. This was the first time I heard from her in nearly a month. I had never known her to be emotional but it was at that moment that I realised that our differences couldn't stop us from caring for each other. It would always be there— the love. Seeing that I had somewhat calmed down and the screaming had dwindled to silent, breathless sobs, she got up and faced the crowd behind, one hand still clutching on to my shoulder in an attempt to show her support, and spoke resonantly with a seriousness of tone that had not known the fashionable and glossy voice of Alisha, 'GO! GET OUT OF HERE! Party's over, there's nothing to see.' Like obedient subjects, they all obeyed the queen's order and departed. One by one, the withdrawing footsteps grew fainter and fainter till none could be heard. Then, I caught the sound of someone approaching me. It was Sasha. She sat down beside me and whispered with almost the love of a mother, 'You cannot just sit and cry, Alaina. You cannot give up hope. He jumped from an altitude of three floors above the ground. That's not high enough. *He's not gone, Alaina.* We can save him. We must take him inside. We *will save* him.'

*****

Alisha's parents arrived within ten minutes. They had already called for an ambulance. They had planned to stay at their penthouse for the night and so had sent their driver away for a leave for the remainder of the night. Clearly, their plan had different prospects for them. At the first instance, they clapped their hands over their mouths on catching sight of the damage, looking disturbed and distraught. But realising that they were the only people we were relying on at this needy hour, they reclothed themselves with composure and approached me. I looked at them, face streaked with tears and limbs trembling. They pulled me into an embrace and assured me that everything would be fine. *How would you know?* I wanted to ask them. *It's my brother who looks lifeless, not yours, right?*

I wanted to say in anger. But I suppressed the rage. Mr. and Mrs. Kumar had some medical supplies with them. With the aid of some of the waiters who were supposedly catering at the party, we lifted his body from the grass and carried him inside. We then rested him on the couch painstakingly, making sure his wound wasn't touched detrimentally. I could spot it. It was a gaping bruise on the head, shedding crimson blood on the brown leather. Mrs. Kumar sat on the floor with some first-aid tools in her hands. She began rubbing off the blood from his skin. Meanwhile, Sasha took the job of calling up my parents. The fact that she had enough courage to break the news to parents that their child had just leapt off a building made my heart swell with reverence for her. I was looking at her expectantly as she conversed with Mom and Dad, although not being able to hear anything. After a short while, she turned her head towards where I was seated and gave me a reassuring nod, then came and sat beside Alisha on the floor. They were trying their best to keep me calm. And I tried my best to *look* calm on the exterior, while inside of me was a tumult in the making. There was angst curdling my blood. I wanted to know what had *exactly* happened that led to this. I knew my brother well enough to be sure that he would never resort to ending his life as a solution to his problems. My head was on my knees and my hands over my head, crying in the most vulnerable way possible. I felt their hands hold on to mine. I lifted my head from my knees and I looked at Alisha and Sasha. They were looking at me with the most encouragement they could force their pupils to produce. But I had easily looked beyond the facade. I saw something that I had never encountered in their eyes before, at least not when they usually looked at me. They looked afraid and pitiful.

The wait felt endless and every passing minute stretched into an hour that only magnified the air of uncertainty and fear that hovered over us. As if some undiscovered divinity had communicated my thoughts universally, I heard a distant siren approaching, the sound growing increasingly louder.

TWENTY

Encountering the World for the very First Time

People were rushing everywhere. I could hear voices but failed to fathom out words. I could catch distant wailing of variable pitches but had not enough focus in my mind to draw observance of my surroundings as I normally would. One hand rested on the white sheet covering his blood-drenched body, failing to mask the redness, being stained in the blood itself. The other clutched on, with every iota of resilience left in me, shuddering mildly, to the lower frame of the moveable bed. As the wheels rolled on and my feet caught up to their pace, I didn't know where I was headed. A smoke of distinctive sterile smell hovered in the air and uncertainty resonated with the hushed whispers and frail gasps that entered my ears as we strode against the clock, ticking away, and the people heading in a direction opposite to ours. Fear lurked up from the concavity of my knees all the way up to my pharynx and kept pounding against my neck, synchronous to my heartbeat. The two nurses leading our way finally came to a halt in front of a big door that appeared to have an even bigger ward behind it. A team of doctors, three in number, walked out of it, and exchanged a few words with the nurses in rapid Hindi which I was unable to capture. My head was lost in the body lying beside me. The barely breathing body.

It had been around ten minutes of Sparsh being admitted into the ICU when I saw Mom and Dad running frantically towards us sitting on the seats outside the room lined up against the wall. Sasha had accompanied us to the hospital and insisted on staying with me till I needed her. But I knew that it was too late and her parents wouldn't be too appreciative of her staying out till so late, although they would understand the gravity of the situation. Plus, the fatigue was too apparent in the way she struggled to keep her eyelids open as we drove to the hospital. So she left soon after we arrived at the hospital. Alisha sat beside me all this while, one arm draped around my back and the other holding my hand, resting softly on the cold metal handle segregating our seats. I hadn't noticed until now that she had thrown a jacket on her as well as on me. Her parents, meanwhile, were nervously pacing back and forth in front of the ICU until their eyes met my parents'. They were immediately riddled with horror. How would they deal with the tension? After all, their best friends' son had jumped off their terrace in their absence. I could see the guilt tinting their eyelids. They must've been thinking: *we should've stayed.*

My parents gradually slowed down their pace as they caught sight of us sitting, coming to a halt on standing opposite us. I noticed that the tip of Mom's nose and the apple of her cheeks were stained in a tender red, the kind which rules over your face from excessive crying. Her eyes were swollen and a few tears were still running down from her pupils. She wiped them off as she regained hold of her breath and said, 'Alaina, baby, are you okay? Where's Sparsh?'. I looked at her bleared eyes and the teary lines that had now dried on her cheek and weakly pointed my hand towards the door to our right. I was not brave enough to deal with the reality of my brother battling against death in the ICU, let alone bring that reality to words. 'What happened, *beta?*', Dad asked with a trembling voice. His eyes were as glassy and clear as water. I could nearly peek into his soul. It was wretched. It was then that I realised that I had never seen him cry. It was then that I also realised that I had yet not asked his question myself. I turned to Alisha. She struggled to open her mouth to form words. Sensing the uneasiness that the question had engendered, Mr. Kumar cunningly and quickly diverted Dad's attention by saying, 'Vaibhav, we need to discuss the charges. If word reaches undesirable ears, the police will be here at any moment.' I thought he was referring to hospital charges and felt instantly outraged. This was definitely not the time to quarrel over who would pay when someone was dying. But why would payment include the police? I looked up at Dad with an air of confusion. He answered Mr. Kumar and me with a nod that read: 'We'll handle it'. They both walked away hastily in an attempt to conceal the worry on their visages. While I was curious to find out where they were headed off to or what charges even implied, my mind was dominated by another thought now: what had actually happened? Meanwhile, Mrs. Kumar had offered her seat to Mom and embraced her in consolation. As if reading my mind, Alisha rose from her seat the moment I did too. We kept pacing grimly in a random corridor, seeking a quieter place for conversation. There was a small cubicle for worship at the end of the corridor. Although religion would be my last resort in any other case, today it seemed to be the only haven I could implant faith on. Shutting the door behind us, we sat down on our knees to bow down to the various godly figures and figurines placed in front of us. We were habituated with this practice of prayer through the several visits to some of the most exquisite temples in the country that our parents had taken us to. So it had become a reflex for us to kneel down, hold our palms together and bow our heads down in submission to the symbolic almighty. As we whispered prayers under our breaths and got up, I noticed that despite its limited capacity, the cubicle was representative of our country's secularity. It promised not to disappoint any worshipper that crossed its threshold. We then relaxed our legs into a more comfortable sitting posture. She looked up at me and let out a deep breath before speaking.

'Some people at the party had started circulating rumours that Sparsh is gay. I was not present in the scene. I was inside at the time. This was happening in the backyard. Most of our friends were in my company so I'm presuming that the kids spreading the word must've been his batchmates. I did spot some faces through the windows and most of them were juniors. I don't know every detail of what led to his trigger but from what Arshiyaa told me—'

'Was she involved in this?', I asked curtly, cutting her off mid-sentence.

'She told me that she saw some nuisance being created by the juniors, but she didn't participate. She sensed something was skeptical when Sparsh ran away from the backyard speedily and headed inside, and upstairs.'

'And she didn't bother to stop them? Or him?'

'Alaina, I know you want to hunt down a single culprit. I know you are devastated and want to ruin the person or the people who did this to Sparsh. And you have every right as his sister to feel vindictive. But hear me out, okay? Listen to the full story, will you?' She was speaking to me in a sisterly tone, trying to calm me down. I nodded in approval and she continued, 'So, Arshiyaa said to me that they were bullying him by calling him a faggot, pushing him around and they even went to the extent of forcing him to play "Spin The Bottle" to prove that he was straight. Apparently, they wickedly forced the bottle to point its ends between him and Ira. They were compelled to make out for around five minutes in front of their entire grade. They made him gulp down shots under the excuse that if he was a *real man*, he needed to drink. And I think after being made to forcefully have three shots, he ran away, his *friends* behind him guffawing at his escape that they deemed cowardly. Arshiyaa didn't run after him because she thought since Ira and he were dating, he was probably upset about being made to drink. I'm sure had she felt the slightest instinct that he would've gone so far, she would've done something.'

'But she was busy groping the DJ,' I blurted.

'Alaina, can you please for once let go of the coldness and talk to me? How are you feeling? Are you okay?'

'Am I okay?', I asked in a rhetorical tone, then realising that I might still be coming off as adamant, I continued in milder words, 'No, Alisha. I am not okay. God damn it, he went through heartbreak just three days ago and I thought it would be a fantastic idea to bring him to your party to cheer him up.'

'He broke up with Ira? But they seemed to be bonding well last ni—'

'He wasn't dating Ira!'

'What do you mean?'

'He *is* gay, Alisha. And he was outed at your party! He was closeted for nearly two years now. I still remember the day he came out to me. He was so scared, Alisha, so scared that I might look at him or think of him differently,' I broke down into sobs on recalling that day, but went on nevertheless, 'He confided in me to protect his identity. Ira knew too, so they put up the pretence of dating to escape peer pressure and hushed floating hearsay about his sexuality. His class is dumped with homophobes, Alisha. It's disgusting. They forced him, Alisha! That's assault! Imagine someone compelling you to kiss a girl when you're straight. Of course, you'll feel beyond uncomfortable. He felt violated, Alisha. I can't deal with this world,' I paused for a breath, then, striking a realisation, continued, 'It all makes sense. He didn't overreact. Don't anyone dare to utter that he overreacted or he just wanted attention! He was drunk, something he never wanted to be. And he was forced to kiss a girl.

Even if it was his best friend, I know how repulsive he must've felt. They are vile, inconsiderate, and condescending. They are not his friends. Hell, they're worse than enemies. I can't deal with this world, A. I can't, I can't,' and I fell into her embrace as I broke down completely. She hugged me tightly and continually whispered, 'Yes, you can.'

'Do you want me to talk about something else?', she asked.

'I do.'

'I suppose you've heard of Ray and me.'

'I have. But I don't know how serious it was.'

'It was pretty serious.'

'Yeah?'

'Yeah.'

'Tell me about it if you feel comfortable.'

'I've always shown myself to be this confident, charismatic, charming girl who always seems to get everything she wants and has her own way in everything, but that's just an illusion. It's an illusion I created for myself as a shelter. I created it to protect myself from vulnerability. I know you and Sash think that I don't have much room in my life for emotions, which is partly true— I never wanted to deal with any emotions. I hated them because I didn't know how to deal with them. I was afraid of showing myself for who I am and figured that the best thing to do would be to display myself with this whole new persona. And over time, I got addicted to it. Addicted to being perceived as powerful, popular, and intimidating. I loved having things be just the way I wanted. I know it sounds toxic. In all honesty, it very much is. You know why I lost my shit when you mentioned that I only care about the sex and nothing else in relationships? Because it was true. And when you said it, it all became so real— the fact that I had a facade. I had been carrying this facade with ease for so long, but in those days, it was beginning to wear off with Ray. I was starting to encounter my emotions, starting to *feel.* And it scared the shit of me. I was scared that I would lose this identity that I had created over the years. I was scared that I would be in a position of vulnerability.' With this, she began sobbing. I had never seen her like this— raw and real, like I was talking to her soul. A part of my heart sank to see her so broken. Pulling her into a light embrace, I whispered into her ear, attempting to pacify her, 'You don't have to talk about it if you don't want to.'

Her sobs receded gradually and recollecting herself, she looked at me, straight in the eyes, and answered, 'But I do want to,' and continued.

'I was beginning to develop feelings for Ray that I didn't want to face or feel. But some parts of me did desire something serious, like an actual emotional connection. In the end, it didn't work out. He was infatuated with this illusion I had created of me, and my blooming feelings for him in their infancy desired him to *like me, not my illusion.'*

'That's so deep. I have also always tried to run away from reality but I can't even begin to imagine what you must've had to go through. I wish I could've been there for you then.'

'You're here now. That's enough.'

'I'm sorry, A.', I said with genuine regret, laying my head on her chest, wetting her dress with my tears which was already drenched in hers. She understood, without the need for additional reasoning, and replied, 'I'm sorry too, A.'

'It's okay. I shouldn't have overreacted that night.'

'And I shouldn't have pettily gossiped about you. In hindsight, I may have used it as a coping mechanism to deal with all of *it.* Gosh, that was so immature of me!'

'Yeah, it kinda was,' I teased.

'Shut up!', she giggled.

As our chuckles resided, I lifted my head from her chest, and looking straight into her eyes, I said, 'But on a serious note, I need to tell you something.'

'Go on, A.'

'Remember how I'd blurted that night that I wanted to explore my sexuality?'

'Yes, I do remember. And I am sorry for reacting the way that I did. That was so not it. It was so dismissive. I'm sorry.'

‘It’s okay. You were not in control of yourself, and I'm over it. What I wanted to tell you was...,’ taking a deep breath and letting it out, I admitted, ‘...I think I am bisexual.’

She raised her eyebrows in surprise.

‘Or queer. I go with queer. I mean to say that I am not straight.’

She was a little taken aback by how suddenly the confession tumbled out of mouth, but responded quickly, ‘That’s amazing, babe! I will always love you, no matter how many fights we have or how immature I might behave sometimes. And if you must know, I don’t think of you any differently as I did before. You’re still a bitch.’

We burst into laughter. It was strange how we, as humans, could manage to find things to laugh about when all the strings within us wear tearing apart. We were roses. Some with more petals than thorns and some with more thorns than petals. We were strings that were barely managing to keep joining their broken ends and we were blooming buds that met with atrocious weather every now and then. What were these roses or strings or buds, I knew not. Perhaps we were more metaphors than we were skin, flesh and blood.

'You know that our parents are conservative, right?', I asked her once our laughs had subsided. We had been in the prayer room for over thirty minutes by now.

'Yes, I think mine are too.'

'Sparsh was always so afraid to reach out to them about his sexuality. He's scared that they will not accept him or love him as much. To be honest, I'm a little afraid too.'

'I know that this is the last thing you'd wanna hear from anyone in this regard, but, conservative or not, they're still your parents. If you don't tell them, they'll find out someday. If you do tell them and their reaction is dramatically different than your expectations, it's okay. You can't do anything about it. I am here to support you. Sasha is here to support you. We will always love you for who you are. This legal normalisation of heterosexuality is humanmade. I read it one day. In fact, I read a few days after the night of our fight when you had mentioned that you wanted to explore your sexuality. I realised the next day that I may have been slightly homophobic. So I wanted to look it up.'

'You're right. But out of genuine curiosity, did you do that research for me or because you'd literally get cancelled next year in college for being homophobic?', I asked in a jocular air.

'A little bit of both,' she admitted with a shameful smile.

'Say no more! Anyway, what did you discover there?'

'I found out that it was the British who criminalised homosexuality in India and in fact Hinduism has nothing against homosexuality. Some Vedic scriptures acknowledge it, even the presence of a third gender.'

'Wow, so Hindus who think that their religion condemns the LGBTQ+ community are a bunch of stubborn idiots.'

'That's one way to put it.'

We talked for another hour in that little cubicle like old companions that had reunited after several years.

This was the first time I was engaging in an erudite conversational exchange with her, and it felt good. I told her about Myra. She looked happy to listen to my tale of love and said, 'Dude, were you two in a movie or what?' but the main area of her interest was the extent of physical contact we had had. I repeated to her several times that we could never go beyond a heated make-out, being interrupted every time we wanted to go further. And maybe we were not ready either. But she refused to believe me until I repeated it for the tenth time. 'You could write a book about it, A! '*The Girl I Met at the Literary Club*'. Woah, did I just sell out a compelling book title? I need my name to be the first on the list of acknowledgements. This story even has prospects to get you into top colleges, haha,' she giggled excitedly.

'Oh, come on, I wouldn't use something so personal as a bait to impress admissions officers,' I said, shrugging off her suggestion. But she wasn't wrong. It was a brilliant love story, at least in my opinion.

'But you could.'

'I'm not that desperate.'

I had almost forgotten that we were at a hospital where only a few metres away my brother was in an ICU until a nurse knocked at the cubicle's door to summon us outside. Suddenly, I started feeling guilty again. We went back to the area outside the ICU and saw that the doctor was intently conversing with our parents. When they spotted us approaching, they beckoned us to speed up.

'He wants to see you,' the doctor said to me, 'He specifically mentioned your name. Note that he is in a very delicate condition. Be careful with your words.'

I nodded in agreement and walked into the room without exchanging a word with anyone else. Inside, I was screaming gleefully. *He is breathing!* At that moment, everything and everyone else seemed insignificant. He was alive and I did not care about anyone or anything else. Everything else around me was spinning as I approached him, his eyes open tiredly, an oxygen mask over his mouth and nose and some pipes extending from his wrists to a cylinder of blood. He had several bandages around his head, piling up over his wound.

I sat down on a stool beside his bed and rested my hand above his. With much strain, he tried to turn his head to look at me but prevented him from doing so immediately. I held his cheek lovingly, the part which was uncovered by the oxygen cylinder. Although it was hazy with the condensation of his breath on the inner surface of the mask, I could tell that he was smiling. I fought hard to suppress the tears, but I couldn't help one or two drops glide down my cheeks.

'Can you talk?'

He nodded in response and took off the mask from his mouth with his right hand, the one which was free of the pipes.

'Hi,' he said, catching his breath.

'Are you sure you can take the mask off?' He nodded slightly in response.

'How are you feeling?'

'I'm feeling okay.'

'Okay.' I didn't know what to say because I feared that anything could trigger him.

'I'm not,' he blurted a few seconds later.

'You can talk to me, Sparsh. I don't wanna push you too far, but just know that you can tell me anything, and I'm all ears.'

'Yes, I know.'

'Whenever you're ready.' He remained silent for a while which crept fret into me. I wasn't ready to be on the verge of losing him again, for knowing why he tried to leap off the cliff was not more important right now than the fact that he was in front of me, alive and breathing. 'If you don't want to, that's also okay. I'm here for you for whatever you want. And I love you,' I said, meaning every syllable I pronounced, and mildly caressed his cheek.

'I am ready.'

'Go on,' I said, with an encouraging smile.

He thought for a while, and as if deciding against his initial thought, he shook his head slightly to himself and asked, 'Do you know what happened?'

‘I do. They are horrible people, Sparsh. You deserve so much better,’ I almost broke down with these words but managed to maintain my composure. I needed to be brave for him.

‘I don’t know, *Di.* The world is wrecked.’

‘I know. It’s unfair.’

‘I don’t even know how they found out! Did they find out through Aarav? Why would he do that? It cannot be. I don’t think it’s him. But that’s not the point. I don’t care anymore how they found out. But they began calling me a faggot and laughed at me. They said I was too “fem” and I had to prove to them that I was straight. I was so terrified, *Di.* It was me against all of them. Ira tried to argue them out of bullying me but this is India, and she was one girl against a gang of hooligan guys. And before I knew it, Rihan pulled me by the collar of my T-shirt. I was this close to his face,’ indicating about a centimetre with his fingers, ‘and I felt so intimidated. I thought he’d spit at me. Or fight me. I don’t know. He started pushing me and some other boys gathered around, supporting him and chanting “faggot”. I have never hated myself more than I did at that moment when they derided my identity. I felt ashamed of who I was. They shoved shots in front of my face and made me drink them because if I didn't, I wouldn't be "man enough". I was dazed. And scared. Ira was crying when we were kissing. I felt a teardrop on my skin. And I felt so repulsive, like my body was fighting against my soul. I didn't know what to do after we broke off. They were still laughing at us, but their voices mingled into nothing but an echo of the word "faggot" in my ears. My vision turned blurry and all I could hear were their bullying and Aarav's words: "a mere distraction".'

My voice had descended from my throat and lingered somewhere at the pit of my belly, curled up in fear and anguish. Every word he uttered was a daunting reminder of my absence to protect him. I couldn't even imagine what he must have gone through in those minutes.

He looked at my distraught face, and releasing a deep breath, said, 'I know what you wanna know. It's okay. I won't be triggered. You wanna know why I decided that ending my life was the only option?' I didn't answer. I wasn't sure what word could turn into a dagger at that moment for the fragile state he was in. I did want to know what pushed him to the edge, but the guilt was overpowering against any concern in that regard. But he continued, 'Partly because the alcohol drained my mind of any rational thought, and partly because I couldn't see anything ahead of me. How would I live? Going to a classroom every day for over two years to be surrounded by people who would disdain me and laugh at my identity. Coming back home to Mom and Dad who were repulsive to the concept of anything other than being heterosexual. I felt humiliated, worthless, and lost. Somebody that I love, and believe me, I mean it when I say that I love him, discarded me as a distraction. If all the people I love cannot accept me, then how can I ever accept myself?'

I didn't know how to answer him, again. This time, I allowed the tears to flow. My heart collapsed and my chest felt empty. How can people treat someone like this? Nobody deserves to feel this way. Nobody deserved to feel discarded, or unwanted, or unloved, or unworthy. Maybe happiness doesn't come to all easily but nobody deserves to suffer through lethal depression. I clenched my teeth to hold back the tears and spoke, hoping that my words could find his torn strings and sew some of them together once more, 'The world is unfair, Sparsh. It is so unfair. I've realised this more in the past few months than I had all my life. But I cannot imagine struggling through what you have. I cannot change people. It is not in my power to make them more progressive or considerate. And you don't deserve this tainted world. You are too kind a soul. People love to fuck up with kind people because they see them as easy targets. But they're deceived. Kind people are the strongest people in existence. You've fought for so long. I'm proud of you. I will not say that what you did today in trying to end the war was erroneous or weak. But I want you to remember the day before yesterday, when we were sitting in my room, reciting the slogan that we are brave. I know you are still brave. Maybe the thorns stung you too deeply but the petals still exist. We'll find them together. Are you with me?'

He finally smiled a little, bringing relief to my heart, and answered, 'Yes, I'm with you. Also, please stop using metaphors in our conversations. Reserve them for your writing endeavours.'

'Okay. I was just trying to be philosophical,' I mumbled.

‘Oh, don’t make that frowning face! You know you triumphed very well in that attempt. You sounded no different than a therapist. But it’s difficult to follow up with your metaphors sometimes. Also, I’m not a big fan of that particular literary device.’

The sombreness dispelled from our surroundings as we continued talking. Although he was telling me about the kind of homophobia he had to struggle with in his class and how dejected those experiences made him feel, he did not shed tears or look upset. Instead, he looked relieved after releasing all the emotions and feelings he’d been bottling up for an unimaginably long period, and I listened to him attentively. Not unlike before, he bedazzled me with his level of maturity once more. The fact that he had borne such an intense mental ruckus till now was unbelievable. I wanted to say to him that he inspired me, refuting the general belief that elders inspire their juniors. But I didn't want to interject him and hence remained silent. He kept talking and I kept listening till a knock at the door interrupted us. Without even asking for permission to come inside, a nurse walked in and said that our parents wished to see him now. Apparently, we had talked for long enough. I was a little annoyed but understood that Mom and Dad had their heads wrapped around uncertainty for too long, and they deserved to speak with their son who had just brushed away with death. As I nodded in agreement to the nurse, beckoning her to invite my parents in, and proceeded to leave, Sparsh held my hand and asked me to say. There was a glint of pleading in his eyes. I understood that he might be nervous to open up to Mom and Dad, so I stayed back.

'Sparsh, my son, you're okay, oh thank you *Krishna!*', Mom uttered in relief as soon as she crossed the threshold and saw that her son was alive. She planted kisses all over his face. Seeing that the oxygen mask lay beside him on the pillow, unused, she looked back and forth from the mask to his face fretfully and placed the mask cautiously over his mouth once more.

'How are you feeling now?', Dad asked with a voice as low as his heart was, caution written all over his face.

'Better.', Sparsh replied.

'Do you think you can come home today?', Mom asked in a way that sounded like she was speaking to an infant, full of compassion and tender concern.

‘I think that the doctors can answer that better,’ I answered after silence hung in the air for a few minutes, although the question was not directed at me.

‘You’re right.’, said Dad while eyeing Mom, as if signalling something. The silence was almost excruciating. I could see their eyes glazed over with worry and fear, a sight not generally caught by sons and daughters in their parents. I knew the question that rested at the bridge of their throats which probably had rolled over to the tips of their tongues by now, but nobody could determine when would be the right time to ask it. Mom backed up from the hospital bed and now stood by Dad’s side, whispering something into his ear and then glaring at the opposite wall mindlessly. Sparsh, as if catching a glimpse of their thoughts, filled the empty void with words that none of us were brave enough to utter, ‘I can talk about it.’

I looked at him sympathetically, trying to communicate through my eyes that he didn’t have to if he wasn’t ready, that things could go horribly wrong and I didn’t want to see him get hurt any further, but he reassured me with a slight nod, which was more of his eyes blinking than his head moving.

'I'm gay,' he announced without warning, the sound of his voice reverberating through the vast space of the hospital ward, striking against walls, tumbling and echoing till it completely settled in. I noticed by quick observance that Mom flinched a little, struggling to keep herself from gasping in shock, so she gasped with her mouth closed. Dad didn't look much taken aback. The same sombreness sat on his countenance. 'Yes, I'm proudly gay,' he continued, 'and I cannot keep it locked somewhere inside my trembling soul anymore. I don't want to lie to you anymore. I realised this two years back but kept myself closeted because I didn't know how to talk about it. But that didn't end up well, quite visibly. You wanna know why I tried to kill myself? Because at that moment in the party, at that moment after being bullied for my sexuality, at that moment after being forced to conform to someone else's rules, at that moment when everyone was laughing at me, I didn't like who I was. I didn't like the fact that being born this way was apparently my fault. I hated the fact that a guy who I had fallen for discarded my feelings ever so complacently. I hated the fact that even if I would go home after the night ended, the struggle would be far from over. And home,' he snarked, 'feels like a trap. What an irony.

There were countless nights when I would huddle down in a corner of my room and weep, shuddering, wishing that I wouldn't wake up the other day. There were days when the bullying would get so bad that I would have to run from class to the washroom because I couldn't breathe. And there were so many other moments when I wished I could be anyone else but myself. Why didn't I speak about it before? Because I never felt safe. Everytime that I tried to muster enough courage to talk about it, to seek help, my mind would spring with all of the worst possible repercussions. I was scared. And I remained silent for so long that I eventually stopped feeling the urge to scream. I simply let it bottle up in me. And don't get me wrong, this isn't a "phase" or me complaining in search of pity, because I know a lot of people have it harder. But it's the truth. So yeah, to sum it up, my home, bullying, getting your heart broken, and feeling disgusted by my own identity do seem like good enough reasons to die.' He let out a long-drawn breath, as if a burden that had been suppressing him suddenly disappeared. My heart sank. But at the same time, I felt proud of him. There was no sign of fright or shame in his voice when he spoke. He spoke *his* truth without feeling that it was his fault. And I felt inspired. I shut my eyes as my vision blurred slowly with the piling tears, took a deep breath before taking the leap, and said, not caring if anybody would listen or approve, 'I want to say something too. I am also, uh, not straight. I know that you both have very conservative beliefs and I know it's difficult for you to budge an inch from them. But I... *we* cannot change ourselves to adhere to your standards. Before you even say it, again, this is not a phase or hormones acting up. This is not just about infatuation. It's about love. Love knows no boundaries. All is fair in love, right? I don't think there's anything wrong with not being heterosexual, although our society has been dictating it for decades: that boys should like girls, and girls should be like boys. The only reason it took me so long to understand my sexuality was because my mind was trained and programmed by default by society to believe that I can only like boys! So, when I had goosebumps sitting next to Drisha in fifth grade or when I kept staring at the actress more than at the actor during movies, I thought that something was wrong with me! That maybe my mind was dysfunctional, and I constantly kept subsiding these feelings thinking I would be violating the golden regulations laid out by society. But who set these rules? People did! So we can change them. Why does there need to be any rule anyway when it comes to love?'. I unintentionally broke down at this point, but wiping off the tears and gulping down the rising nervousness, I continued in a quivering voice, 'So yeah, that's it. I think I'm bisexual, or maybe pansexual, I'm not sure yet. But I know that I'm definitely not straight and I'm not going to force myself to be just because that's the *normal* path everyone *should* follow.'

The room filled with a deafening silence once more. It was blindingly dark until I realised that I was speaking this entire time with my eyelids fastened. Perhaps I was still a little afraid of my identity. I opened my eyes to look at Dad in tears, looking from me to Sparsh, and with a weary smile on his visage. Mom's face was hidden behind Dad's. She emerged to the front, cheeks streaked with tears and an unsettling shock shining in her distraught eyes. 'I don't know what to say,' she uttered, glaring into zilch. She didn't make eye contact with any of us. She stood there, frozen, as if allowing our confessions to sink into her petrified soul and waiting to hear the echo of her own voice. Without another word, she turned around and proceeded to leave with slow and heavy steps. Dad didn't follow. He turned to me and held my hand. We walked towards the bed and he sat down on the stool. He now took Sparsh's hand into his, all three of our hands held together, and spoke, in a voice that resurrected the little girl in me who was once being rocked in the cradle by her father, 'Sparsh and Alaina, I love you both so much. You have no idea. I will continue to love you no matter what. What you both said was definitely a lot to take in at once. But I want you to know that I do not look at you or think of you both any differently than before. You know that your mother is a staunch follower of societal conventions and is very pious. But trust me, this won't diminish her love for you. She just needs some time. I'll talk to her.'

'You promise?', I asked.

'I will, bacha. Hang in there,' he said to both of us, patting our heads affectionately.

We sat there silently for a while till Sparsh eventually fell asleep. But this was not a painful silence. It was relieving. Dad got up to leave, saying that he would speak with Mom and then come back to stay here for the rest of the day. He suggested I go home but I insisted against it. Something told me that he already knew about us, or at least me. But I couldn't figure out how. As he was exiting the door, I asked him, 'Dad, what charges were you talking about earlier?'

'Nothing significant, beta,' he answered, trying to dodge the question.

'Please, Dad!', I attempted further, not ready to surrender just yet.

'Attempt to commit suicide is a punishable offence in our legal system. But we've dissolved the charges; nothing to worry about.'

I was confounded. My mind was brimming with an array of follow-up questions: shouldn't the law care about the mental health of the suicidal person than punish them for it? How was that reasonable? But I fought the urge to ask them. This wasn't the time.

TWENTY ONE

Till the 'Night Lives

'Yes,' I overheard the doctor say to Mom as they tried their best to converse in whispers, on the status of Sparsh's condition, 'he can leave in a week or so. Considering that the level of intoxication was just above average, we believe that rehab is not the need of the hour. But I'll recommend seeing a therapist for at least two months.'

I thought about the idea of sharing all your problems with someone without the fear of being judged and with the comfort of being understood. It would feel relieving and safe. But therapist or not, we are all still humans; it's difficult to resist the spontaneous judgement from setting in. I wondered what amount of schooling and training could ever truly make a human exceptionally considerate, understanding, and helpful.

While Alisha's family left at around four in the morning, Mom, Dad, and I stayed over at the hospital. It was currently seven in the morning and I had barely slept. I stayed seated on the stool beside the bed, in the same position as was when Dad had left us. Sparsh and I talked for a while till he dozed off. We spoke about how a weight had been removed off of our shoulders, and despite not having received the ideal response, we acknowledged that it could've been a hundred times worse than what we got. We laughed over the fact that in spite of our tireless efforts of pretence, Dad knew. I told him that I was proud of him for being brave enough for saying what he said. He inspired me. He inspired me not only to speak my truth but also to come face to face with it myself. And when his eyelids had shut, his nose was drawing air of renewed life from the oxygen mask, I whispered into his ear that from that moment onward, I would always be there for him. I meant it too.

But as the dawn of a new morning rose, still waiting for the first rays of light to shine, the afterthought hung in my head for long: what if we hadn't made it in time?

My parents told me to return home because apparently the skin under my eyes had been swallowed by the sockets beneath and I was beginning to look sick. I tried to resist initially but when it became too exhausting to even whisper words, I understood that indeed I needed some rest. The driver was waiting outside with the engine on as I walked out, looking at me sympathetically. As soon as I got inside the car and the softness of seat cushions hit my back, I closed my eyes slowly. I could still catch sight of his pitiful glance and resolutely tried to ignore it, wondering all the while what the pity was directed at. But after a point, I was too tired to think any further.

Vigorous shaking of my shoulders was what woke me up when we arrived home. Apparently, the loud honking had failed to interrupt my sound slumber. I walked inside with a hazy vision, not looking where I was going. Since I grew up here, I knew every nook and corner, every edge and turn. So I didn't really need the assistance of sight to guide me to my room. As soon as I entered my room, I flung myself down on the bed, not caring that I was clothed in what now stank with the obnoxious mixture of blood and alcohol. The house felt peculiarly desolate. I had been alone in the house, of course. And our house-helpers were always present. They were present today too. But the house felt empty, or perhaps, I did. Something dark, almost ominous, was spreading across my chest. It felt cold and shivery. But once more, sleep took over the better of me. So, I allowed the fatigue to dissolve from my head, knowing that the darkness had only begun to set in.

*****

I woke up to the sound of mellow drizzle murmuring against the casements. Twilight had fallen and the sky was turning purple. I turned over to my right to grab my phone only to see twelve missed calls from my parents, one from Alisha, three from Sasha and two from Myra. I suddenly felt a lump of anxiety rise to my throat. Hardly preventing my mind from imagining the worst, I clicked on their names and called them back, one after another. To my relief, Mom and Dad had called me only to inform me that they would probably be returning home late at night and so if I felt scared of staying alone till that hour, I could sleep over at Alisha's. The suggestion was promising but I didn't feel acquiescent to consider it. The conversation was brief and I assured them that if I felt the need, I would definitely ring up the Kumars. The thing is, I just wanted to be alone for a while. Although Alisha and I had somewhat buried the hatchet between us yesterday, I didn't want to go crawling back to her. I still felt a certain degree of discomfort. Things would definitely revert to normal, or someplace near normal, but it would take time. Sasha had called only to check in on me, said she had received the news of Sparsh's recovery from Alisha and suggested that she could come over to my place if I liked. On any other occasion, I would like that, of course. But something in me prompted me to respectfully decline the offer, convincing her that I needed an unadulterated headspace to think. She said that she understood but still insisted that if I changed my mind, she would be just a call away.

There was something dreadful spreading in my gut. I've read and heard a lot about how humans can sense a forthcoming action by their sixth senses, although there has been no proven existence of a sixth sense till present. But intuition warned me through, its soldering negative thoughts, that while there may be nothing to mourn over, there was nothing to derive mirth from either.

When I called her, Myra made me wait for five rings to pass. She then picked up, silence stretching between us for a couple of moments until I whispered into the empty space, 'Hello?'

'Hi,' she answered with a voice that lacked the excitement it carried everytime it heard mine.

'How are you feeling? How is Sparsh?'

'He's okay. I'm okay too.'

'Are you sure?'

'Mostly.'

'Are you still at the hospital?'

'No, I returned home this morning and dozed off. I couldn't sleep all night. Mom and Dad are still there. They'll be returning late.'

'So, you're alone at home now?'

‘Yes, except for the house-helpers and security.’

‘Are you sure you wanna be alone?’

‘Actually, solitude is precisely my craving at the present moment.’

‘Oh, I completely understand,’ she answered in a tone that announced disappointment.

‘Don’t worry, I’ll be fine,’ I answered, assuming that her fret was brewing from my being alone.

‘Okay, if you say so. Umm, I actually wanted to talk to you.’

‘But we are talking, aren’t we?’

‘No, like, *talk* talk.’

‘What do you mean?’ I knew exactly what it meant. Or partially, at least. Something ill was dancing toward my path.

'I know you want to be alone and I don't intend to invade your privacy. But I really need to talk to you, as soon as possible. So let me know when you feel better and we'll meet somewhere.'

'You can come over,' I blurted involuntarily.

'But don't you want to be alone?' I did. But a part of me was also longing to see her.
'Not anymore,' I said, changing my mind spontaneously once more.

'Okay,' she responded in a shallow voice, 'I'll see you in ten.'

And she did. She arrived exactly ten minutes after we hung up— a rare phenomenon. My heart was thumping nervously. I didn't know what was coming or what it was that she desired to '*talk*' about but it was certainly not going to be pleasant to my ears. Or so indicated the tone in which her voice almost backed away from talking like we used to. I was sitting in the living room, reading a magazine I'd randomly picked out from the shelf, and crunching on almonds. I was taken by surprise as she cleared her throat abruptly. Lifting my eyes from the page whose words were travelling over my head, her figure came into the focus of my vision. She smiled at me but I couldn't help but notice the absence of enthusiasm in it, the one which it always carried when we were together. It was more of a smile born out of the habitual greeting. I placed the magazine on the table in front of me and ran up to her, still holding the bowl of almonds in my hand. I pulled her into a tight hug and she requited. It was at that moment that our bodies crashed against each other and I could once more smell daisies and jasmine from her hair that I realised how much I had missed her, and how much I needed that hug. From the curves along my waist, she glided her hand up to my head and caressed it lovingly. The hug lasted for longer than I had expected it to. Three minutes into the hug, she grabbed the bowl from my hand and placed it on the table. As soon as my hand was free of the travail, I ran it through those messy curls that I had fallen in love with before I could even fathom what love was. Before I knew it, I was sobbing into her shoulder. They were finally unbridling: the emotions, the agony, the torment, and the anguish that had afflicted my soul; that I had been bottling up and ignoring for the past nineteen hours. Words weren't needed for me to explain what was going on or how I was feeling or what about her visiting me triggered me. She seemed to understand it all. As I raised my head from her shoulder, looking her in the eyes, I caught a glint of sympathy glimmering in her pupils. She cupped my face in her palms and caressed my cheeks lovingly, then delicately wiping off the tears from my face. Her fingers travelled all across my countenance, from lining my eyebrows to tracing my lips to gliding along the bridge of my nose, then finally landing on my eyelids and mildly closing them. I felt her lips brush against my eyelids, one after another, which then proceeded to kiss my lips. It was not a passionate kiss; rather a soft one brimmed with hallowed affection and love. I once more buried my head into her shoulders. The tears came running down again. But I was not crying this time with the release of the same emotions of agony, torment, and anguish as before. I was crying because I had never experienced love like this before. Crying because I had never thought I would meet someone who would know me better than I know myself. Crying because I had never imagined knowing someone so well that I felt like it was my soul living in her body and hers in mine. Crying because when I thought I could neither love nor be loved, she told me that I mattered. Crying because I was afraid to lose her, for if I did, I don't think I would ever be able to find myself in someone else again as I did in her.

And so we held ourselves in each other's embrace for over ten minutes, each knowing that something was about to break. The string between us was stretching farther, with such tension that it would only be mere seconds before snapping apart. But we clung on till we could.

There eventually came a point when our bodies felt numb and stiff, so we broke off. We sat down on the couch and nibbled on the almonds for a few minutes. There was no exchange of words. Although the sound of chewing echoed through the otherwise forlorn atmosphere, every moment that passed by without a word stretched the string only more. We allowed the silence to rule till we ran out of almonds to lighten the glumness.

'So... you wanted to talk?', I said to her, looking at her face which was resolutely trying to look away from mine.

'Yes, but not now,' she answered, finally looking me in the eyes.

'Why?'

'I've come over to stay, dumbass. Didn't you notice my bag?'

I turned to search around the room for her bag until I finally spotted it, resting on the floor behind the table. It was the same bag she had brought when we had first gone to Rosé Café together. The same one which she brought with her nearly every time we hung out.

'I didn't realise!', I answered ardently. But a part of me felt guilty. I turned down Sasha and Alisha's considerate efforts on the premise that I wanted to be alone. I still wanted to be alone. But something prompted me to let her stay with me. There was a strange uneasiness brewing at the pit of my stomach.

'Are you okay?'

'Now I am.'

She looked down at her fingers fidgeting at her lap, and her eyebrows were slightly creased in a way that a person does when they're guilty. I noticed a blob of tear swelling up in her eye but she managed to gulp it down, restraining it from escaping the periphery of her lids.

'What's wrong?', I asked as the silence between us was growing uncomfortable once more.

'Nothing, actually. Trust me, it's nothing. Talk to me, Alaina. I know you said that you're okay but you know that you can tell me how you're feeling. I'm here to listen, baby.', She was still staring at her fingers.

Yes, I did know that I could tell her explicitly about how I was feeling and she would understand immediately. But I also knew that it wasn't 'nothing' that made her avoid eye contact with me.

'I'm sorry,' she blurted out just as I was about to speak, catching me off-guard.

'Why are you sorry?'

'I shouldn't have gone. I really shouldn't have left you alone there. I just freaked out. And my parents would've lost it if I didn't return home. I really am sorry, Alaina. I wasn't there for you when you needed me the most. I fucked up. I'm really sorry.' She began sobbing, covering her face with her hands.

‘It’s okay, babe. It’s okay. I get it. You don’t have to be sorry.’

‘I understand if you don’t forgive me—’

‘Shush! Look at me’, I interjected, placing my index finger on her lips in an attempt to silence her. She kissed my finger and I began laughing at how ticklish it felt. ‘If you apologise any more, I will then be mad at you.’, I added.

‘Okay, sorry, Alaina. I mean, not sorry, Alaina.’

‘I like it when you say my name.’

‘Alaina.’, she repeated. Her uttering my name consoled my heart.

‘Myra.’

‘Alaina.’

‘Myra. I need to tell you something. Before getting mad at me, just hear me out,’ I noticed that her face had distorted in confusion, wondering how the roles had reversed, ‘I think that Alisha and I are on good terms again. I mean, we aren't exactly best friends again, of course. It's natural for us to outgrow people as we grow through the journey of life. But deep down, I still love her and care for her and I cannot deny that. We have grown up in each other's company. Yesterday, I realised that she felt that too. That the love and friendship between us could diminish but never completely die. We may not be there for each other at our best but I know for a fact that we'll definitely be there for each other at our worst. And I think that's all that matters.'

She looked reflective at the end of my monologue, remained quiet for a few moments, as if utilising them to gather her thoughts, then said, 'You're right. I am a little annoyed because I know how many nights you've cried for her, and I cannot help but entertain the thought that she might hurt you again. Or instead, you both might hurt each other again. But I know what you're referring to. *Some bonds are evergreen.*'

I smiled at her, warmth spreading across my chest at her comprehension of my perspective. I looked at her eyes, the ones that beamed with a spiral of passion and emotions behind those spectacles, at her cheeks that turned into apples every time she smiled, at her heart-like lips that swayed so perfectly with mine, and at every other feature that sat on her beautiful body, and thought to myself: I love her so much.

*****

When we were having dinner, I sensed some unrest in her. She wasn't eating like she normally would, joyously and at a regular pace. Instead, she seemed to be nervously taking each bite, once more avoiding eye contact with me, staring at the blank wall behind us.

'You seem to be feeling uneasy,' I told her when we were heading to the sink to load our used dishes. She started a little, a little taken aback, then answered, 'I don't know why but my mind keeps spiralling back to irrational thoughts.'

'Like?'

'Just, you know, arbitrary ones.' Our conversations had never been so vague and restricted, even when we had first talked. It was strange.

It was when we entered my room and she banged the door behind us louder than usual that the ordeal of waiting was over.

'Alaina,' she uttered in a way that I no longer liked the sound of it.

'Myra?'

'I think it's time.'

'For what?'

'To talk.'

'Right,' I said, not knowing what exactly I could expect to hear from her but knowing well enough that it wasn't going to render me mirthful.

'I can't do this anymore!', She exclaimed in frustration, and I noticed that her voice had slightly raised. A lump of anxiety rose to my throat.

'Can't do what?', I asked, my voice almost trembling.

'I can't lie to you anymore. I need to tell you the truth. You deserve it.'

'What truth?' I asked, having absolutely no clue about what she could be talking about. 'You didn't cheat on me, did you?' My words were broken at this point.

'No, I would never, babe,' she said with a reassuring glance, then pausing for a moment, she continued, 'but, this might be worse. I don't know how to say this and I'm afraid about how you'll react.'

'What is it? I'm sure nothing can be worse than cheating, right? Tell me. You know that I'll *understand.'*

She hesitated a little, then taking a deep breath, she confessed, 'The reason why I freaked out was that... I knew that my friends are homophobic and the rumours about Sparsh's sexuality had been floating around our grade and his grade for a while. But I never asked you because I figured that if you had to tell me, you would. I kind of guessed, when I saw him lying on the ground and you weeping in agonising affliction, that it might have to do something with those rumours... and I just freaked out. Only if I had told you, this might've never happened.'

I remained silent for a while, registering everything that she had just said. I didn't know how to react. I could feel some anger levitating from the tips of my toes but my mind reminded me to comprehend her point of view. Had I been in her place, I would've also felt uncomfortable asking something like that, considering how sporadic our conversations have been on the theme of our families. I had been to her place a few times and she to mine, but we had always been friends in the eyes of our parents. We had never talked to each other about family problems, or anything explicitly with respect to our families for that matter. At the same time, it was difficult for me to let go of the thought that things may have turned out differently had she told me, if not before, at least at the party. The regret glimmering in her eyes was palpable. While forgiveness lay stuck at the tip of my tongue, my heart restrained it from rolling out. I couldn't say that it was okay because I myself didn't know if it was. Everything was okay just a while ago. Everything was in place when we were eating and sitting on the couch and talking, even if the strangeness in her demeanour was inordinate all the while. Why couldn't it have remained okay? I wanted to un-hear it all, if that was even possible. I wanted to go back to when we were on call and say to her that I didn't desire for her to come, that I wanted to be alone for some time. But I didn't. And now her words hung in the thick air like footsteps engraved on the moon, never to disappear. Not for long, at least.

'Alaina, you must know that I do feel guilty, and I wish I had done things differently, and I totally get it if you don't wanna speak with me, or,' she continued providing numerous elucidations for her actions but I was too far away from her to hear anything. I was back on the cold, hard ground, sitting beside Sparsh, wondering how many breaths he had remaining till losing them all. The scene was more vivid than ever. Her words twirled into my ears and morphed themselves into my own. I had promised to cheer him up at that party. I had told him that I would need his company, but ended up leaving him alone. I was satiating my hormonal desires while he was finding reasons to live. *If only I had not followed her up to the room*, I thought, *none of this would've happened. If only I would've stayed with him like I promised...*

I climbed on the bed and turned to one corner, staring at zilch as my mind struggled to keep pace with my thoughts, and as my ears felt deafened by all the voices reverberating in it. At one point, she stopped talking, probably realising that I had stopped listening a long time ago.

'I'm scared,' she said, breaking the silence that floated around for longer than forty minutes.

'I'm scared too,' I answered, knowing exactly what she was talking about.

I turned around and saw that she was now laying on the bed too, turned over to the other side, her back facing me. I reached out with my arm to tap her on the shoulder, and she turned to face me. Both of us were trying to hold back tears in vain. But we kept trying till we could. She grabbed my hand in hers and entangled our fingers together.

'I know you can't forgive me easily,' she said between silent sobs.

'I know,' I answered, not knowing what else to say.

‘But I don’t wanna let go of you yet.’

‘The night still lives.’

‘I hope this night never comes to an end.’

But it would. Everything is mortal. If there is a start, there must be an end too. We knew that, but at that moment, holding on to each other for the few hours that remained, holding on to the idea of an everlasting night, seemed to make everything okay. We did not want to think too deeply about what would happen when she got out of this room, the one that had seen so much of us, the one that would throng with memories of our laughter and our tears. But even without thinking, we knew it wouldn’t be a beautiful sight after she left.

We kept glaring into each other's pupils till all the energy drained out of them and sleep took over like an unwelcome escape. Every second felt like a prolonged eternity of pain, but I was still grateful for being with her till I could. I saw in her something I would probably never see again: my rain. From stealing glances in the school corridors, wondering if it was infatuation or detestation that always seemed to pull us together even when we were apart, to now looking at each other like this was the last time, in an attempt to heal our wounds with glances that were already bleeding, time really flies away quickly. I was on the verge of falling asleep when she scooted closer to me till our eyelids touched each other and our breaths once more synced. She whispered, ‘Alaina, I do not care if you forgive me or not, but please forgive yourself. You didn’t do anything wrong.’

‘How did you know?’, I asked in a frail voice.

‘I know you. I understand you. Without words spoken, remember?’ Yes, of course I did, but I never thought that there would actually come a point when we would no longer speak with each other.

I leaned in and our lips brushed against each other in such tender, raw emotions as never before. Every stroke was an agonising pinch on my heart. Between the tears and the gasps for breath, we kissed each other with the most love we could ever invest and express in a kiss, continuing till our lips felt numb and her taste sat on my tongue to last long enough for reminiscence.

‘I will always love you, Myra,’ I said as our lips were still stationarily touching each other.

‘I will always love you too, Alaina.’

Four Months later...

'Just a few inches down, yes! Perfect!', Mom exclaimed as she stood behind me, resolutely trying to get the dress to perfectly hug my body. She said that there was an elegance in body-fitting clothes that loose clothes failed to compete with. Today was going to be a big day. It was the performance day, after all. Our school's magazine, 'Artem: Reconnecting with Ourselves', had won the national magazine competition. We didn't secure the first position, but we were the runner's up team. I had nearly forgotten about the magazine complctcly till Mrs. Whayton summoned Myra and me to her office, just like the first time, only this time to break the news that we'd won the second position. But the real deal was, the founders of the competition were specifically fond of a poem in our magazine— the one Myra and I had composed together— and they wanted us to perform the poem in the felicitation ceremony. Apparently, it was a way bigger deal than we'd imagined while applying. Renowned artists from the country would be attending it and felicitating the winners. My parents had gone absolutely bonkers over the news and Mom had asked a designer to make an outfit for the occasion.

Once the blue silk sat flawlessly curved parallel to the curves along my waist and hips, and the pads underneath were suffocatingly pressed against my breasts, Mom finally gave up tightening the strings at the back. I had initially decided not to paint my face with heavy makeup but Mom seemed to have other intentions. I ended up wearing a pound of blush on my cheeks and a thick maroon matt shade tinting my lips. I curled only the tips of my hair but straightened the remaining. I felt pretty after a long time. We had an hour until we were supposed to leave. The event would begin at seven. Actually, the venue was hardly ten minutes from home but Mom's inextinguishable enthusiasm was not prepared to wait for more than an hour, and she had been insisting on leaving within thirty minutes until Dad somehow managed to allay her excitement. I opened my laptop and skimmed through the piece one more time in an attempt to reassure myself that I had all the sentences running fresh in my memory. I then decided to walk out and get some fresh air because the atmosphere inside was too irksome. My brain felt like it was shrinking into a knot. I simply needed to clear my head.

In another warp of space-time, I would've gone to *her* when it came to clearing my mind. But that warp seemed like a memory long lost, or even a fantasy. I had never been more confused, agonised, and fickle in my life as I had been in the past four months. There came a point when I had to go to therapy. Not that there was anything wrong in seeking help, but I never thought, at least four months back, that something worse could coerce me to seek therapy. It did feel relieving to talk to someone about thoughts and feelings that seemed so unusual and crazy to me that I would've never otherwise collected the guts to talk about them. Sparsh changed schools and even if I wanted to go along with him ever so desperately, it was deemed as an unwise decision to make with college waiting on the other side of the threshold. But the battle for justice hadn't been over for me. I made sure to make noise till the silence was broken. All the boys and girls who were involved in the heinous bullying that night were punished by the school after countless appeals from my, Alisha's, Ira's, and Sasha's parents. The punishment was nowhere near fair to weigh out what they'd done but beyond a certain point, there wasn't much we could do. But we didn't give up. We persevered till the school agreed to organise a series of sex education sessions and inaugurate a department that would deal with issues regarding sexual harassment and bullying. While this wasn't, again, justice being served, I learned to view it as a step towards justice someday.

Therapy had its own costs (besides the obvious ones, of course). When you talk about why you feel traumatized, you must recall the trauma. That was not plain sailing for me. But I persevered. I discontinued therapy a month ago when my therapist told my parents that 'signs of healing are noticeable'. But then came the day when Mrs. Whayton called *us* into her office. Before that day, for the last three months, we saw each other only seldomly, mostly in areas of large crowds: the cafeteria, the corridors, the field. Never alone. It sounds juvenile of me not to forgive her yet. I know. In truth, she was forgiven in my mind. And I wanted to talk to her so desperately. There were nights when her number was a digit away from being dialled, as I kept wondering if it was time yet to call her.

Everything was okay but it also wasn't. It wasn't as much about forgiveness as it was about distance. Within two weeks or so, her confession to me from that night was almost forgotten. But if you ask me what can change in two weeks between two people, I would say it would be more than you'd anticipate. We went to school. Every moment of seeing her rendered bitter nostalgia; a feeling of indifference. The first few days were difficult, of course. I struggled to keep my mind focused on studying for exams when all the time, the image of my brother running to end his life while I was smooching under the same roof made me feel sick. No, not just sick. It made me feel disgusted. In the struggle of trying to convince myself that I had not done it deliberately, that if I had known, I'd have protected him, I ended up consoling myself with this: it was her fault. But somewhere in the back of my mind, I very well knew that it wasn't. I also knew that the winding thoughts around my mind would soon disentangle themselves and allow me to hit the epiphany that it was neither's fault— that life sometimes flings you into a dumpster and you can't blame the non-existent wind instead of blaming life; that sometimes things are simply not under your control. But by the time the epiphany struck me, there were over fifty missed calls and over seventy messages from her that I had ignored. I read them all, cried at some even, but always ended up putting the phone away, thinking that a day would come when I would call her, reply to all of the things she'd said, when her dulcet voice would once more make me feel serene as it once did, that her hearing her words would make everything okay again, but that day never came. Over a hundred times, I was on the verge of clicking on that last digit and ringing her up, but my finger could never make it. It hid away nervously every time. So I kept procrastinating on calling her, kept avoiding eye contact with her, kept pretending like I couldn't hear her when she'd call out my name when we were alone in the washroom or at the bus stop, and kept ignoring her messages till it was too late to hold up the pretence any longer. She had hurt me and I hurt her back. We hurt each other while we never intended to. Perhaps our own strings were too broken for us to stitch a new one together. Our roses had thorns that overpowered the love of the petals. And so, tinkling nervousness no longer made my toes curl or my heart pound at the sight of her. The flame of passion no longer burnt my chest when she was even only a few centimeters away from me. I knew that all things are mortal and our paths might bifurcate soon. And maybe they already had. But to live in oblivion, or at least in the act of oblivion, was more agreeable, delightful even, than the contrary. I also realised by now that things happen. Life is dynamic. Things happen that tear you apart from the people you once believed you had been permanently hot-glued to. Things happen that are way too beyond your sway. And you don't feel the presence of these things when they begin to bloom. They cultivate long before you start taking observance of them and you are clueless of what they can lead to. They grow perniciously, punching you on the face only when they arrive at their zenith, allowing the collapse to occur not gradually but all at once— like the flash of lightning before the thunder roars, like the clamour of thunder before the hurricane ensues, like the last few seconds before the descending raindrop strikes the earth.

And then the flood wreaks havoc.

So, when we were at Mrs. Whayton's office, me having to lock eyes with her for the first time in three months, the collapse repeated itself. We entered awkwardly inside, presuming that it would be something about our club. But when she announced the good news, we were in raptures. Out of human instinct, we beamed with wide smiles on our faces and hugged each other.

For the first few seconds, it was only the celebratory trumpets and cheer that were ruling over my mind and body till they dissolved, and I felt her little fingers clasp my shirt wistfully, smelling jasmine and daisies in her ponytail that had swung over to her left shoulder. I know she felt it too: the bittersweet nostalgia. I know she wanted to hug longer too, perhaps sempiternally. And if we were in a different warp of space-time, it would've happened. But we weren't. So, we broke the embrace sooner than it had commenced, our cheeks brushing against each other. The flame of passion had almost risen but we put it out. But when Mrs. Whayton further explained the impact that our writing had engendered and that we were invited to perform, I wanted to hug her again, kiss her even. But I managed to subside the feeling.

At home that day, I balled out like I had never before. Tears were running down my cheeks and snot down my nostrils. I wailed like a parent who had lost their child, like a simpleton who had been betrayed by a friend whom they considered most loyal, like a child who had lost their parent, and like a girl who realised she had lost herself again, just when she thought she may be heading towards finding herself. I was not crying because I missed her, which I did. I was not crying because she had hurt me. I was crying because we had something out worldly, something that you would think only exists in novels, and that something had been annihilated. I was crying because I knew that no matter how much I wanted it back, it would never happen. Crying because I knew that this wouldn't be the last loss I'd face.

We had to practice our recitation a couple of times but since we did it during school hours at the convention of all members of the Literary Club, we could escape exchanging any words between ourselves. We lied to Mrs. Whayton that we practiced together after school hours. The club met twice a week and we prepared for three weeks. Six rounds of practice may not be the ideal amount to guarantee a mind-blowing performance, but our voices seemed to perfectly sync together. We would recite with the same emotion that we had written it with, but on the last day of practice, which was three days ago, I failed to find my voice. I could not feel my feet on the ground. Along with my mind, they had drifted away to the scene of us composing it together. I rushed to the washroom as soon as we finished the recitation and sobbed helplessly. I knew that I was probably acting immaturely, that it was futile to cry over spilled milk, but not always can you retain control of your emotions. Like a godsend, Sasha happened to be in one of the stalls at that time. Not that her presence could bring my breakdown to an end, but crying in her embrace felt better than listening to my gasps echo as I struggled to breathe.

*****

The wind was brisk and light. It washed all the tension away from my head as it whooshed past my cheeks and rustled through my hair. I stood at the side of the street and looked around at our neighbourhood. I had not acknowledged its elegance previously. The houses and apartments were aligned adjacent to each other in near perfection, and the imperfection generated by the alternating heights of the structures only added to the glory of the view. Most of the houses were painted in neutral tones. A few deciduous trees were flanking the street on either side, lined up along the edges in discontinuity. The diminishing sunlight glowed refreshingly on the antiquated paints of the buildings. The sky almost matched the hue of the leaves, amber, and auburn. I reminisced how a few months ago, just a few paces from where I stood, there had been standing Alisha's car, her screaming on the verge of losing her voice, for Sparsh and me to hurry up. It seemed like an event from years ago. These were the streets I had often walked along when I needed to ground myself. Today, I needed just that. I was not so much looking forward to performing as I was to make my verses be heard to an audience who probably loved words as much as I did. To make *our* words be heard.

I heard a vehicle slowing down behind me. I turned around to see the spectacle of Pranul Bhaiya decelerating our car as he made way to stop in front of our house.

'Why are you here so early, Bhaiya?'

'Madam told me to arrive in thirty minutes to six.'

'Oh, okay,' I said and turned around to roll my eyes. I screamed upward to my window, 'WE'RE LEAVING AT SIX AND SIX ONLY!!'. I then turned back to him again, caught by quick observance that he sat with a weirded-out expression which changed to normal instantly, and told him, 'You can park the car and walk around for a while. We'll leave in half an hour.' He nodded his head and proceeded to park the car beside our gate. As I walked on, I stepped on something that cracked louder than the dry and dead leaves I had stepped on earlier. I looked down to see a piece of white paper, double-folded, lying beneath my heel. I picked it up and rubbed the dust from its surface away. Unsure if I was invading someone's privacy, I hesitated to unfold it. I looked around to find Pranul Bhaiya, thinking that maybe he'd know about the origin of the paper. But he seemed to have taken my words too seriously and walked away to a distance where my voice would be out of his earshot. I thought to myself that I would only look for a name, if there is one, and immediately give it to the person it belonged to. It must be for someone from our neighbourhood. No sooner had I unfolded the piece of paper than I recognised the handwriting. At first glance. On the top left corner, it read: 'My Lovely Alaina,'. My heart picked up pace in its beating immediately. I began perusing the letter:

My Lovely Alaina,

My sentences are probably trembling in your grip presently. And this is probably the first and last letter I'll ever write to you. So, I'll try to make it worth your read.

I must admit to you that there hasn't been a day since that night that I haven't thought of you. In fact, at this instant, as I write to you, the sketch of you runs in my mind. Those plump, pink lips carving into a smile at the sight of the simplest of things. Those dark brown eyes glistening softly against the sunlight. Your face is flawless and the more I look at it, the more baffled I get by how insanely beautiful someone can be. Your body's a blessing and so is your soul. I have never felt safer anywhere else than I have in your embrace. Truth is, I miss you. A lot. I know that I have disturbed some part inside of you, shaken probably, by the things that I said. I know that things have changed tremendously in the past four months, and I blame you not. But I'd be lying if I said that my heart didn't shatter a little every time you turned a deaf ear to my calls, every time you turned away when you caught my glance, every time you chose to pretend I do not exist when I stood right in front of you. We both broke each other's hearts a little, did we not? Or perhaps, as you would say, we pulled the wrong strings. I guess that's the circle of life. Everything is ephemeral. But even the limited time that I got to spend with you will live infinitely in my mind. Although I cannot remember the last time we spoke, I still imagine us in my mind. At that spot on the beach. Or wandering through the viridescent valleys of the ghats. Or sipping hot chocolate at the cafe. Or dancing at your rooftop. Or cackling in my house. You are everywhere. I see you in sunrises and in sunsets. I see your reflection glimmering on sea waves. I hear your words dancing along with the wind and the rains. Maybe this is what longing for something that you've lost feels like. And I'm embracing the pain. Don't get me wrong— this is not a letter of me accusing you of messing up something beautiful we had. Because we both fucked up a little, and maybe me, a little more.

I'm sorry. You were right. I was still not ready. I was somewhat ashamed to introduce you to my friends because I was not even ready to acknowledge my own feelings.

That day when we hugged, I felt the butterflies all over again, just like the first time. But I also felt a sense of relief, a sense of home. We now exist only in my memories, and I hope I never forget the sound of your voice or the glimmer of your eyes. I wonder if things could ever truly be over between the two of us. Because I know that I cannot completely forget about you nor refrain myself from finding you in everyone else. If it's not your voice, I don't wanna hear it. If it's not your poetry, I don't wanna read it. If it's not your smile, I don't wanna see it. If it's not your skin, I don't wanna feel it.

You have no idea how rapturous I felt when Mrs. Whayton told us that we won the second position. This magazine was more than a school project for me. It was the beginning of us. I still have the tattered piece of paper where you'd scribbled your phone number for me. That's where it all started, from the exchange of numbers to the cafe, two strangers sipping hot chocolate, the synergy of creativity erupting between them along with sparks of infatuation. But it grew to so much more than infatuation so quickly. The magazine will always occupy a special room in my heart. I cannot let it be the end of us. I know you were really excited about tonight's performance but I don't think I can make it. I know that you'll understand and I hope that you can forgive me.

I love you,
Myra.

P.S. In case you're wondering, our prints are still up on my wall. <3

Letters definitely rank second after physical touch among the ways of expressing affection. At least in my world, they do. It felt wonderful to catch a glimpse of her handwriting again. Those words had tumbled down from her fingertips with that blue fountain pen she always went gaga about. I wanted to drop to the ground, scream and cry. But I didn't. I knew where she was coming from and she was right, I *understood* her. I didn't want this to be the end of us either. I didn't want us to be over yet, or ever. No matter how hard I might try to suppress these feelings, I don't think they'll ever disappear. They can be forgotten, but my soul refuses to part with them. If this were a movie, I would've gone running back to her, scrambling to her house, not caring about the show or about the worry my abrupt disappearance would render my parents, then jump into her arms, kiss her passionately and longingly, and we would live happily ever after. But this wasn't a movie. This was my life. And although we may get back up after we collapsed, it takes time to heal wounds. Stones flung at you don't bounce back. They leave stains behind. And these stains, too, take time to be mended and washed away.

There wasn't much time to think. I heard Mom's heels clicking behind and Dad's slow footsteps approaching too. In reflex, I crumpled the piece of paper in my grip, gulped down some saliva in my throat in an attempt to pull back in the tears that were beginning to form, and turned around to see them with a blithe demeanour. They smiled back at me. I caught from my peripheral vision of Pranul Bhaiya walking toward us from a distance, picking up pace as he noticed that my parents had come out.

The drive to the venue was shorter than I had estimated. We arrived way too early and so were asked to sit at the reception till the auditorium would be unlocked. I had managed to slide the paper into one of the seat pockets in the car without my parents noticing. I was currently tapping my feet in anxiety. The more I tried to filter my mind of the contents of the letter, the more nervous I felt. My stomach curled up into a ball and I could feel sweat dripping down my forehead. Dad asked me if I was doing okay. I told him that I was. After sitting there for around twenty minutes, a lady signalled us that we could go in. My Mom whispered good luck to me while dad said out loud, 'Break a leg!'. This seemed like the perfect family moment, or at least as close to perfect as we could get. Only Sparsh was missing. He was studying for his midterms and promised me that he'd try to arrive during the time of my performance which was fifth in number. 'Thank you,' I said to both of them, to which Dad responded with a pat on my back and Mom intertwined her fingers with mine. I looked at their faces, their smiley faces beaming with happiness. I felt so grateful. How far we had come from those nights of soulless conversations at dinner. How far from them not having enough time to make it to our school conferences. How far from that morning in the hospital when Mom had lashed out. She was yet to become a complete ally. She also has not entirely gotten rid of her conservative beliefs. But she was trying her best to fight her homophobia. She didn't look at me or Sparsh differently, nor did she think of us differently. She loved us the same and she was making an effort to learn every day. That's all that mattered.

The wait seemed way longer than its actual duration. Despite trying to keep my ears alert to the voices of the other speakers, my thoughts ended up being louder than them. Plus, it was not so easy to hear from backstage. My mind was in a conundrum. From the moment of getting into the car to the moment of coming into the green room, I had not once opened space for the thought: how would I perform alone? Although I had the entire piece memorised by heart, I knew very well that the same magic couldn't be created by myself alone as it would've been if she was here. But it was too late to brainstorm ideas then. I heard my name being called, 'Alaina Kaur', loud and clear, resonating through the silence that fell after the applause for the previous performance. It took me a few seconds to register that I'd have to get up and go to the stage. Then I did. I didn't know what I was thinking. In fact, I didn't know if I was thinking anything at all. I could hear the sound of my nervous footsteps creating a disturbance in the deafening silence that enveloped me. A thousand eyes seemed to be fixated on my figure. But I could see nobody. The spotlight shone over me and everything else was dark. I shut my eyes and took a deep breath in. And let it out. Grabbing the microphone with my hands, while I could feel my heartbeat at the peak of my throat, I spoke, 'Good evening, everyone. I hope you're keeping well and don't have your expectations set too high by the mind-blowing performances that preceded mine. I know that you heard two names being summoned to the stage but looks like only one showed up. Don't worry, my name's not that long. There was supposed to be another person, my partner, Myra, who couldn't make it today due to some personal emergencies. You may not have signed up for a single-person show but I'll try to give you all the best that I can,' there were cheers from the audience, probably from students and teachers who came to attend as representatives of our school, 'Before I begin, I would like to add a little back story. When Mrs. Whayton told me that I would be the student editor for this year's magazine along with a new student whom I had never spoken to before, I immediately felt repulsive. Firstly, I had no idea how I'd get along with a stranger and secondly, I was baffled how a new student got so much preference not even three minutes inside the school. Yeah, I was being petty. But if it weren't for Mrs. Whayton, I wouldn't have gotten to know one of the most talented, beautiful, and magnanimous souls to walk the face of earth. The creative energy between Myra and me was astronomical. We just clicked and from our synergy was born this gorgeously-crafted magazine. I was myself amazed by the outcome of our creativity. But I have this bad habit of underestimating myself, so I never thought we'd win this competition. But we did, and now here I am standing to recite to you a piece composed by Myra and me. This piece is very close to my heart and I hope that it finds a way to touch all your hearts too. Okay, so, here I go:

I crush dry leaves in the heart of my fist
as a brisk autumn zephyr chills down my spine.
the ground is cold,

and my feet, colder.
My fingertips feel crisp against the touch of stevia;
an unrest churns in my belly;
a thousand thoughts wind round my mind at once
but my lips remain resolutely affixed to themselves.
These thoughts will never find voices to be heard.

I can feel every part of myself—
every touch of the sand grains against my skin,
every salty breath of air rustling through my hair,
every lump of bile rising to my throat—
as I hear them chant, watch them dance, and feel them
walk farther away from me.
But I cannot feel myself.
I'm exhausted from running; let me catch my breath.
I'm exhausted from trying; make the race end.
I'm exhausted from questing; why can't I be found?

As the clock strikes three and I attempt my best at silence,
love tells me to relinquish my sleep for exchange of words
with a stranger who I might not recall in a month.

On the brink of twilight, while I glare at pages and click my pen away in anxiety,
love tells me to push my mind just one more time
for receiving approbation from someone who couldn't care less about me.

As my mind dwells in a clamour over the next steps of life,
love tells me to plant faith in ma and pa's amorous visages once more
and wake myself up from the dream I hitherto couldn't do without.

But what does love tell me in those tenebrous hours when I lose grip over my breaths?
what does love tell me when I lose myself in perpetually trying to be someone else?
what does love tell me when that stranger has vanished from my memory,

when that approbation reduces to mere sentences said out of habit,
when that dream has gone too far away for me to keep seeking it anymore?

Love remains shushed within my lips.
Love crushes like the dry leaves in my fist.
Love shivers fretfully like my spine.

But love finds me this time.

The stretches across my thighs— I am not ashamed of them anymore.
The strange soreness in my voice— it doesn't scare me from listening to myself anymore.
The dancing couple to my side—I don't imagine myself in them anymore.
The waves swaying in the distance—I don't want to be washed away with them anymore.

My feet are cold and my fingertips are sore,
so I pull them closer and huddle up in an embrace.
As I unwind my fingers, I let go of the broken pieces of leaves—
I let go of the broken fragments in me.

the wind whooshes them away.

Autumn shall revisit these cold grounds and trembling limbs;
dried leaves shall shatter in my grip once more,
but I know this time that if I fall,
I shall rise again.
if We fall,
We shall rise again.'

When I finally stopped to catch my breath, I was pretty sure I had gone overtime. I was also mostly sure that I had stuttered somewhere or said some of the words wrongly. But I couldn't tell if it was the post-performance anxiety or intuition. My heartbeat slowed down and I regained touch with my senses. Silence hung in the air for a couple of moments after I stopped speaking, but was soon replaced with booming hosannas from the audience— an amalgamation of claps and cheers. The hall got lit up in yellow lamps and I could now see everyone in front of me. I noticed Sparsh giving me a standing ovation with my parents. It immediately brought a smile to my visage. 'You came!', I mouthed to him. Surprisingly, he spotted that and mouthed 'YES!' in response. I saw a couple of other people standing for me, including the teachers from my school, Alisha, Sasha, and Kiara.

About a dozen people came running towards me as I exited the auditorium. Among the ones in the front were my parents, my brother, and my friends. Before I could process it, they were congratulating me and praising me for my performance. All their words jumbled up into an indistinct murmur hovering over my head. My eyes were scurrying around, looking at the grinning faces surrounding me. Some of them took me by surprise. Somewhere at the back, I saw Arj. Our eyes met and he waved at me, mouthing 'celebrity'. I giggled. It felt good to see him after so long. It was not like I had not seen him at all since we broke up. He studied in my grade, after all. But social interaction to me had become a voluntary leap into a treacherous engulfing sea after a terrible heartbreak. The crowd soon dissolved and each went their own way, some sailing towards the buffet, some towards the restroom to fix their mien, some just wandering around and others headed home. Mom whispered to me that I could hang out with my friends for a while and go for the food whenever I felt like it. Sparsh was also about to make his way to the buffet when I placed my right palm on the shoulder. He turned around and raised his eyebrows, asking, 'What?'

I smiled at him and answered, 'Thank you!'

'No biggie, sis. You were amazing, there. You've deranged everyone.'

'I don't think that's the correct use of the word.'

'Oh, c'mon. You get it!'

'Yeah, whatever,' I said, rolling my eyes. Then he left, making his way towards the buffet. Sasha and Alisha were still standing beside me, chuckling away.

'What are you two laughing about?'

'This bhaiya,' Sasha began explaining but was too riddled with laughter to utter more words.

'So, there was a waiter', Alisha continued, 'he looked like he is a part-time student who works here,' they simply couldn't stop giggling.

'Okay, and?', I asked, confused.

'And he asked Sasha out. She replied to him saying, 'No bhaiya, I don't roll like that.' And he didn't get what she implied, so he left with an unsettled look on his face. Then a few moments later, he came back with a chicken roll for her!' they burst out laughing even more energetically after the recall of the anecdote. It was hysterical, not going to lie. I burst out too.

'And then?', I asked between guffaws.

'We took the roll and said, 'Thank you bhaiya ji, but this is what I meant,' and then she pecked me in front of him!' Alisha answered. As I was laughing, I caught from the side of my eye a figure standing but a few paces from me. I turned around to see, still laughing, Arj standing, as if waiting to talk to me. I looked back at Alisha and Sasha and gave them a look, signalling them to look at Arj but in a way that wasn't conspicuous. They understood me and headed towards the buffet, leaving Arj and me alone to talk.

'Hi,' he said. It was a familiar voice, yet at that instant, it felt strange, like an old childhood memory that rings a bell but you still can't quite get yourself to remember the specifics. I realised then how much I had missed talking to him.

'Hey,' I answered. I was already feeling nostalgic.

'You did so well! I just wanted to say how proud I am of you. I had always known you to be a writer but I never thought you had a knack for spoken word too!'

'Oh, looks like you don't know me so well after all!' We chuckled lightly. How long it had been since we had laughed together. It felt tranquil to reconnect like this with an old friend. We may outgrow people but somewhere in our strings, the connection never dies. The stitches never completely tear apart.

'How've you been?'

'Oh, that's a good question that I don't know how to answer.'

'I get it. I saw you that day at Alisha's party, by the way. I was too scared to approach you.'

'Scared? What are you even talking about?'

'Wrong choice of words. Not ready, I meant. I was not ready.'

'And are you, now?'

'Yes, maybe. But don't get me wrong, *ha*. I'm not a creepy stalking ex or anything.'

'Shush. I know.'

'You always do, don't you?'

'It's you, Arj.'

'You're getting me emo now.'

'School's getting over soon. I guess we need to start getting the hang of it,' I said in a jocular tone, but it didn't seem to have the desired effect. He was tearing up and I regretted my words immediately. 'I'm so sorry, I didn't mean to make you more emotional. Fuck!'

'It's okay,' he said with an evil smile and started laughing.

'Asshole! Go pursue acting, na! You made me feel so guilty.'

'Come on, can't friends tease each other?'

'The real question is: are Arj and Alaina ever gonna stop teasing each other?'

'Right. You just say the right things at the right time.'

'It's a talent,' I said, raising my eyebrows and closing my eyes, trying to act vain but failing miserably. He began laughing again. So did I. His laughter was contagious.

'I'm gonna miss you, though, for real,' he said in a sombre tone once we ran out of breath from laughing.

'Me too.'

'But you're gonna miss her the most, aren't you?'

'Miss whom the most?' I asked, confused.

'You know who I am talking about.'

'You know?'

'Yes, I know. Don't ask me how. And don't worry, it's not a publicly known matter.'

'Okay, but why do you say that?'

'I saw it, Alaina. It was in your eyes. The way they shined when you were speaking about her in your introduction. You mirrored how I felt about you.' It stung a little to hear him say 'felt'. I hated endings. I hated change.

'Wow. What exactly did you see?'

'Love,' he answered with a smile. It was a bittersweet moment. I wanted to cling on to it. Ten years from now, he'd probably become a distant memory somewhere in the back of my brain, being remembered every once in a blue moon.

We hugged and promised each other to hang out once before we'd leave for college, just the two of us. We also promised to try and remain in contact as much as possible. I told him that college decisions weren't out yet and we still had a faint probability of attending the same institution, to which he answered that we still couldn't strike off the other possibilities. I then headed off to the buffet and he headed home. The food was scrumptious but my mind was more focused on his words. If he said that I mirrored what he *felt* about me in talking about Myra, did it mean that love was mortal too?

The way back home was quite enjoyable. I felt content. Dad had sent our driver back home a couple of minutes after we'd arrived because he wanted to drive today on his own. I guess this would make our first family ride in the true sense of it. We were cracking jokes about everything and nothing at the same time. But we had soon run out of jokes to say, so Mom broke the silence by asking me, 'Why didn't Myra come, though Alaina? What kind of personal emergency showed up?'

'Umm', I mumbled, clearly not expecting this question to be shot at me but also baffled that nobody had asked this till now, 'her mother's sick,' I lied. Like a godsend, Dad sensed the discomfort in my voice and soon diverted the topic, saying, 'Today, I feel very proud of both my children. I know I say it every day but you must still hear it: I love you both. And I love you, Ammu. So, tell me, where should we go today? Name any place in the city and we'll go there!'. I wondered if he knew about Myra and me just like he knew about my sexuality before I came out. Maybe he just had this supernatural power of reading people's minds. Or actions. Or eyes, perhaps. Whatever it was, I'm glad he used it in my favour.

'The beach?', I said, looking at everyone in request of their consent.

'Yes!', Mom and Sparsh said unanimously.

'Okay then!', Dad replied cheerfully, then suddenly accelerated the car. We all screamed and began laughing.

With dad's insane driving skills, we arrived at the beach within seven minutes. I waited for everyone to get down so that I could take the crumpled paper out of the seat pocket and read it once more at *our* spot. The four of us looked like we came from a fancy dress competition in contrast with all of the other people there dressed in casual attire. But nobody was really bothered, except a handful of judgemental eyes being cast at us. I loved that about the people here. Most of them didn't care about how others looked or behaved or dressed or talked. They just let them be on their own. They were too busy with their own lives to spare any bothering. Mom, Dad, Sparsh, and I scattered away in different directions, each in search of our spaces of serenity. We had learnt when to give space to each other and when not to.

It was the inception of fall. The sky glistened with an auburn sun, preparing to plummet into the waves. I was laying down on the sand on my stomach, face toward the sea, beholding the endless beauty in front of me. It felt just like old times when I used to come here alone. I then realised that this was probably the first time that I came here by myself since introducing Myra to this spot. The oscillating waves rang with memories of us and of my past wool-gatherings here.

I opened the paper once more and laid it down on the sand, trying to straighten the creases with my hands. I read it once more, and then again. I kept reading it till her sentences were flashing right across my mind. I wanted to weep. I wanted to shout. I wanted to scream at the world for being unfair, at my mind, and my life for always being so chaotic. Why did things have to be so complicated? I wanted to tell her that I still loved her, that I believed, too, that I could never stop loving her, that she was everywhere for me too. I didn't want ours to be one of those summer loves that ends before it starts, that you can never imitate with any partner ever again, that you keep clinging on to even when you're in someone else's embrace, that keeps you up on nights when you wonder what if your paths hadn't bifurcated after all, or what if, even after the bifurcation, they'd cross again. I didn't want us to live in my head. If I wanted to, I could have torn up the paper into a hundred pieces and thrown them into the sea. I could've convinced my mind that it was all a dream, or that it in fact was one of those unforgettable summer romances, and attempted my best to forget about it. But I didn't. There was something about the waves rumbling at the shore and the sky dissipating into navy and the subtle zephyrs rustling through my hair that told me to feel it. Not to run away anymore, because, in fact, I was tired of running away.

I was so desperate to paint the canvas of my life with stolen hues that I never realised that I could have hues of my own. But now I did. I lost myself multiple times in trying to be someone else. I lost my identity multiple times in trying to find it in others. But I knew now that I could just be me— and that would be enough. It wouldn't be easy for me to strongly and wholly believe that. But every pace away from those stolen hues would be a pace towards myself.

There would be many drizzles. There would be many tempests too. Then there'd be sunrises and sunsets.

When would they be? I knew not. But until then, I would keep going— away from the stolen hues towards my own— towards the rain.

A Letter to My Readers,

If you have made it this far, then I would first like to thank you for having faith in my words and delving into the story of Alaina, which is somewhat my own too. This was my first experience with writing a full-length novel and in all honesty, it was one hell of a ride. After several rounds of editing and countless nights of contemplating whether I should publish this story or not, here I am today. I hope, from every corner of my soul that not long back was not brave enough to make its voice heard, that this story stays with you. It was written to evoke some emotion in you— be it love, remorse, spite, envy, despair, sympathy, empathy, or even numbness, whatever you name it— to make you feel more human. And I really hope I was able to do that.

Nevertheless, there is always room for improvement, especially since this is my very first time. I would like to hear from you about how you think Alaina's story continues: do you see her story entering a sequel or the open-endedness is what holds the tale's value? How did the story make you feel?

I would also highly appreciate constructive criticism from you so that better stories can be written and new voices can be made heard. Email me your thoughts at ruchika.121504@gmail.com or you can also reach out to me via Instagram, @ruchikaa___15.

Once again, thank you for living this journey with me. I hope to hear from you soon.

Until next time,
Ruchika.

9 789354 725470

Printed by Libri Plureos GmbH in Hamburg, Germany